120 PATTERNS FOR TRADITIONAL PATCHWORK QUILTS

MAGGIE MALONE

Virginia Star (116), p. 227

Sterling Publishing Co., Inc. New York

Distributed in the U.K. by Blandford Press

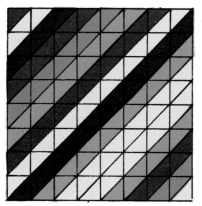

Barn Raising (2), p. 21

Storm at Sea (105), pp. 208–209

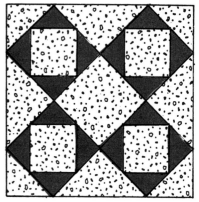

Block & Star (3), pp. 22–23

The number within the parentheses in each caption of the Color Index refers to the number of the pattern. The page numbers which follow are the pages on which the patterns are to be found.

Library of Congress Cataloging in Publication Data

Malone, Maggie, 1942–
    120 patterns for traditional patchwork quilts.

    Includes index.
    1. Patchwork—Patterns.   2. Quilting—Patterns.
I. Title.   II. Title: One hundred twenty patterns for
traditional patchwork quilts.
TT835.M346   1983   746.9'7041   82-19671
ISBN 0-8069-5488-4
ISBN 0-8069-7716-7 (pbk.)

Edited and designed by Barbara Busch

Copyright © 1983 by Sterling Publishing Co., Inc.
Two Park Avenue, New York, N.Y. 10016
Distributed in Australia by Oak Tree Press Co., Ltd.
P.O. Box K514 Haymarket, Sydney 2000, N.S.W.
Distributed in the United Kingdom by Blandford Press
Link House, West Street, Poole, Dorset BH15 1LL, England
Distributed in Canada by Oak Tree Press Ltd.
% Canadian Manda Group, P.O. Box 920, Station U
Toronto, Ontario, Canada M8Z 5P9
Manufactured in the United States of America

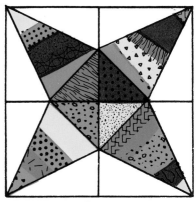

Rocky Road to Kansas (89),
pp. 175–176

Moon Over the Mountain (74),
pp. 146–147

Lily of the Valley (64), pp. 128–130

Contents

Swing in the Center (106), pp. 210–211

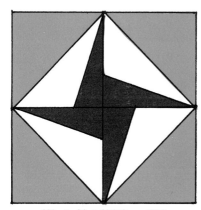

Waste Not (117), p. 228

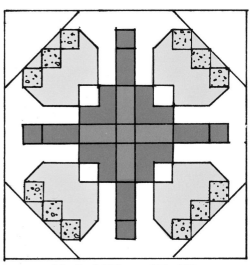

Lily Pool (65), pp. 131–132

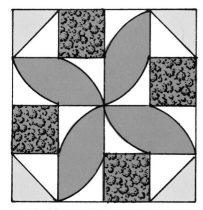

Windflower (122), pp. 236–237

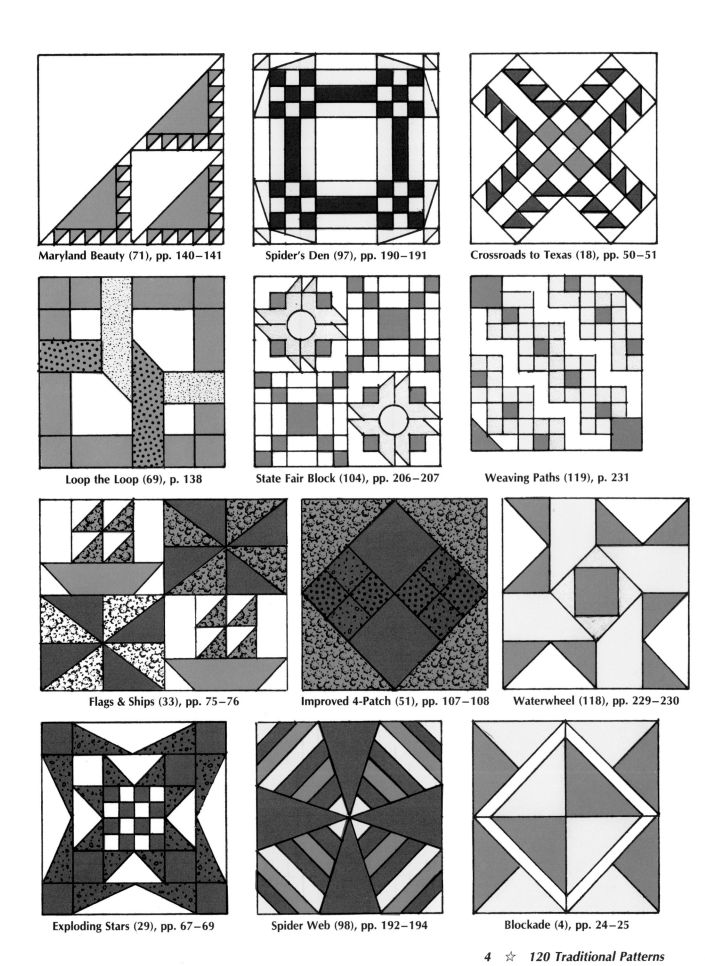

Maryland Beauty (71), pp. 140–141

Spider's Den (97), pp. 190–191

Crossroads to Texas (18), pp. 50–51

Loop the Loop (69), p. 138

State Fair Block (104), pp. 206–207

Weaving Paths (119), p. 231

Flags & Ships (33), pp. 75–76

Improved 4-Patch (51), pp. 107–108

Waterwheel (118), pp. 229–230

Exploding Stars (29), pp. 67–69

Spider Web (98), pp. 192–194

Blockade (4), pp. 24–25

Pine Tree (83), pp. 161–163

Diamond 9-Patch (22), p. 58

Friendship Star (40), pp. 86–87

Railroad Crossing (88), p. 174

Hunter's Star (50), pp. 105–106

Morning Glory (75), pp. 148–149

Prosperity Block (86), pp. 169–171

Triple Irish Chain (113), pp. 222–223

Pickle Dish (80), pp. 63–64

Seven Sisters (93), pp. 182–183

Pinwheel Square (84), pp. 164–165

Turkey Tracks (115), p. 226

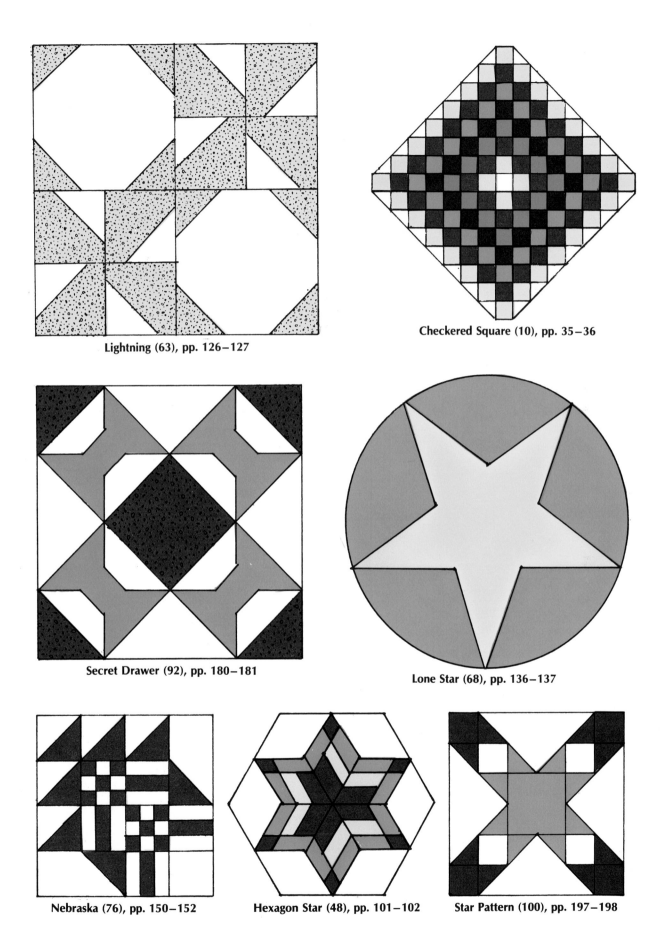

Lightning (63), pp. 126–127

Checkered Square (10), pp. 35–36

Secret Drawer (92), pp. 180–181

Lone Star (68), pp. 136–137

Nebraska (76), pp. 150–152

Hexagon Star (48), pp. 101–102

Star Pattern (100), pp. 197–198

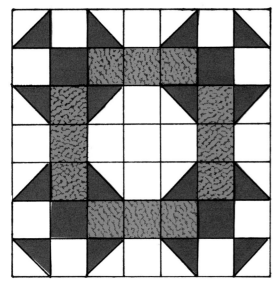

Greek Cross (46), pp. 97–98

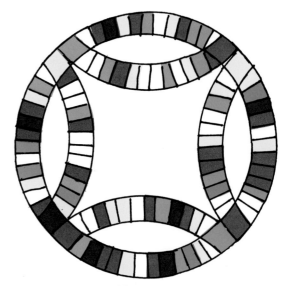

Double Wedding Ring (27), pp. 63–64

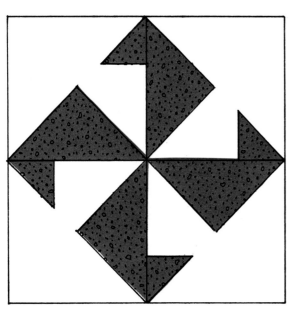

Lindy's Plane (66), p. 133

Bridal Path (6), p. 28

Snake's Trail (96), pp. 188–189

Flying Bats (37), pp. 81–82

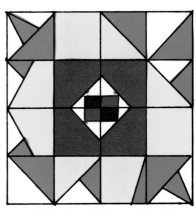

Cubist Rose (20), pp. 54–55

Altar Steps (1), pp. 19–20

Country Roads (15), pp. 44–45

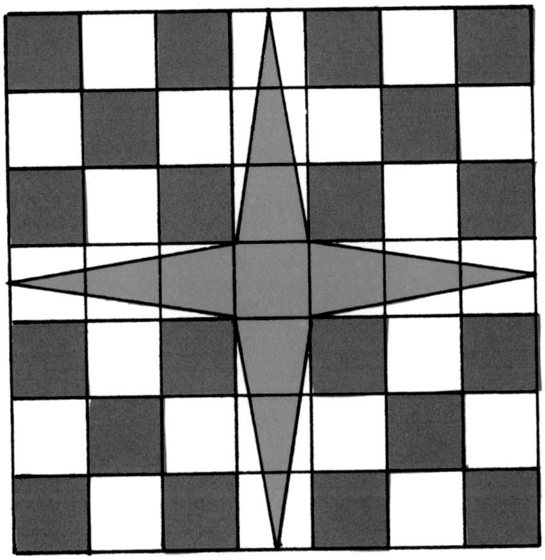

Nosegay (79), p. 157

Shadows (94), pp. 184–186

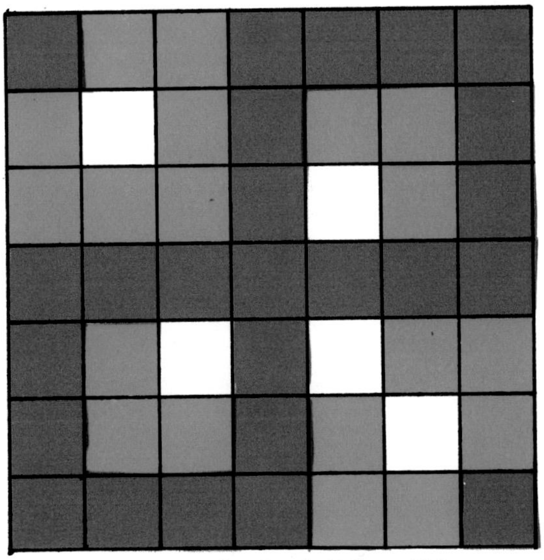

Leavenworth 9-Patch (61), p. 124

9-Patch Star (77), pp. 153–154

Chrysanthemum (11), pp. 37–38

Diamond Chain (21), pp. 56–57

Jig Jog Puzzle (55), pp. 113–114

Three Cheers (109), pp. 216–217

Fair & Square (30), pp. 70–71

Fantasy Flower (31), p. 72

Geometry (41), p. 88

1904 Star (78), pp. 155–156

Flower Garden (35), p. 78

Flywheel (38), p. 83

God's Eye (42), pp. 89–90

Gothic Windows (44), pp. 93–94

Feathered Star (32), pp. 73–74

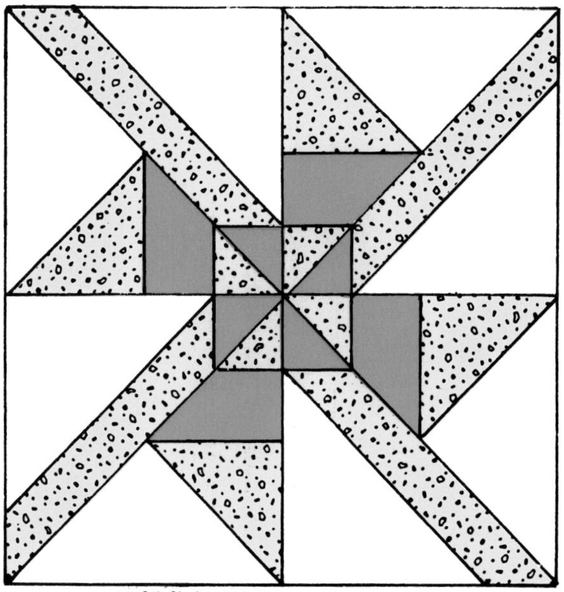

Whirligig (121), pp. 234–235

Heart's Desire (47), pp. 99–100

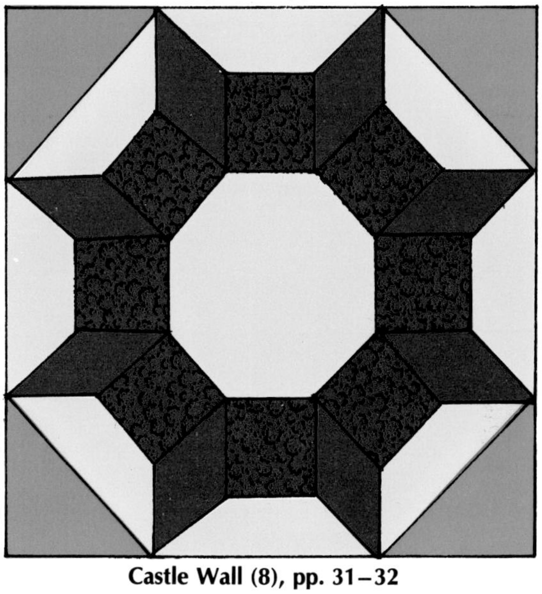

Castle Wall (8), pp. 31–32

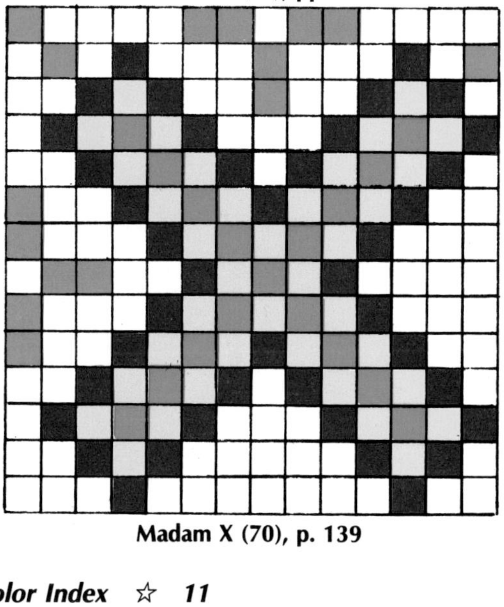

Madam X (70), p. 139

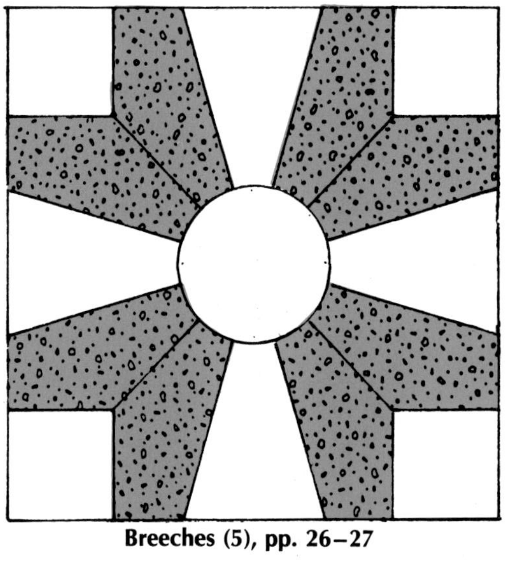

Breeches (5), pp. 26–27

Cobwebs (14), p. 43

Hourglass (49), pp. 103–104

Kitchen Woodbox (59), pp. 120–121

Scottish Cross (91), p. 179

State Fair (103), pp. 204–205

Grandma's Hopscotch (45), pp. 95–96

Tic Tac Toe (110), p. 218

Starry Pavement (102), pp. 201–203

Lady of the White House (60), pp. 122–123

Tangled Lines (108), pp. 214–215

Golden Stairs (43), pp. 91–92

Tulip & Star (114), pp. 224–225

County Fair (16), pp. 46–47

Topsy Turvy (112), pp. 220–221

Little Star (67), pp. 134–135

Cowboy Star (17), pp. 48–49

Indian Patch (52), pp. 109–110

Evening Star (28), pp. 65–66

Double Irish Chain I (25), pp. 61–62

Kaleidoscope (56), pp. 115–116

Dogwood Blossoms (23), pp. 59–60

Shooting Star (95), p. 187

Climbing Roses (13), pp. 41–42

King's Crown (58), pp. 118–119

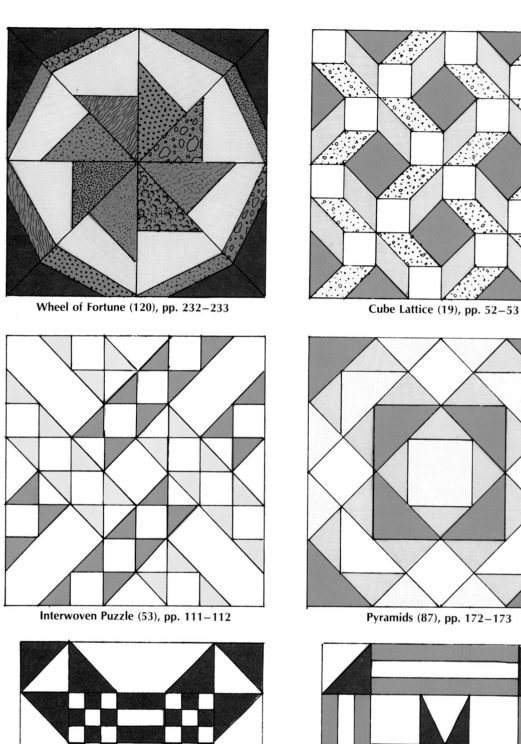

Wheel of Fortune (120), pp. 232–233

Cube Lattice (19), pp. 52–53

Interwoven Puzzle (53), pp. 111–112

Pyramids (87), pp. 172–173

Missouri Puzzle (72), pp. 142–143

Burnham Square (7), pp. 29–30

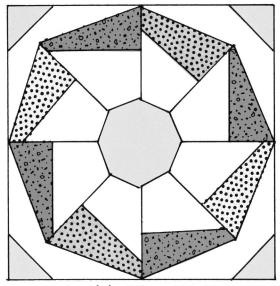

Saw Blades (90), pp. 177–178

World's Fair (123), pp. 238–239

Kansas Dust Storm (57), pp. 116–117

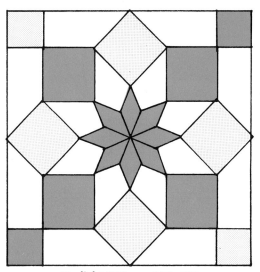

Starlight (99), pp. 195–196

Tangled Garter (107), pp. 212–213

Mollie's Choice (23), pp. 144–145

Pilot Wheel (82), pp. 159–160

Flower Basket (34), p. 77

Starry Path (101), pp. 199–200

Cathedral Window (9), pp. 33–34

Folded Star (39), pp. 84–85

Light & Shadow (62), p. 125

Circle & Star (12), pp. 39–40

Postage Stamp Baskets (85), pp. 166–168

Tile Puzzle (111), p. 219

Flyaway Feathers (36), pp. 79–80

Pigeon Toes (81), p. 158

Introduction

Whether you're a quilter or a collector, the quest for new patterns is unending. My collection numbers in the thousands, culled from such sources as the Ladies Art Company, the *Kansas City Star*, *Godey's Lady's Book*, *Hearth & Home* and other needlework magazines that were published up to the early part of this century. Choosing 120 patterns from this collection was difficult, and as my editor, Barbara Busch, pointed out to me, I got carried away and wound up with 124. Fortunately, in the final editing she only had to omit one.

The patterns range from easy to hard; from well-known designs such as Double Wedding Ring to more obscure patterns such as Spider's Den. Some of the patterns you may have never seen before since they were reproduced from museum quilts.

The book is broken down into two sections. In the first section you will find color pictures of 120 of the patterns given. The second section gives you the full-size patterns and piecing directions for each quilt. The colors used for the quilts in this section may not correspond to those used in the color section. This was done to offer you alternative color schemes. And if you don't like either one, make up your own. When choosing your own color scheme keep in mind the light and dark values. You can change a print to a plain or use all plain colors if desired as long as you maintain the balance of light and dark. Otherwise your design will get lost.

Most of the patterns do not include a seam allowance. How you cut your template is a matter of choice. Some people like to include the seam allowance so that when they trace around it they have a cutting line to follow. Others prefer that the seam allowance not be included so that when they trace around it they have a visible seamline to follow when sewing. With the second method you must remember to provide for the seam allowance when placing the template on the fabric.

In the instructions you'll find that many of the patterns call for the blocks to be set solid, or set without lattice strips or alternating plain blocks. This is a personal preference of mine. Some of the designs do have to be set solid to bring out an overall design that comes only when the blocks are joined together. But the vast majority of patterns can be set with alternating plain blocks or lattice strips and if you think a design would look better that way, go ahead and do it. You won't have to piece so many blocks either.

The quilting itself is another matter of personal preference. When the individual pieces are fairly small I prefer outline quilting, or quilting 1/8" on each side of all seams, to bring out the pattern. If the pieces are large, I shadow quilt 1/4" or 1/2" from the seamline quilting to fill the area. However, there are many ways you can quilt the top. You can ignore the pattern and make the quilting an allover design of scallops, diamonds or straight lines. You can work a circular design on the blocks if you think it will better set off the pattern. Or make up your own design to finish the quilt top.

Keep in mind that there is no right or wrong way to make your quilt. Feel free to experiment with colors, patterns, and techniques. If it doesn't turn out the way you thought it would, you still have a serviceable bedcover. Or, you may wind up with a masterpiece quilt.

Happy quilting!

METRIC EQUIVALENCY CHART

MM—MILLIMETRES   CM—CENTIMETRES

INCHES TO MILLIMETRES AND CENTIMETRES

INCHES	MM	CM	INCHES	CM	INCHES	CM
⅛	3	0.3	9	22.9	30	76.2
¼	6	0.6	10	25.4	31	78.7
⅜	10	1.0	11	27.9	32	81.3
½	13	1.3	12	30.5	33	83.8
⅝	16	1.6	13	33.0	34	86.4
¾	19	1.9	14	35.6	35	88.9
⅞	22	2.2	15	38.1	36	91.4
1	25	2.5	16	40.6	37	94.0
1¼	32	3.2	17	43.2	38	96.5
1½	38	3.8	18	45.7	39	99.1
1¾	44	4.4	19	48.3	40	101.6
2	51	5.1	20	50.8	41	104.1
2½	64	6.4	21	53.3	42	106.7
3	76	7.6	22	55.9	43	109.2
3½	89	8.9	23	58.4	44	111.8
4	102	10.2	24	61.0	45	114.3
4½	114	11.4	25	63.5	46	116.8
5	127	12.7	26	66.0	47	119.4
6	152	15.2	27	68.6	48	121.9
7	178	17.8	28	71.1	49	124.5
8	203	20.3	29	73.7	50	127.0

YARDS TO METRES

YARDS	METRES	YARDS	METRES	YARDS	METRES	YARDS	METRES	YARDS	METRES
⅛	0.11	2⅛	1.94	4⅛	3.77	6⅛	5.60	8⅛	7.43
¼	0.23	2¼	2.06	4¼	3.89	6¼	5.72	8¼	7.54
⅜	0.34	2⅜	2.17	4⅜	4.00	6⅜	5.83	8⅜	7.66
½	0.46	2½	2.29	4½	4.11	6½	5.94	8½	7.77
⅝	0.57	2⅝	2.40	4⅝	4.23	6⅝	6.06	8⅝	7.89
¾	0.69	2¾	2.51	4¾	4.34	6¾	6.17	8¾	8.00
⅞	0.80	2⅞	2.63	4⅞	4.46	6⅞	6.29	8⅞	8.12
1	0.91	3	2.74	5	4.57	7	6.40	9	8.23
1⅛	1.03	3⅛	2.86	5⅛	4.69	7⅛	6.52	9⅛	8.34
1¼	1.14	3¼	2.97	5¼	4.80	7¼	6.63	9¼	8.46
1⅜	1.26	3⅜	3.09	5⅜	4.91	7⅜	6.74	9⅜	8.57
1½	1.37	3½	3.20	5½	5.03	7½	6.86	9½	8.69
1⅝	1.49	3⅝	3.31	5⅝	5.14	7⅝	6.97	9⅝	8.80
1¾	1.60	3¾	3.43	5¾	5.26	7¾	7.09	9¾	8.92
1⅞	1.71	3⅞	3.54	5⅞	5.37	7⅞	7.20	9⅞	9.03
2	1.83	4	3.66	6	5.49	8	7.32	10	9.14

MODERATE

in color p. 9

BLOCK SIZE: 14″

QUILT SIZE: 84″ × 98″

NO. OF BLOCKS: 42

PIECES PER BLOCK:			PER QUILT:
A	1	Pink Print	42
B	4	Pink Print	168
	4	Red	168
C	16	Pink Print	672
D	4	Red	168
E	4	Red	168

FABRIC REQUIREMENTS:

Pink Print—8 yards
Red—6 yards

Make full-size template for Part A. Add 1/4″ seam allowance to all templates. Pattern pieces are on p. 20.

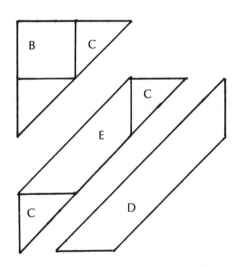

Cut out fabric. To assemble the block, follow the diagrams below:

Seam these completed units together to form the corners.

Stitch the completed corners to the diagonal edges of Part A.

This is the hardest step. Set in the pink Part B to complete the edges of the block. An easier method would be to turn under the seam allowances on three sides of Part B. Lay over the seam allowances of D and A and whipstitch in place.

The center of the A piece gives you a 10″ area for a feather motif or other fancy quilting.

Bind edges to complete.

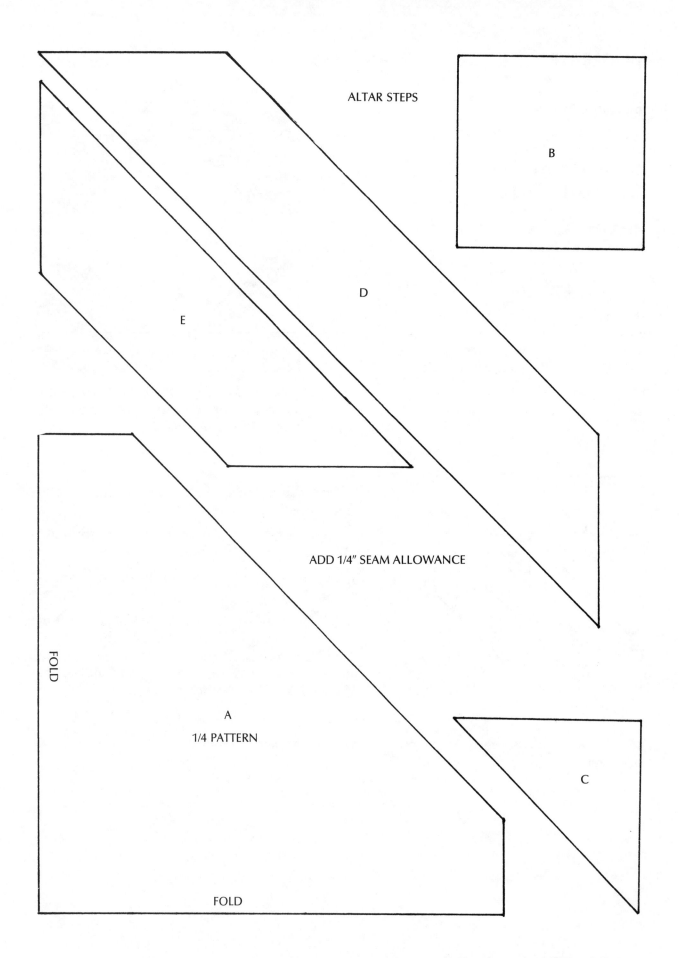

ALTAR STEPS

B

D

E

ADD 1/4" SEAM ALLOWANCE

FOLD

A
1/4 PATTERN

C

FOLD

in color p. 2

Scrap Fabrics

This Pennsylvania pattern dates from at latest, 1885. The entire top is made up of 5″ half-squares of light and dark scrap fabrics. The center is the only area that carries out the same colors.

The finished quilt is 87″ by 87″, 16 squares across by 16 squares down, with a 4″ border all around.

For the center, piece four squares using red and yellow. Then use a solid blue for the squares surrounding this center square. For the other squares, simply alternate light and dark fabrics, and set them together so that they form diagonal lines as shown in the above drawing.

Outline quilt along all seams.

ADD 1/4″ SEAM ALLOWANCE

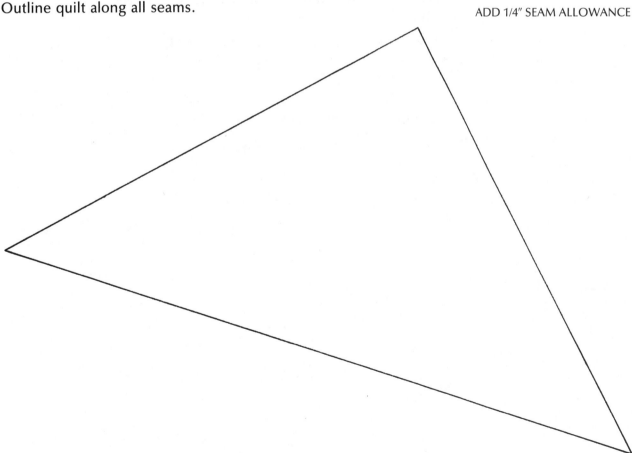

3. Block & Star

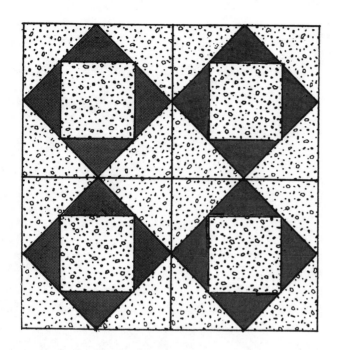

A Ladies Art Company pattern.

EASY

in color p. 2

BLOCK SIZE: 16″

QUILT SIZE: 80″ × 80″

NO. OF BLOCKS: 25

PIECES PER BLOCK:			PER QUILT
A	4	Print	100
B	16	Dark	400
C	16	Print	400

FABRIC REQUIREMENTS:

Print—3 3/4 yards
Dark—3 1/4 yards

This is a very easy pattern and should work up quickly. Pattern pieces are on facing page.

Start with the A-print center, add the dark B pieces to each side. Add the C-print pieces to form a square. Sew four completed squares together to form a block.

Since these are very large pieces, I recommend that you use an overall quilting pattern of diamonds or circles, ignoring the seams.

Bind the edges to complete the quilt.

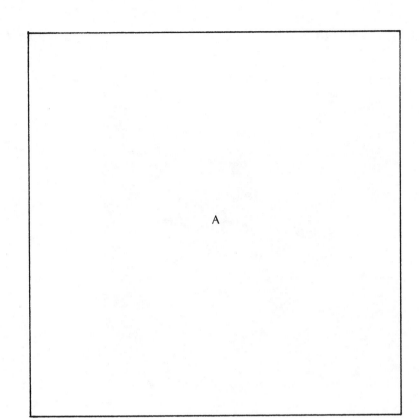

A

BLOCK & STAR

ADD 1/4″ SEAM ALLOWANCE

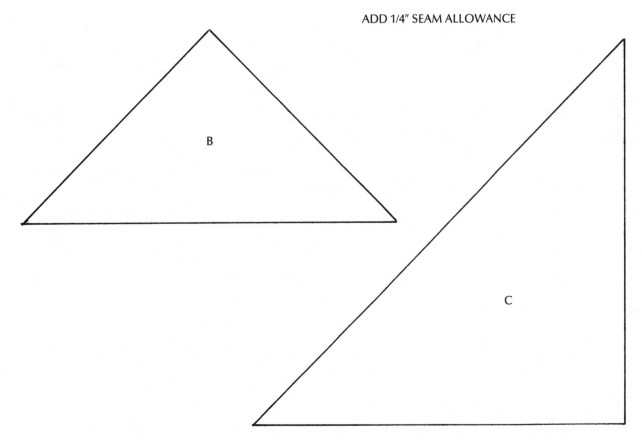

B

C

4. Blockade

A *Kansas City Star* pattern from 1938.

EASY

in color p. 4

BLOCK SIZE: 12″

QUILT SIZE: 80″ × 92″

NO. OF BLOCKS: 42 with a 4″ border

PIECES PER BLOCK:			PER QUILT:
A	4	Yellow Print	168
	4	Blue Print	168
B	4	White	168
C	4	Yellow Print	168
	4	Blue Print	168

FABRIC REQUIREMENTS:

Yellow Print—3 1/2 yards
Blue Print—3 1/2 yards
White—2 yards
Solid Yellow for Border—3 yards

The pattern given on p. 25 shows 1/4 of the block, and how it goes together. Stitch A to A, add B and C. Make four for each block and set together.

BORDER: Cut fabric into 4 1/2″ wide strips. You need two strips 73″ long and two strips 85″ long.

QUILTING: Quilt along each seamline, then space the lines of stitches 1″ away from each seam, filling the block.

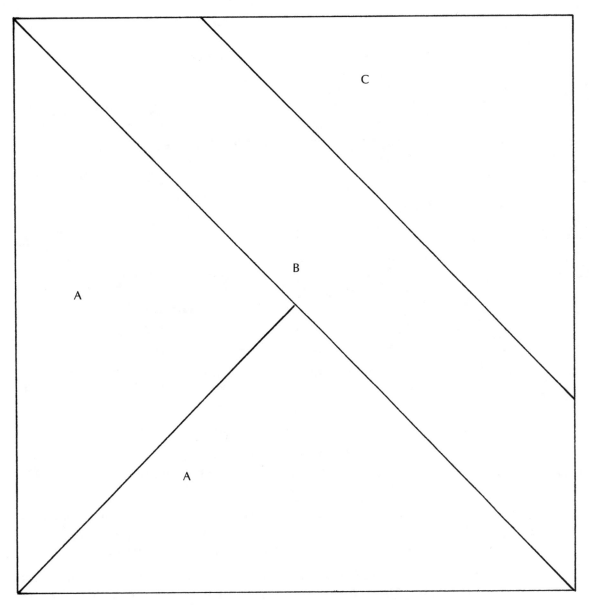

1/4 of the block, showing how it is set together

5. Breeches

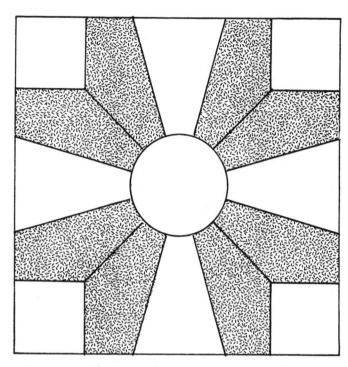

This is a somewhat difficult block because of the circular center.

in color p. 11

BLOCK SIZE: 10″

QUILT SIZE: 86″ × 96″

NO. OF BLOCKS: 36 Pieced
36 Plain

with a 3″ border

PIECES PER BLOCK:			PER QUILT:
A	1	White	36
B	8	Print	288
C	4	White	144
D	4	White	144

36 White 10 1/2″ squares

FABRIC REQUIREMENTS:

White—7 1/4 yards
Print—2 1/2 yards
(This can also be made up as a scrap quilt with different fabrics for each block.)

Cut out the pattern pieces adding 1/4″ seam allowance. For Part B, be sure to reverse 1/2 of the pieces needed or cut 144 with the template face up; turn it over to cut another 144 pieces.

Follow the pattern layout on p. 27 for placement of the pieces. This shows 1/4 of the block. To simplify sewing, piece the BCD pieces to form a square, then lay the circular center in and treat as an appliqué.

To turn under the seam allowance evenly, use the following method: Cut a template 3 1/2″ in diameter. Lay it in the center of the circle and run a basting stitch along the seam line. Pull the thread tightly around the template and press so that you have a sharp crease on the seamline. Remove template and sew down.

Set the completed blocks together, alternating a pieced and plain block, 8 across and 9 down.

For the border you need two strips 3 1/2″ × 87″ and two strips 3 1/2″ × 97″.

The plain blocks allow you to use a variety of quilting motifs. For the pieced blocks, outline quilt along each seam.

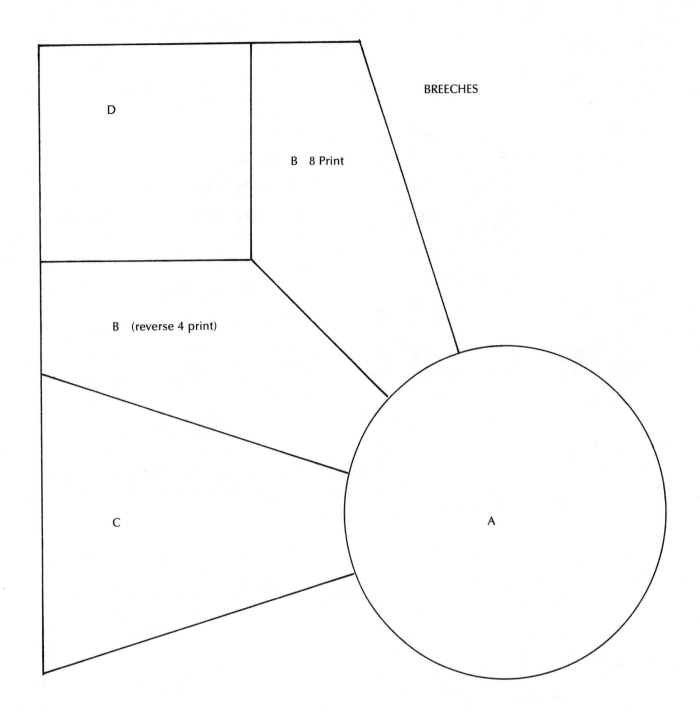

BREECHES

D

B   8 Print

B   (reverse 4 print)

C

A

ADD 1/4″ SEAM ALLOWANCE

6. Bridal Path

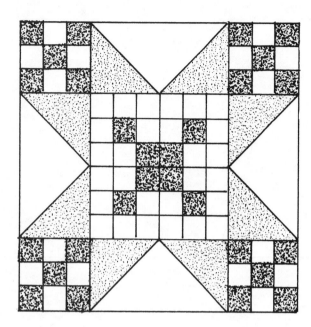

A *Kansas City Star* pattern, 1935.

EASY

in color p. 8

BLOCK SIZE: 12″

QUILT SIZE: 72″ × 84″

NO. OF BLOCKS: 42

PIECES PER BLOCK:			PER QUILT:
A	28	Dark	1176
	44	White	1848
B	4	White	168
C	8	Medium Print	336

FABRIC REQUIREMENTS:

White—5 1/2 yards
Dark—1 2/3 yards
Medium Print—1 3/4 yards

This is a very easy pattern to piece. Piece the nine-patch corner blocks and the center square. Make four units of BC and assemble following the diagram.

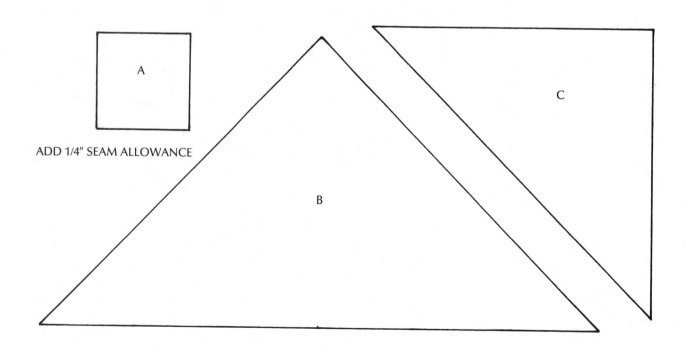

ADD 1/4″ SEAM ALLOWANCE

in color p. 14

BLOCK SIZE: 15″

QUILT SIZE: 75″ × 75″

NO. OF BLOCKS: 25

PIECES PER BLOCK:			**PER QUILT:**
A	4	White	100
	1	Dark	25
B	8	Dark	200
C	4	White	100
D	8	Print	200
	4	White	100
E	4	White	100
	4	Dark	100

FABRIC REQUIREMENTS:

White—3 2/3 yards
Dark—2 1/2 yards
Print—1 2/3 yards

This is another easy pattern that will work up quickly on the sewing machine. Pattern pieces are on p. 30.

TO ASSEMBLE: For center square, sew together four units of BCB. Rows one and three: Add the A square to each side of completed BCB unit. For center add BCB unit to each side of dark A unit.

Sew together four light and dark E pieces, and four print, white, print D pieces. Add one E unit to each end of D. Make two. Sew other two D units to each side of center square. Add ED units to top and bottom to complete block.

A small, circular quilting motif can be used in each 3″ square of the center block. Outline quilt along seams.

No border is necessary.

BURNHAM SQUARE

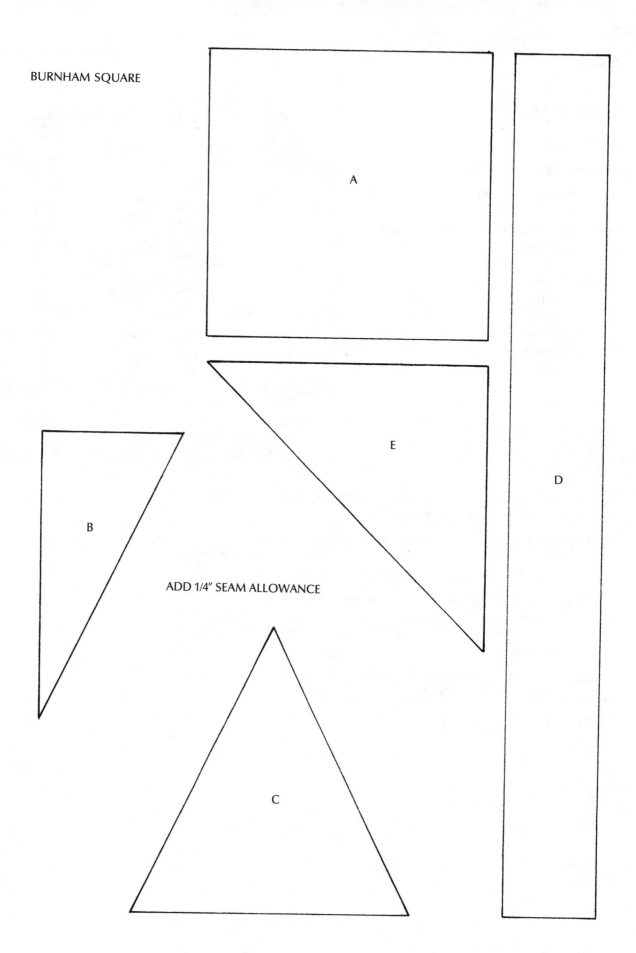

A

E

B

D

ADD 1/4" SEAM ALLOWANCE

C

in color p. 11

BLOCK SIZE: 12″

QUILT SIZE: 84″ × 84″

NO. OF BLOCKS: 49

PIECES PER BLOCK:			**PER QUILT:**
A	1	Light	49
B	8	Medium Print	392
C	8	Dark Plain	392
D	8	Light	392
E	4	Dark Print	196

FABRIC REQUIREMENTS:

Light—4 1/4 yards
Medium Print—1 2/3 yards
Dark Plain—2 1/4 yards
Dark Print—2 1/3 yards

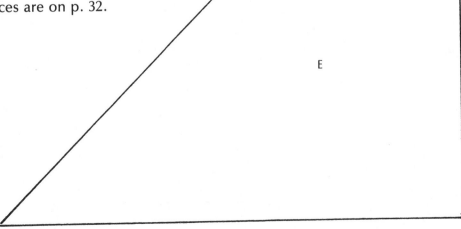

This is difficult to piece, but well worth the effort.

The easiest way to tackle this pattern would be to assemble the outer rows then lay the A piece in to complete.

Stitch the B and C pieces together. Set in the D pieces; add the corner E pieces. Turn under the seam allowance on the A piece and pin in place over the seam allowance of the BC pieces. Stitch in place.

Use a small decorative motif for the center A piece, then outline quilt around the remaining pieces.

No border is necessary for this quilt, but if you want one you could eliminate some blocks and add a border using one of the colors of the quilt top.

Remaining pattern pieces are on p. 32.

E

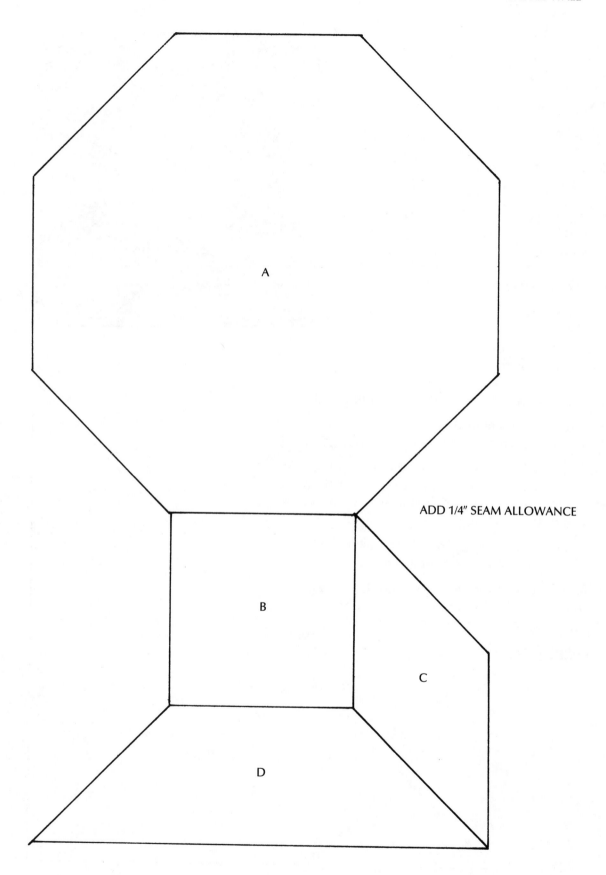

ADD 1/4″ SEAM ALLOWANCE

in color p. 16

BLOCK SIZE: 11″

QUILT SIZE: 77″ × 88″

NO. OF BLOCKS: 56

PIECES PER BLOCK: **PER QUILT:**
A 16 Plain   896
B 24 Print   1344

FABRIC REQUIREMENTS:

Plain—2 1/3 yards
Print—Assorted scraps or 2 yards

This is a lovely pattern when made up and lends itself to infinite variations in color. It is usually done with unbleached muslin for the background and scraps of cloth to fill the "windows." It can also be carried out in a color-coordinated fashion. For example, you could use a dark blue for the background squares and fill in the windows with one or more color-coordinated prints.

The real beauty of this quilt is that it requires no filling, no backing and is finished when you take the last stitch on the last window. No quilting is required.

TO CONSTRUCT THE QUILT: Cut a 6″ square. Turn under a 1/4″ seam allowance on all sides. Mark the exact center of the square by measuring diagonally from corner to corner and placing a small mark where the lines intersect.

Fold each corner to the center point and press. Fold the resulting corners to the middle again. Press and pin down. Stitch the points down securely.

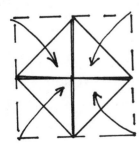

Square now measures 2 3/4″

Complete 16 such squares to make one block. When all squares are ready, join them side by side with a slipstitch.

Lay one of the 1 1/2″ squares over the seam of two adjoining squares. Fold the free edges over the "window fabric" and stitch. This will form a curved frame around the window.

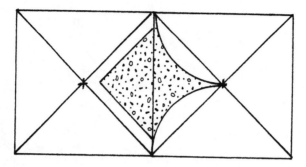

The edge can be filled in with a half "window" or left flat, forming a border around the quilt.

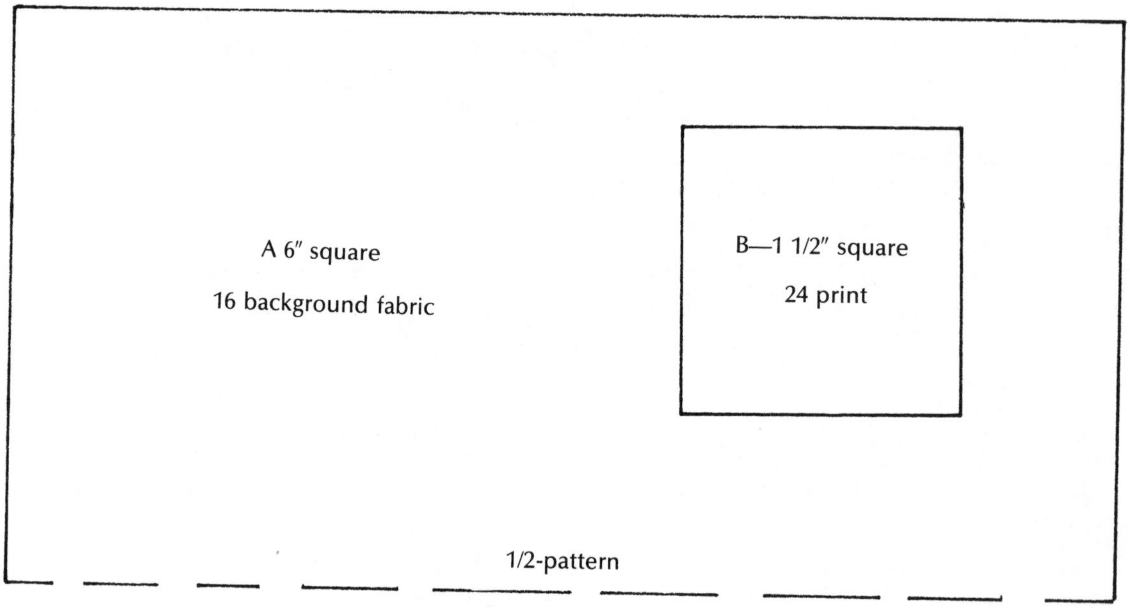

A 6″ square

16 background fabric

B—1 1/2″ square

24 print

1/2-pattern

[SEAM ALLOWANCE IS INCLUDED IN PATTERN]

Cathedral Window is the most common name for this pattern, but, among other names, it has been called Stained Glass Windows and Attic Windows.

in color p. 7

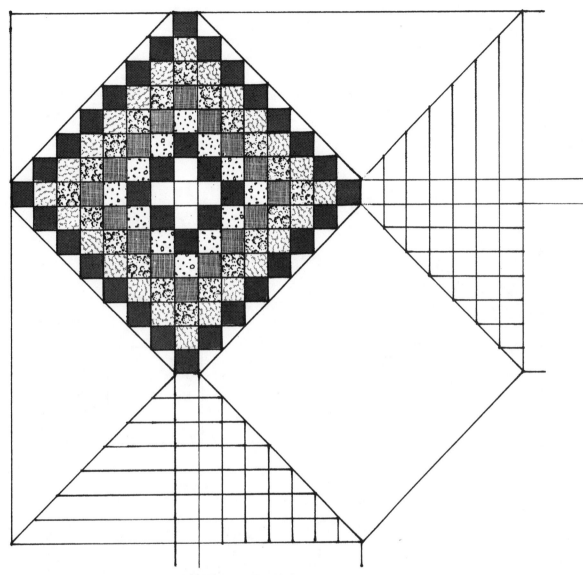

QUILT SIZE: 75″ × 90″

NO. OF BLOCKS: 30
pieced, 20 Plain

FABRIC REQUIREMENTS:

White—4 2/3 yards
6 different fabrics
per block for Part A

This pattern dates to at latest 1870 and you should have no trouble piecing it if you follow the drawing.

For the plain blocks, cut a 10″ square, adding 1/4″ seam allowance or a finished size of 10 1/2″. For the half-blocks, enlarge Part C as indicated.

Outline quilt along each side of each seam, carrying the lines of stitching across the plain blocks. Or you can work a fancy design in the plain blocks.

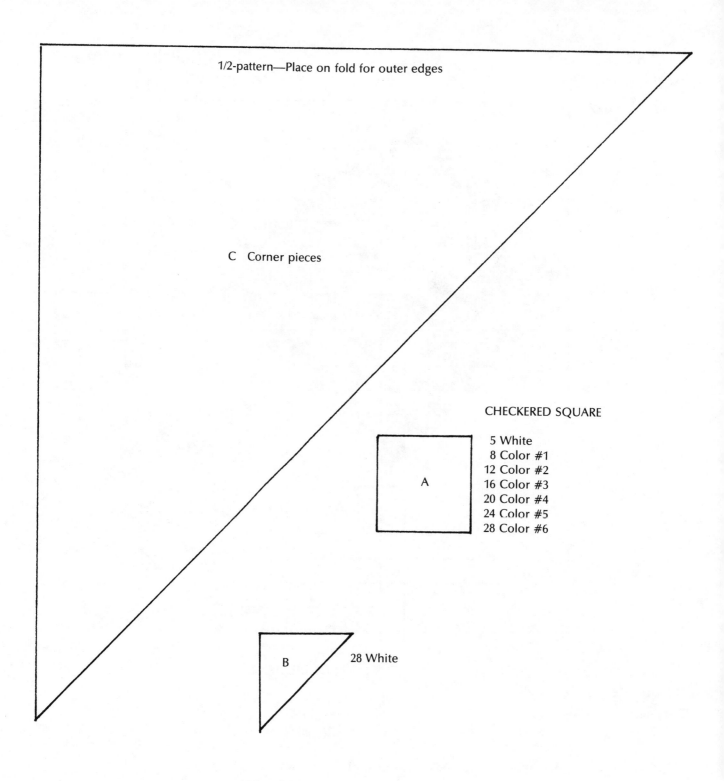

1/2-pattern—Place on fold for outer edges

C   Corner pieces

CHECKERED SQUARE

A

5 White
8 Color #1
12 Color #2
16 Color #3
20 Color #4
24 Color #5
28 Color #6

B   28 White

ADD 1/4″ SEAM ALLOWANCE

Plain blocks are 10″ square plus seam allowance

in color p. 10

BLOCK SIZE: 16"

QUILT SIZE: 84" × 100"

NO. OF BLOCKS: 20
Plus border

PIECES PER BLOCK:			PER QUILT:
A	24	Green	480
	16	Dark Yellow	320
	8	Medium Yellow	160
	8	Light Yellow	160
	4	Red	80
B	8	Medium Yellow	160
C	8	Light Yellow	160
D	4	Green	80

FABRIC REQUIREMENTS:

Green—3 yards
Dark Yellow—1 1/2 yards
Medium Yellow—1 yard
Light Yellow—1 yard
Red—1/3 yard

FABRIC FOR BORDER:

Green—3 3/4 yards
Yellow—1 1/2 yards

This is a fairly easy pattern to piece once you get the color placement firmly in mind.

Cut out pattern pieces on p. 38, adding 1/4" seam allowance. Be sure to reverse half of the Part A, Part B and Part C pieces before cutting.

For ease in piecing, divide the block into quarters and stitch each quarter following the diagram. Join the completed quarters to form the whole block.

BORDER: The border is made up of an 8" wide strip of plain green and a 2" wide sawtooth strip of green and yellow.

Cut four strips of green measuring 8 1/2" wide by 80 1/2" long. Sew one strip to each of the 80" sides of the quilt. Sew the other two strips across the top and bottom.

Cut out 180 green Part A's and 180 yellow Part A's. Stitch together to form a square. Sew two strips of 48 squares and two strips of 42 squares. Sew the 48-square strips to the sides of the quilt and the 42-square strips to the top and bottom of the quilt.

Quilt along the seams of each block and use a wide cable pattern for the 8" green strip in the border.

CHRYSANTHEMUM

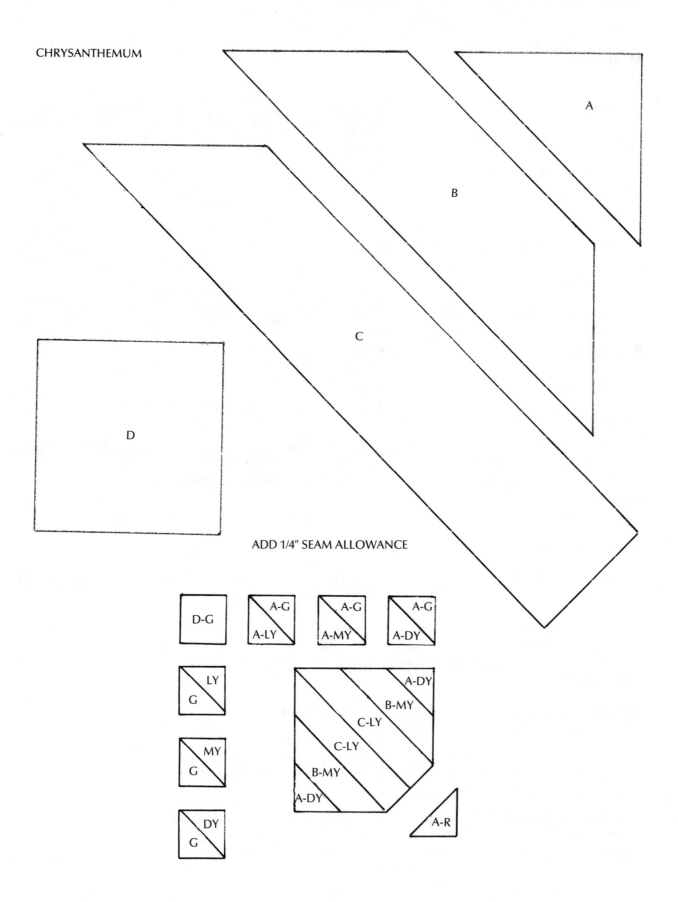

A

B

C

D

ADD 1/4" SEAM ALLOWANCE

D-G

A-G
A-LY

A-G
A-MY

A-G
A-DY

LY
G

MY
G

DY
G

A-DY
B-MY
C-LY
C-LY
B-MY
A-DY

A-R

in color p. 16

BLOCK SIZE: 12″

QUILT SIZE: 72″ × 72″

NO. OF BLOCKS: 36

PIECES PER BLOCK:			PER QUILT:
A	4	Print	144
B	8	White	288
C	4	Dark	144
D	4	White	144
E	8	Dark	288
F	4	White	144
G	4	White	144
H	4	Dark	144

FABRIC REQUIREMENTS:

Print—1/2 yard
White—3 3/4 yards
Dark—6 3/4 yards

This pattern appeared in *Hearth & Home* magazine in 1927.

This is a difficult pattern to piece because of all the curves.

Begin in the center and work outward in rows. The pattern on p. 41 shows how the pieces go together.

Outline quilting along each seam would show the design to best advantage.

If desired, a border could be added to enlarge the size of the quilt. A 12″ border would be a good size, bringing the finished quilt to 84″ by 84″. You could embellish this with a scallop design along the edge to tie into the quilt top.

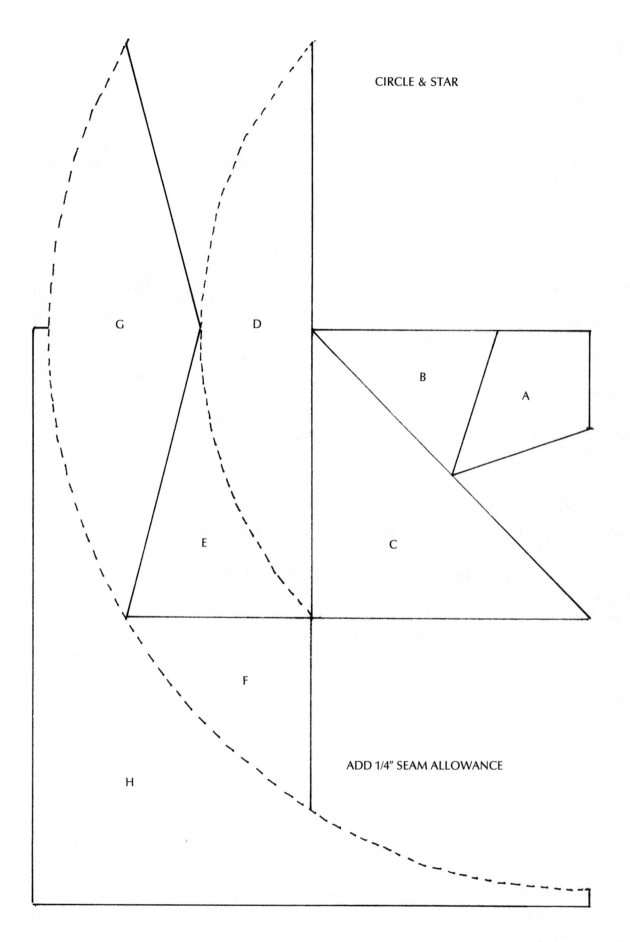

CIRCLE & STAR

B

A

G

D

E

C

F

ADD 1/4" SEAM ALLOWANCE

H

in color p. 13

BLOCK SIZE: 15″

QUILT SIZE: 75″ × 75″

NO. OF BLOCKS: 25

PIECES PER BLOCK:

			PER QUILT:
A	6	Light Green	150
	6	Dark Green	150
B	4	White	100
C	3	White	75
	4	Red	100
	2	Pink	50

FABRIC REQUIREMENTS:

Light Green—2 1/4 yards
Dark Green—2 1/4 yards
White—2 3/4 yards
Pink—1/2 yard
Red—1 yard

This is a Nancy Cabot pattern which appeared in the *Chicago Tribune* during the 1930's.

Add 1/4″ seam allowance and cut out pattern pieces. For Part A, reverse 1/2 of the required pieces. This is a fairly easy pattern to piece and you shouldn't have much trouble if you just follow the diagram. The diagram shows four blocks set together. Note that each block reverses the pattern.

A border could be added to the completed quilt but is not necessary. A simple binding is sufficient.

Quilting should follow the seamlines of each piece.

CLIMBING ROSES

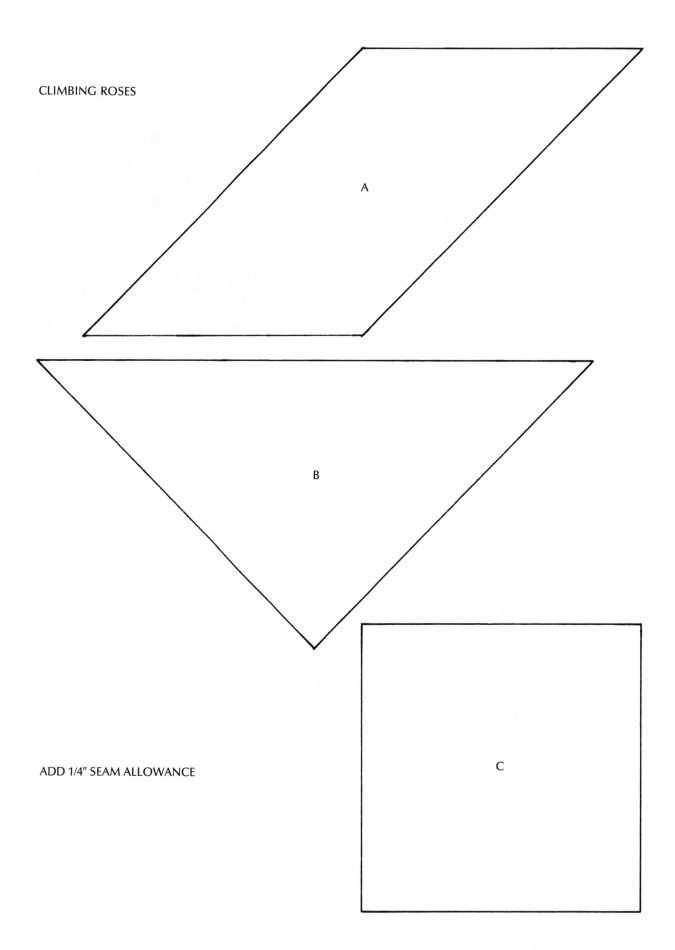

A

B

ADD 1/4" SEAM ALLOWANCE

C

in color p. 12

BLOCK SIZE: 12″

QUILT SIZE: 84″ × 96″

NO. OF BLOCKS: 56

PIECES PER BLOCK:			PER QUILT:
A	2	Yellow Print	112
	2	Blue Print	112
B	4	Blue Print	224
C	6	Red Plain	336
	6	White Plain	336

FABRIC REQUIREMENTS:

Yellow Print—1 1/4 yards
Blue Print—2 1/2 yards
Red Plain—2 1/4 yards
White Plain—2 1/4 yards

ADD 1/4″ SEAM ALLOWANCE

TO ASSEMBLE: Set aside the yellow and blue A pieces. Seam the plain red to plain white C pieces; add the corner B blue print to form a square, following the color placement in the above diagram.

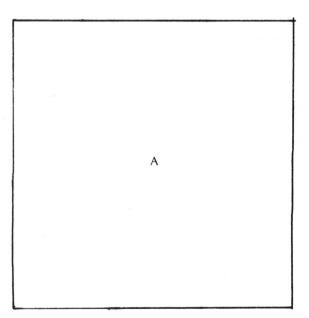

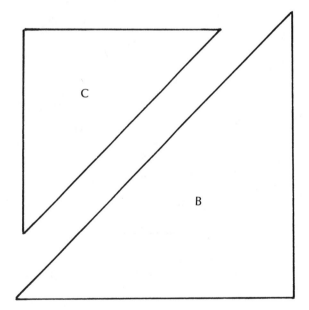

Stitch the completed small squares to form the larger block. In setting the quilt, I have rotated every other block a quarter turn to create more movement in the finished design.

This quilt requires no border, just a narrow binding around the edges. Outline quilt along each seam.

15. Country Roads

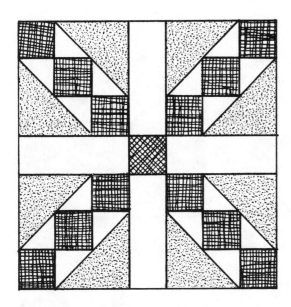

in color p. 9

BLOCK SIZE: 14″

QUILT SIZE: 84″ × 84″

NO. OF BLOCKS: 36

PIECES PER BLOCK:			PER QUILT:
A	4	Yellow	144
B	13	Brown	468
C	16	Yellow	576
D	8	Green	288

FABRIC REQUIREMENTS:

Yellow—5 yards
Brown—2 2/3 yards
Green—3 1/2 yards

This is another easy pattern.

Cut out pattern pieces on p. 45, adding 1/4″ seam allowance. Piece the four corner squares then set together with the center strips.

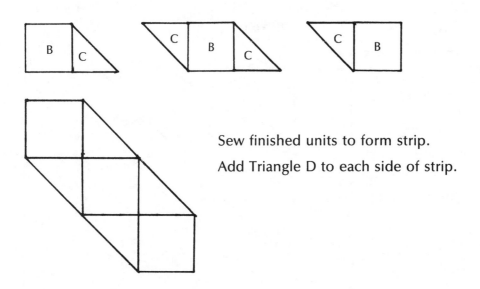

Sew finished units to form strip.

Add Triangle D to each side of strip.

A border is optional and the quilt can be bound off.

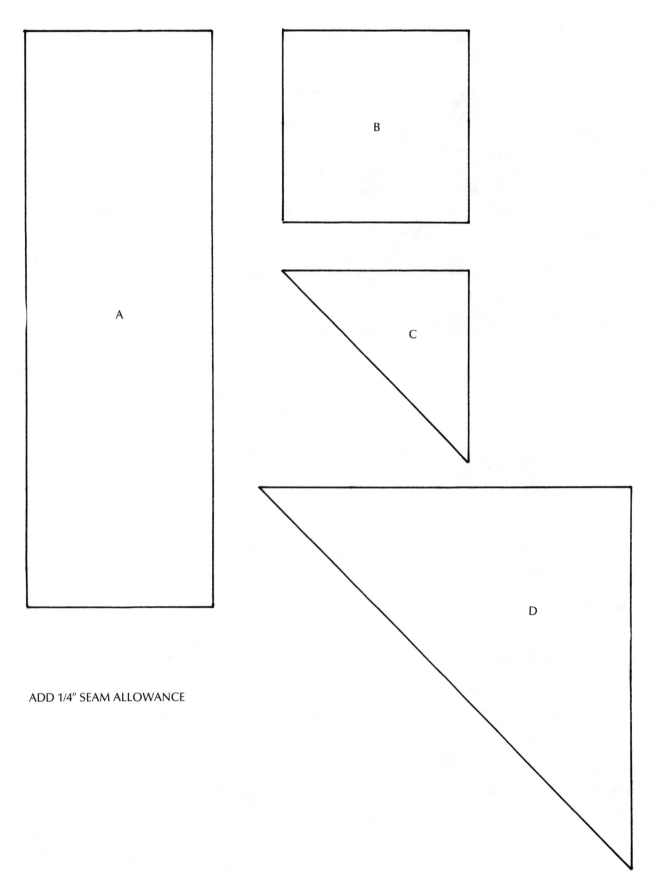

ADD 1/4″ SEAM ALLOWANCE

16. County Fair

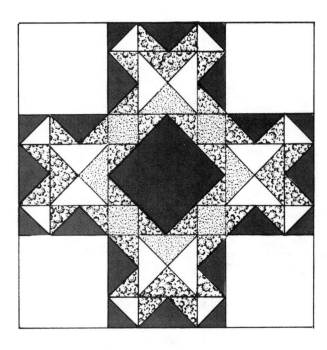

MODERATE

in color p. 13

BLOCK SIZE: 15"

QUILT SIZE: 90" × 90"

NO. OF BLOCKS: 36

PIECES PER BLOCK:			PER QUILT:
A	1	Blue	36
B	32	Dark Print	1152
	8	White	288
	8	Blue	288
C	4	Yellow Print	144
D	4	Dark Print	144
	8	White	288
	4	Yellow Print	144
	12	Blue	432
E	4	White	144

At first glance this pattern may appear a trifle intimidating, but it's more busy than difficult. Just break it down into its nine basic squares, assemble each one, then set them together. It's all straight-seam sewing. Your only difficulty may be in keeping the colors straight.

If you wish, you could alternate pieced and plain blocks rather than using all pieced. This would cut down the amount of work involved and give you some plain blocks for your fancy quilting.

To carry out the theme of the title, I thought yellow, white and blue would be most appropriate, but you could use any color scheme.

Other pattern pieces p. 47.

E

FABRIC REQUIREMENTS:

White—4 1/3 yards
Dark Print—3 1/2 yards
Blue—3 1/4 yards
Yellow Print—1 yard

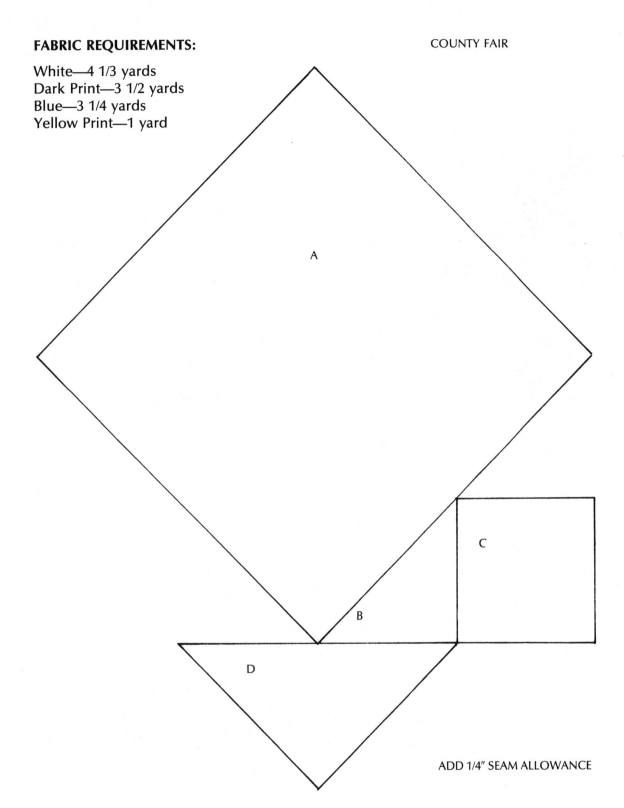

A

B

C

D

ADD 1/4" SEAM ALLOWANCE

17. Cowboy Star

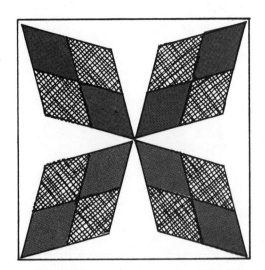

A Nancy Page pattern dating from about 1860. It is also known as Arkansas Traveller and Travel Star. Pattern pieces are on p. 49.

MODERATE

in color p. 13

BLOCK SIZE: 10″

QUILT SIZE: 80″ × 80″

NO. OF BLOCKS: 72

PIECES PER BLOCK:			PER QUILT:
A	8	Plain	576
	8	Print	576
B	4	White	288
C	4	White	288
D	8	White	576

FABRIC REQUIREMENTS:

Plain Dark—3 1/2 yards
Print—3 1/2 yards
White—5 yards

This is a fairly easy pattern to piece. A secondary star pattern emerges as the blocks are joined.

Piece the large diamonds using Part A as shown. Add Part D to the outside edge of the completed diamond. Piece C to B, then join two diamonds together with CB.

Quilt 1/8″ on each side of the seam of the diamond shape. The secondary star pattern could be quilted using a shadow pattern. To shadow quilt, quilt 1/8″ from the seam, then space rows of stitching 1/2″ apart to fill in the space.

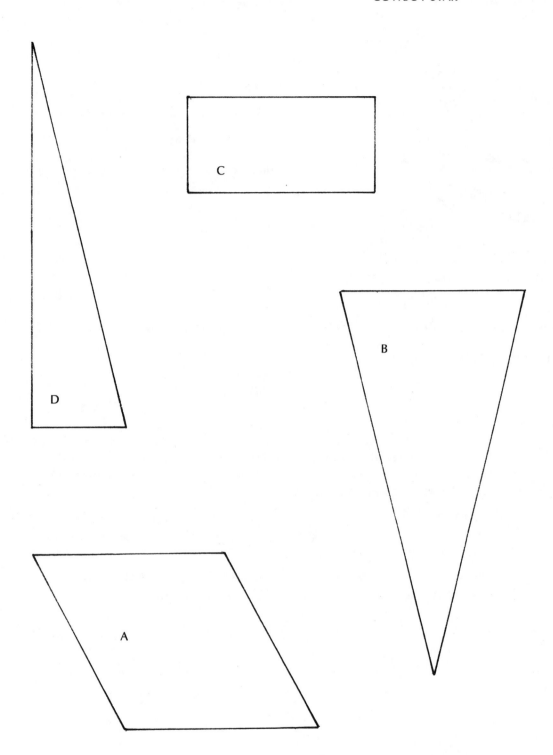

ADD 1/4" SEAM ALLOWANCE

18. Crossroads to Texas

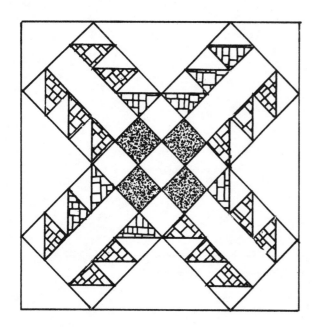

A Ladies Art Company pattern. Pattern pieces are on p. 51.

MODERATE

in color p. 4

BLOCK SIZE: 12 3/4"

QUILT SIZE: 76 1/2" × 89 1/4"

NO. OF BLOCKS: 42

PIECES PER BLOCK:			PER QUILT:
A	4	Dark	168
	5	White	210
B	24	Print	1008
	24	White	1008
C	4	White	168
D	4	White	168
E	4	White	168

FABRIC REQUIREMENTS:

Dark—1/4 yard
White—8 yards
Print—3 yards

Piece the nine-patch center, using Part A. Piece the print and white Part B into a square, then sew into a strip. Set two with a plain white C between. Sew two such completed strips to each side of the center square. Add E to each end.

For the remaining two BC strips, sew Part D to each side, and add the corner E piece. Sew these two completed units to each side of the center strip you have already formed.

An overall quilting design could be used, or you could quilt along each seam and place a fancy motif in the square formed by the joined blocks.

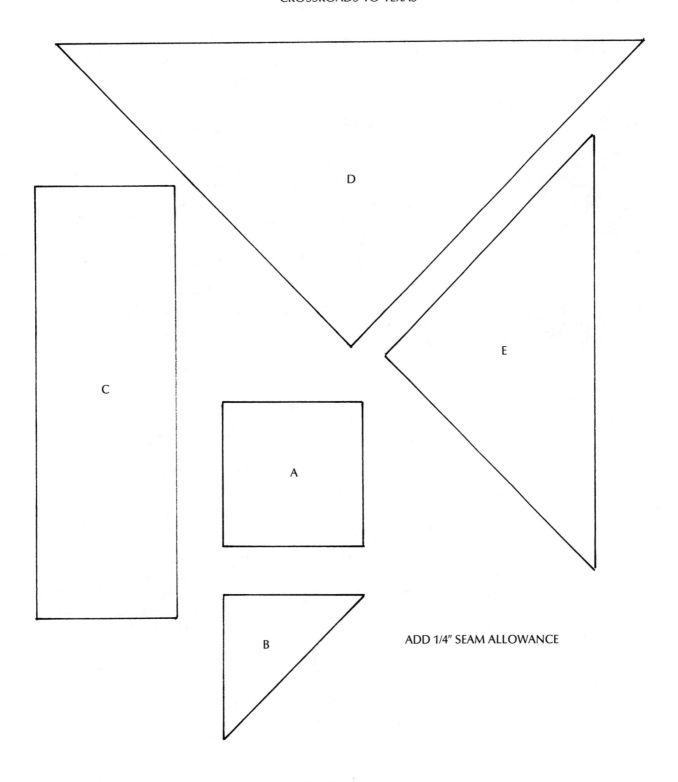

ADD 1/4″ SEAM ALLOWANCE

19. Cube Lattice

A Ladies Art Company pattern. Pattern pieces p. 53.

MODERATE

in color p. 14

BLOCK SIZE: 16″

QUILT SIZE: 80″ × 80″

NO. OF BLOCKS: 25

PIECES PER BLOCK:			PER QUILT:
A	16	White or Light	400
B	16	Light Print	400
	16	Dark Print	400
C	4	Dark Plain	100
D	8	Dark Plain	200

FABRIC REQUIREMENTS:

White or Light—1 2/3 yards
Light Print—2 1/2 yards
Dark Print—2 1/2 yards
Dark Plain—2 1/4 yards

This is a very striking quilt when made up in harmonizing shades of light and dark, print and plain. It's a moderately difficult pattern to piece, mainly because of the number of pieces that have to be set in and the corners that must be pivoted. Great care in sewing is necessary so that the pieces will lay flat and line up evenly.

Sew together the light and dark Parts B, then set in the A,C and D pieces, following the diagram.

If you prefer, you can convert this pattern to all straight-seam sewing for piecing on the machine. In this instance, you will use only Part A and the part designated "for simplified piecing." The block now becomes a series of Part A and two half-square triangles, sewing in the appropriate colors to form a square. The completed squares are then set together, following the diagram.

The illustration below shows the top row:

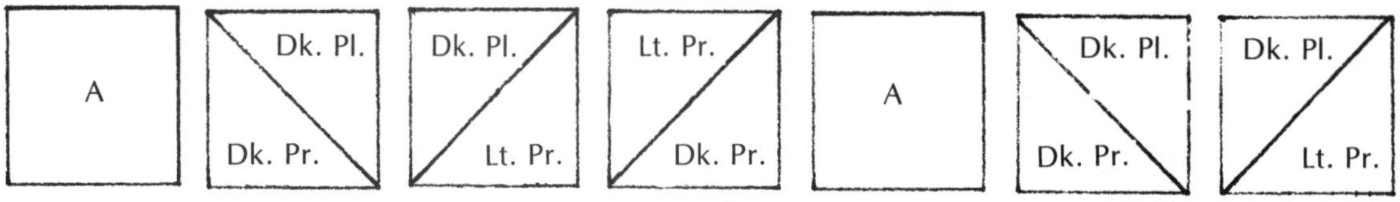

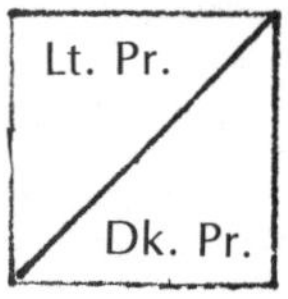

A border can be used if desired.

Outline quilt along each seamline.

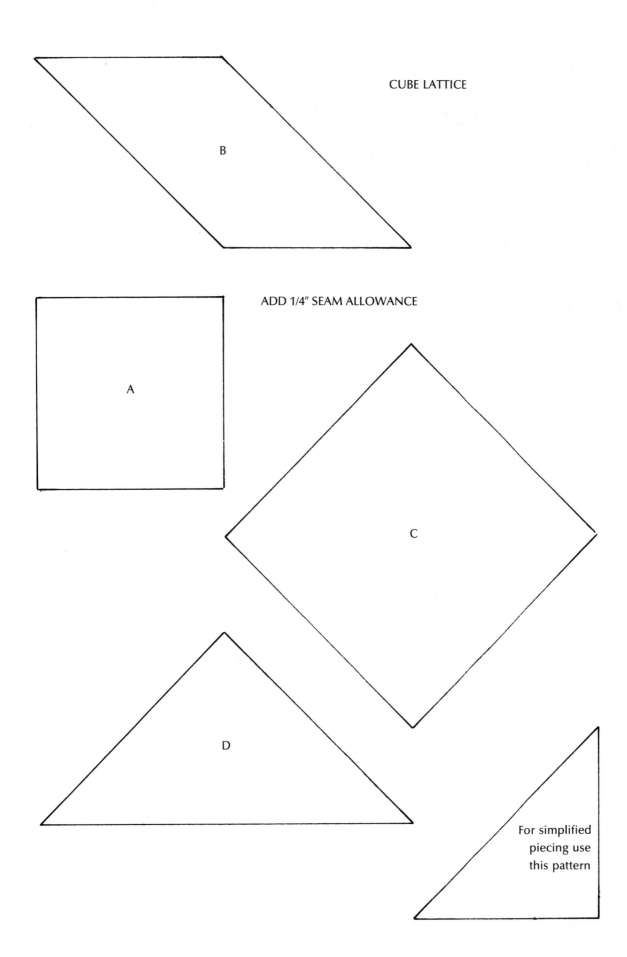

CUBE LATTICE

B

ADD 1/4" SEAM ALLOWANCE

A

C

D

For simplified
piecing use
this pattern

20. Cubist Rose

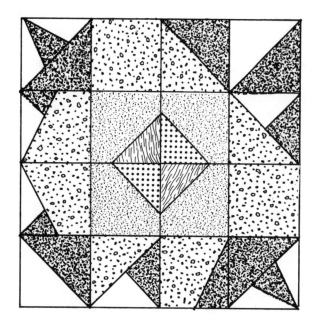

A Nancy Cabot pattern.

This pattern has a lot of pieces but is easy to put together. Break the block down into twelve 3″ squares and assemble each square. Then set the squares together. It is all straight-seam piecing. Pattern pieces on p. 55.

in color p. 8

BLOCK SIZE: 12″

QUILT SIZE: 96″ × 96″

NO. OF BLOCKS: 36 with a 12″ border

PIECES PER BLOCK:			PER QUILT:
A	5	Green	180
	2	White	72
	3	Yellow	108
B	2	Green	72
C	4	White	144
D	1	Green	36
E	1	Yellow	36
F	2	Green	72
	2	White	72
G	2	Yellow	72
H	2	Green	72
I	2	White	72
J	4	Pink Print #1	144
K	2	Pink Print #2	72
	2	Pink Print #3	72
L		Yellow 3″ Square 2	72

FABRIC REQUIREMENTS:

Green—2 1/4 yards
Yellow—2 yards
Pink Print #2—1/3 yard
White—1 1/2 yards
Pink Print #1—1 1/4 yards
Pink Print #3—1/3 yard

For border you will need 3 1/4 yards of one of the colors you use in the top.

BORDER: Cut two strips 12 1/2″ × 72 1/2″ and two strips 12 1/2″ × 96 1/2″.

Quilt along each seamline. For the border, you can use a floral or cable pattern for quilting.

CUBIST ROSE

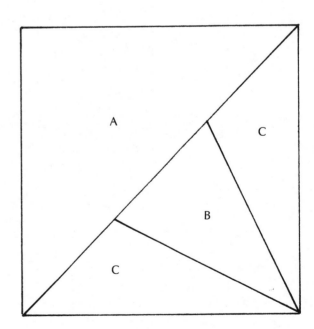

ADD 1/4" SEAM ALLOWANCE

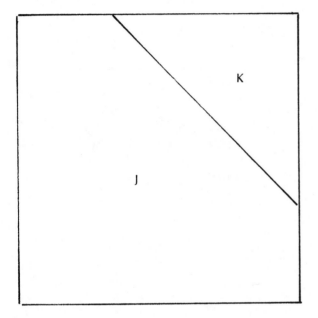

PART L is a 3" square

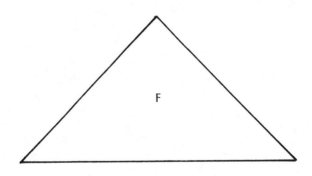

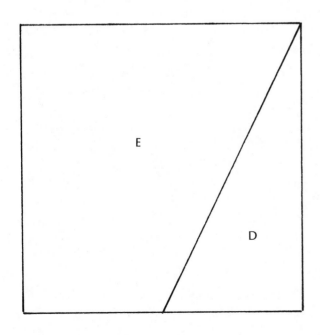

21. Diamond Chain

This pattern is a variation of World Without End or Kaleidoscope, the main difference being that this version is made up entirely of scrap diamonds. Pattern pieces on p. 57.

MODERATE

in color p. 10

BLOCK SIZE: 8″

QUILT SIZE: 80″ × 80″

NO. OF BLOCKS: 100

PIECES PER QUILT:
A   81
B   100   White
C   40

FABRIC REQUIREMENTS:

81 assorted fabrics, print and plain, measuring 8 1/2″ × 4 1/2″
40 assorted fabrics, print and plain, measuring 8 1/2″ × 2 1/2″
6 1/4 yards white

Cut templates, adding 1/4″ seam allowance. Part B as given is only 1/2 of the pattern, so trace this half onto your template material, then turn it over, match the fold lines and trace again. Part C is 1/2 of Part A, as shown by the dashed line.

The design is pieced in rows rather than as blocks. Begin with a Part C, join to B, then add AB, AB, across the row until you have ten Part B's. End with another C. Set in Part C's across the top of the row, then Part A's on the bottom and begin another row, joining the rows as each one is completed.

If you have any difficulty pivoting at the center points (the fabric puckers instead of lying flat) you might want to try this method. Mark seamline on all fabric pieces. Turn under seam allowance on diamond shapes. Line up folded edge of diamond with seamline on Part B. Pin in place. Whipstitch pieces together as for appliqué.

DIAMOND CHAIN

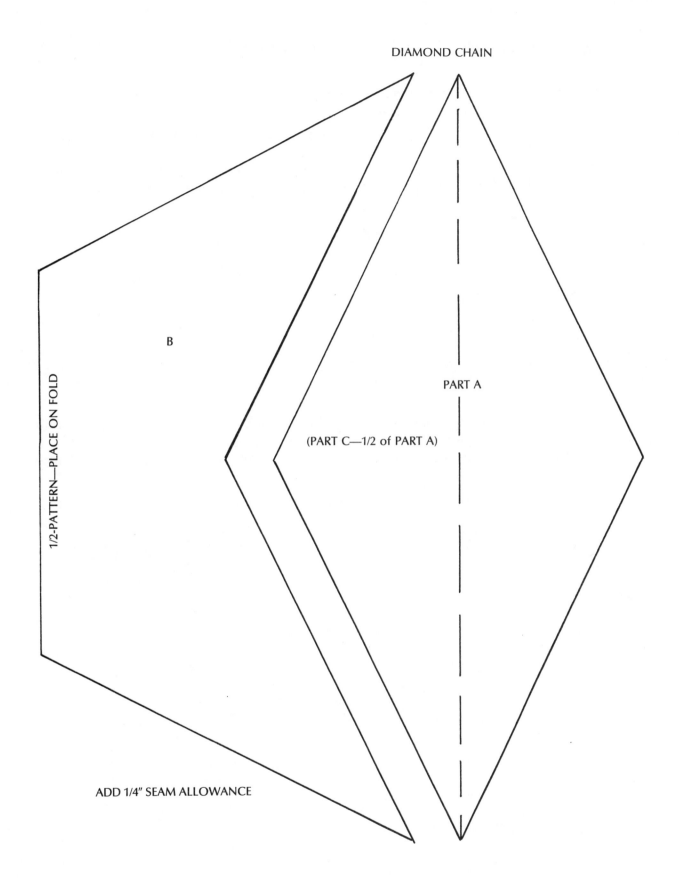

B

1/2-PATTERN—PLACE ON FOLD

PART A

(PART C—1/2 of PART A)

ADD 1/4″ SEAM ALLOWANCE

Diamond Chain ☆ *57*

22. Diamond 9-Patch

MODERATE

in color p. 5

This is a marvelous pattern for using up all those odds and ends of fabric scraps. Each diamond is made up of print and plain fabrics, with continuity provided by using the same color throughout for the squares.

Piece the diamonds, and join to **a** square. Just keep adding units until the quilt is the size you want. The edges are going to be jagged, so it will be necessary to measure each side to the desired size, mark it and cut it off square. Bind the edges.

Outline quilt each diamond shape or work parallel lines over the entire top.

One 7″ square.

ADD 1/4″ SEAM ALLOWANCE

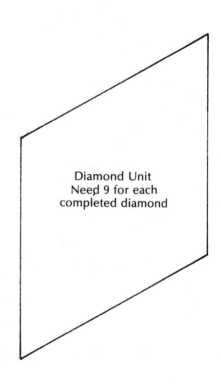

Diamond Unit
Need 9 for each
completed diamond

MODERATE

in color p. 13

BLOCK SIZE: 20″ (both the curved and square)

QUILT SIZE: 80″ × 80″

NO. OF BLOCKS: 16

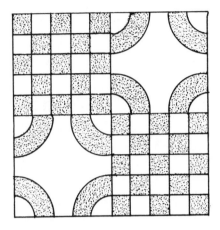

PIECES PER BLOCK:			PER QUILT:
A	26	Pink or Green	416
	42	White	672
B	8	White	128
C	8	Pink or Green	128
D	8	White	128

FABRIC REQUIREMENTS:

Pink—3 yards
White—4 yards

A pattern combining elements of both patterns appeared in the *Kansas City Star* in 1934. This pattern was more elaborate than either of these two, and I would assume that over the years various quiltmakers worked with the pattern, devising both these variations.

Both patterns consist of two blocks, one curved, the other set with the square pieces. Domino Chain adds strips between the blocks for a totally different effect. Dogwood Blossoms is very easy if you will just follow the diagram for piecing. Pattern pieces are on p. 60.

Domino Chain appears a little confusing, but if you remember that the main block is made up of nine 2″ squares you should have little trouble.

MODERATE

24. Domino Chain

BLOCK SIZE: 18″

QUILT SIZE: 84″ × 84″

NO. OF BLOCKS: 16

PIECES PER BLOCK:			PER QUILT:
A	20	Print	320
	21	White	336
B	8	White	128
C	8	Print	128
D	8	White	128

FABRIC REQUIREMENTS:

Print—3 1/4 yards
White—4 1/4 yards

DOGWOOD BLOSSOMS

DOMINO CHAIN

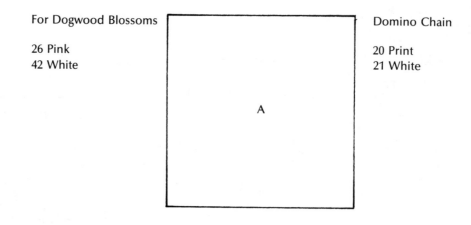

For Dogwood Blossoms

26 Pink
42 White

A

Domino Chain

20 Print
21 White

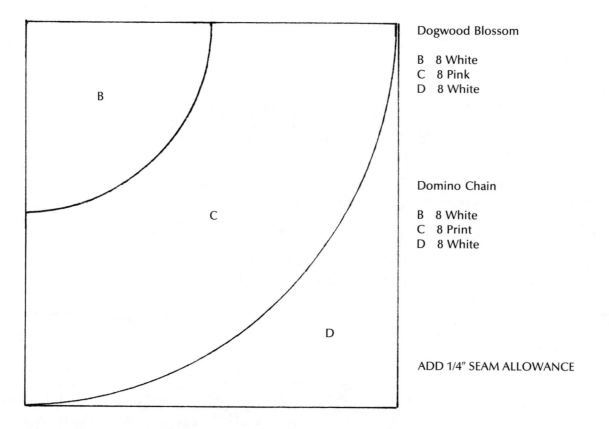

B

C

D

Dogwood Blossom

B   8 White
C   8 Pink
D   8 White

Domino Chain

B   8 White
C   8 Print
D   8 White

ADD 1/4" SEAM ALLOWANCE

FOR DOMINO CHAIN: When doing the joining strips, instead of using
9 Part A, you can make one long strip measuring 2" × 7", then use Part A
for the 9-patch section, thus cutting Part A down to 2.

DOUBLE IRISH CHAIN VARIATIONS

EASY

in color p. 13

BLOCK SIZE: 10″

QUILT SIZE: 90″ × 90″

NO. OF BLOCKS: 81

25. Variation I

PIECES PER BLOCK:			PER QUILT:
BLOCK A—need 41			
A	9	Print	369
	12	Plain	492
	4	White	164
BLOCK B—need 40			
A	4	Plain	160
B	8	Print	320
C	1	White	40

FABRIC REQUIREMENTS:

Print—2 3/4 yards
Plain—2 2/3 yards
White—4 yards

Both of these patterns are very easy to piece and each will make up into a striking quilt. By changing the colors you can come up with an almost infinite variety of quilts from either of these patterns.

26. Variation II

EASY

PIECES PER BLOCK:			PER QUILT
BLOCK A—need 41			
A	9	Dark Print	369
	4	Plain	164
	4	White	164
B	8	White	328
	8	Light Print	328
BLOCK B—need 40			
B	4	White	160
	8	Plain	320
	4	Light Print	160
C	1	White	40

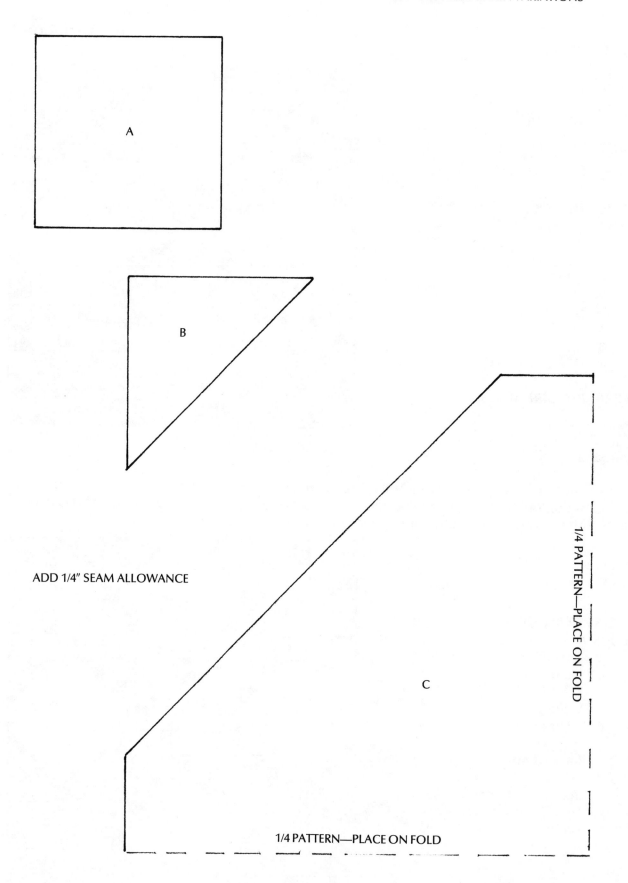

A

B

ADD 1/4" SEAM ALLOWANCE

C

1/4 PATTERN—PLACE ON FOLD

1/4 PATTERN—PLACE ON FOLD

in color p. 8

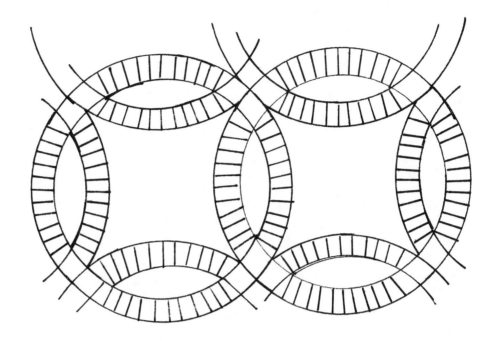

Double Wedding Ring is the ultimate challenge for the quiltmaker. It is difficult to piece. The easiest way seems to be to piece complete circles, then set them together. Each segment of the arc is made of scrap pieces with the center and oval shapes carried out in the same color through the quilt.

Pickle Dish goes a step further by cutting the segments into triangles. Make the segments the same color throughout the quilt. You can change the color of the background from block to block.

Pattern pieces for both are on p. 64.

DIFFICULT

80.   Pickle Dish

in color p. 6

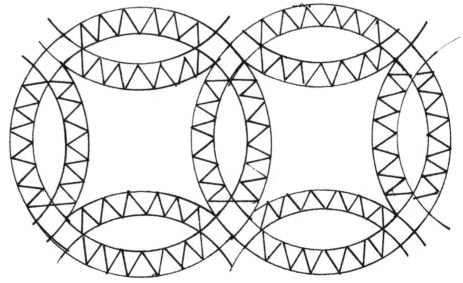

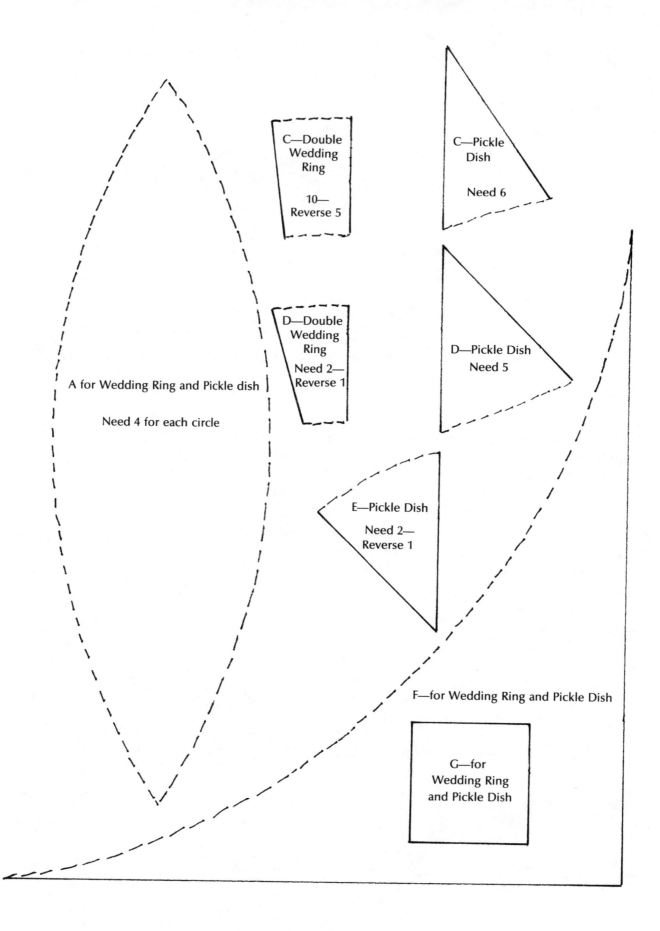

C—Double
Wedding
Ring

10—
Reverse 5

C—Pickle
Dish

Need 6

D—Double
Wedding
Ring

Need 2—
Reverse 1

D—Pickle Dish
Need 5

A for Wedding Ring and Pickle dish

Need 4 for each circle

E—Pickle Dish

Need 2—
Reverse 1

F—for Wedding Ring and Pickle Dish

G—for
Wedding Ring
and Pickle Dish

MODERATE

in color p. 13

BLOCK SIZE: 10"

QUILT SIZE: 82" × 82" with 6" border

NO. OF BLOCKS: 25 Pieced
24 Plain

PIECES PER BLOCK:			PER QUILT:
A	8	Yellow	200
	8	White	200
	8	Light Blue	200
	8	Green	200
B	4	Light Blue	100

FABRIC REQUIREMENTS:

Yellow—1 1/3 yard
White—1 1/3 yard
Light Blue—2 1/3 yard
Green—1 1/3 yard
For Plain Blocks: 2 yards
   (select one of the above colors)
BORDER: 2 strips 6 1/2" × 70 1/2"   1 1/2 yards
   2 strips 6 1/2" × 82 1/2"

From the *Kansas City Star*, 1931.

This pattern appears complicated but is easy to piece. On p. 66 you will find a diagram showing how the pieces are set together. The main design is made up of one pattern piece set in alternate colors.

Assemble each four-piece triangle and set it with the next one. Add the corner blocks B to finish the block.

For quilting, outline quilt along each seam. In the plain blocks, you could repeat the star design or go to a circular feather pattern.

A small cable design can be used for the border.

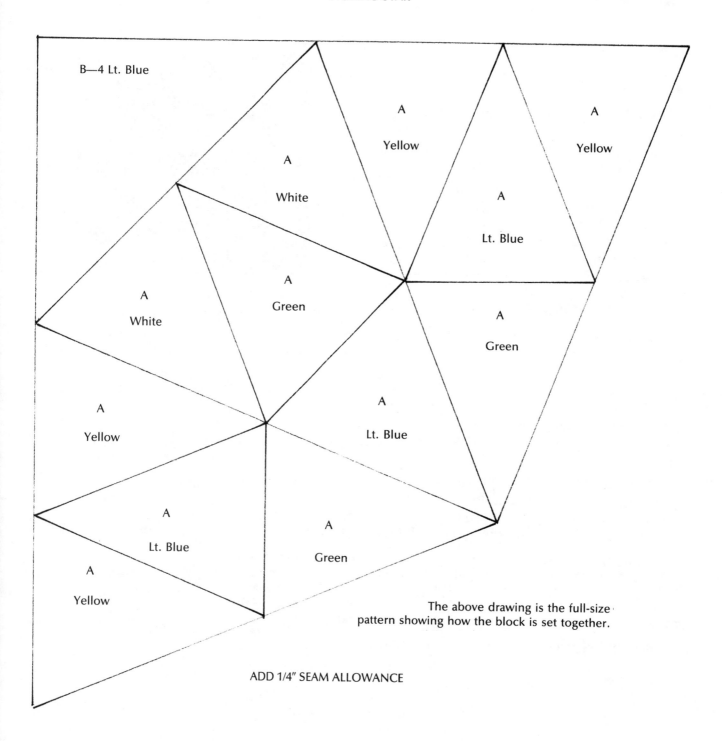

B—4 Lt. Blue

A
Yellow

A
White

A
Yellow

A
White

A
Green

A
Yellow

A
Lt. Blue

A
Yellow

A
Lt. Blue

A
Green

A
Lt. Blue

A
Green

The above drawing is the full-size pattern showing how the block is set together.

ADD 1/4″ SEAM ALLOWANCE

in color p. 4

BLOCK SIZE: 12″ and 8″

QUILT SIZE: 88″ × 88″

NO. OF BLOCKS: 16 12″ blocks
25 8″ blocks
40 8″ × 12″ strips

PIECES PER BLOCK:			**PER QUILT:**
12″ Block:			
A	8	Print	128
B	8	Red	128
C	4	White	64
D	4	White	64
E	8	Red	128
F	8	Print	128
	8	White	128
8″ Block:			
A	4	Print	100
D	4	White	100
E	8	Red	200
F	8	Print	200
	8	White	200
8″ × 12″ strips			40

FABRIC REQUIREMENTS:

White—7 yards
Print —1 1/2 yards
Red—2 yards

This is a striking quilt and extremely easy to do. Assemble the 12″ and 8″ blocks then set together with the 8″ strips, using the diagram on p. 69. Pattern pieces are on p. 68. The design makes its own border.

The large white spaces can be used for some fancy quilting motifs, or you can use a diagonal overall quilting design, with rows spaced approximately 1″ apart.

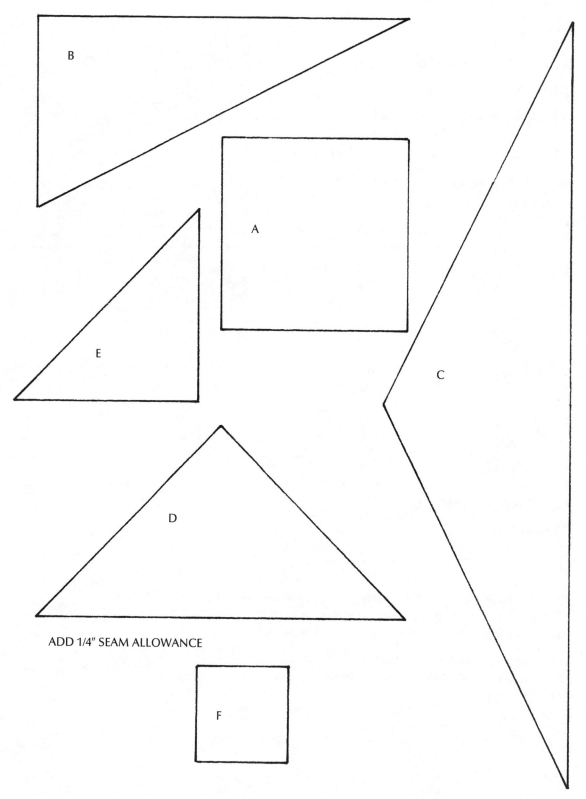

B

A

E

C

D

ADD 1/4″ SEAM ALLOWANCE

F

G—strip measuring 8″ × 12″ plus seam allowance

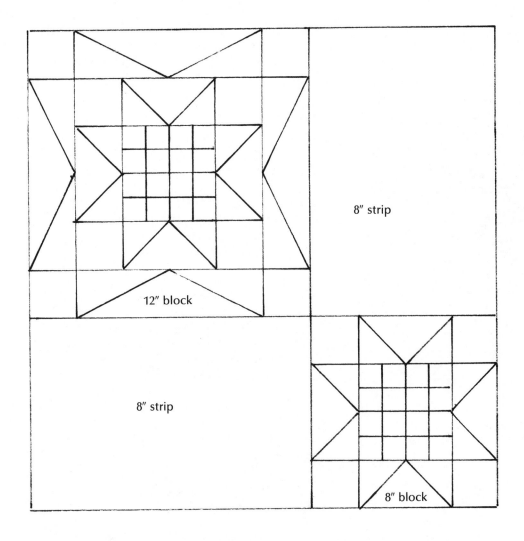

8″ strip

12″ block

8″ strip

8″ block

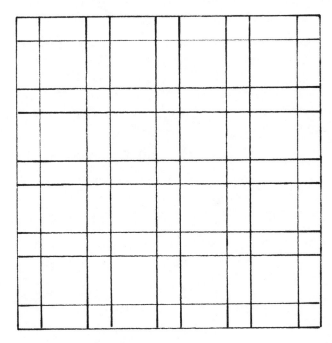

Layout of the quilt top

30. Fair & Square

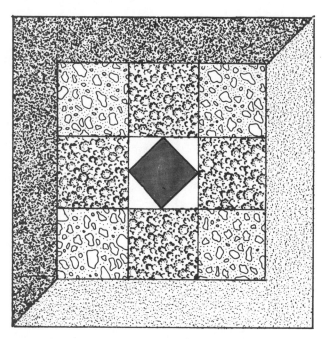

This pattern was published in the *Kansas City Star*. Pattern pieces are on p. 71.

in color p. 10

BLOCK SIZE: 13"

QUILT SIZE: 78" × 78"

NO. OF BLOCKS: 36

PIECES PER BLOCK:			PER QUILT:
A	4	Orange or Red Print	144
	4	Yellow Plain	144
B	1	Brown or Blue	36
C	4	White	144
D	2	Beige or Blue	72
	2	Brown or Yellow	72
E	2	Beige or Blue	72
	2	Brown or Yellow	72
F	1	Beige or Blue	36
	1	Brown or Yellow	36

FABRIC REQUIREMENTS:

Orange or Red Print—1 1/4 yards
Yellow—1 1/4 yards
Brown or Blue—2 yards
Beige or Blue—1 3/4 yards
White—1/2 yard

It's a simple pattern to piece and I have changed the border pattern so that you will have only straight seams to sew.

Begin in the center and stitch the C pieces to the center B. Add an A piece to each side of this completed center. Stitch two strips of A, alternating print and plain. For the strips around each block, cut out two Part E's in each color. Piece a light and dark Part D and add to one end of Part E. Add Part F to other end, matching color of strip. Now just sew these straight strips to the completed center block.

No border is required for this quilt as the blocks form their own border.

Since the pieces of this block are somewhat large, an overall circle or diamond design might be best to use for quilting.

FAIR & SQUARE

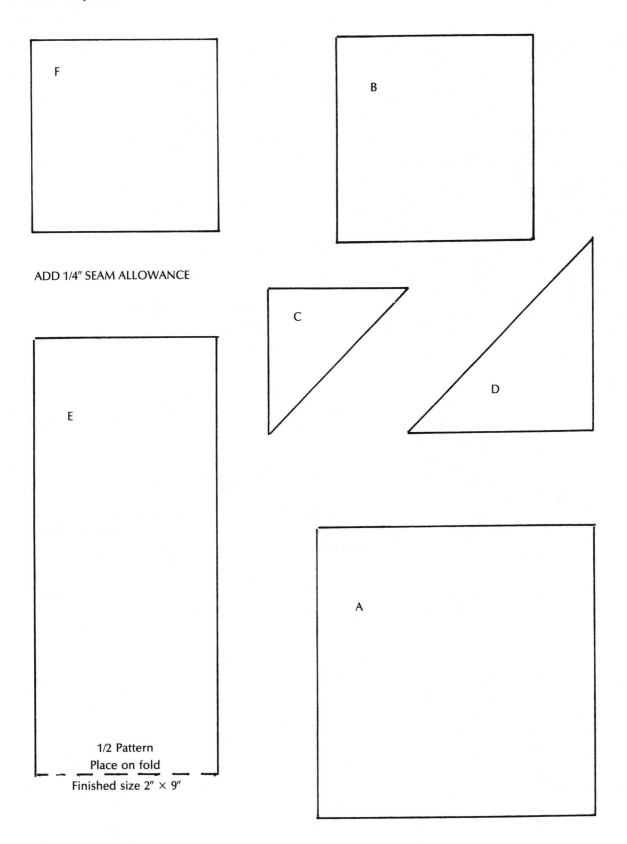

F

B

ADD 1/4" SEAM ALLOWANCE

C

D

E

A

1/2 Pattern
Place on fold
Finished size 2" × 9"

31. Fantasy Flower

in color p. 10

BLOCK SIZE: 8″

QUILT SIZE: 80″ × 80″

NO. OF BLOCKS: 100

PIECES PER BLOCK:			PER QUILT:
A	33	White	3300
	6	Green	600
	7	Print	700
B	16	White	1600
	13	Green	1300
	5	Print	500

FABRIC REQUIREMENTS:

White—8 yards
Green—3 1/2 yards
Print—2 yards

A very easy pattern. The design is made up of 1″ squares and half 1″ squares.

I've given the piece count and fabric requirements for a quilt set solid with pieced blocks, but you could also alternate pieced and plain blocks.

Another way to set the top would be to piece half the blocks following the diagram above, and the other half in reverse order, or starting from the left side. Then set the blocks in groups of four with all the flowers facing inward.

You can also eliminate the outer row of blocks and substitute an 8″ border all around.

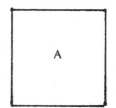

A

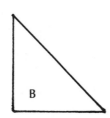

B

ADD 1/4″ SEAM ALLOWANCE

in color p. 11

BLOCK SIZE: 16″

QUILT SIZE: 94″ × 94″

NO. OF BLOCKS: 16 set with 6″ lattice strips and borders

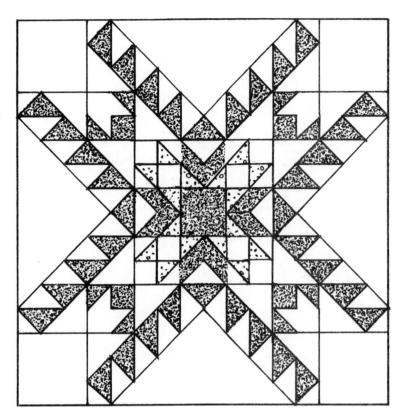

PIECES PER BLOCK:			**PER QUILT:**
A	4	White	64
B	24	White	384
	16	Dark	256
	16	Print	256
C	40	Dark	640
	36	White	576
D	16	White	256
E	8	White	128
	4	Dark	64
F	1	White	16
G	4	White	64

FABRIC REQUIREMENTS:

White—7 3/4 yards
Dark—3 yards
Print— 1/3 yard

The Feathered Star patterns date from the mid-1800's, if not earlier, and there are many variations. The primary variation is the treatment of the center of the block. Each quiltmaker seems to have come up with her own version so in keeping with that tradition I've altered the center of this pattern so that it is different from any of the examples I have patterns for. Pattern pieces are on p. 74.

TO SET THE QUILT: Complete all 16 blocks. Cut 12 strips of white (included in fabric requirements) 6 1/2″ × 16 1/2″. Set the blocks in rows of four across with a strip separating them. Cut five strips 6 1/2″ × 82 1/2″ (this includes top and bottom border) and set the completed rows together with the lattice strips. Cut two strips 6 1/2″ × 94 1/2″ and sew to the sides to complete the border. If desired, a contrasting color can be used for the lattice strips and border.

You have large white areas for fancy quilting designs. The star itself should be outline quilted along each seam.

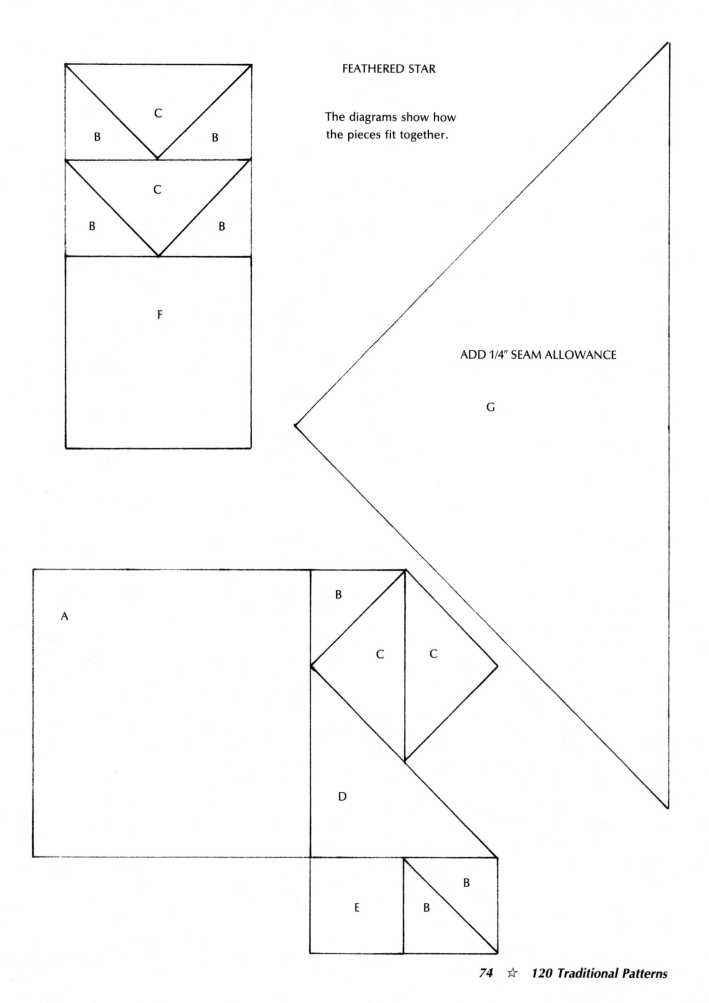

FEATHERED STAR

The diagrams show how
the pieces fit together.

ADD 1/4" SEAM ALLOWANCE

in color p. 4

BLOCK SIZE: 8″ × 6″

QUILT SIZE: 90″ × 90″

NO. OF BLOCKS: 108 **with an inner red border of 3″ and an outer blue border of 6″**

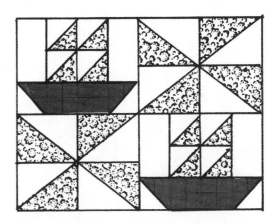

This is an unusual block in that it is rectangular rather than square. It's easy to piece and works up beautifully in red, white and blue.

PIECES PER BLOCK:			PER QUILT:
BLOCK A: 54			
A	2	White	108
B	6	White	324
	4	Red Print	216
C	1	Blue	54
BLOCK B: 54			
D	4	White	216
	4	Red Print	216

FOR BORDER:
2 strips Red Print 3 1/2″ × 72 1/2″
2 strips Red Print 3 1/2″ × 78 1/2″
2 strips Blue 6 1/2″ × 78 1/2″
2 strips Blue 6 1/2″ × 90 1/2″

FABRIC REQUIREMENTS:

White—4 1/4 yards
Blue—3/4 yard
Red Print—3 1/4 yards

BORDER:

Red Print—1 yard
Blue—1 2/3 yards

Pattern pieces are on p. 76.

BLOCK A: Piece four squares using white and red print B. Set these with two Part A's. Sew white B to each side of blue C.

BLOCK B: Piece four red print and white Part D's. Set together.

TO SET THE QUILT: Alternate Block A and Block B across the quilt, 9 across and 12 down.

Sew the 72 1/2″ border strips to each side of the completed top. Add the red 78 1/2″ strip to top and bottom. Sew the 78 1/2″ blue strip to each side, then add the 90 1/2″ strip to top and bottom.

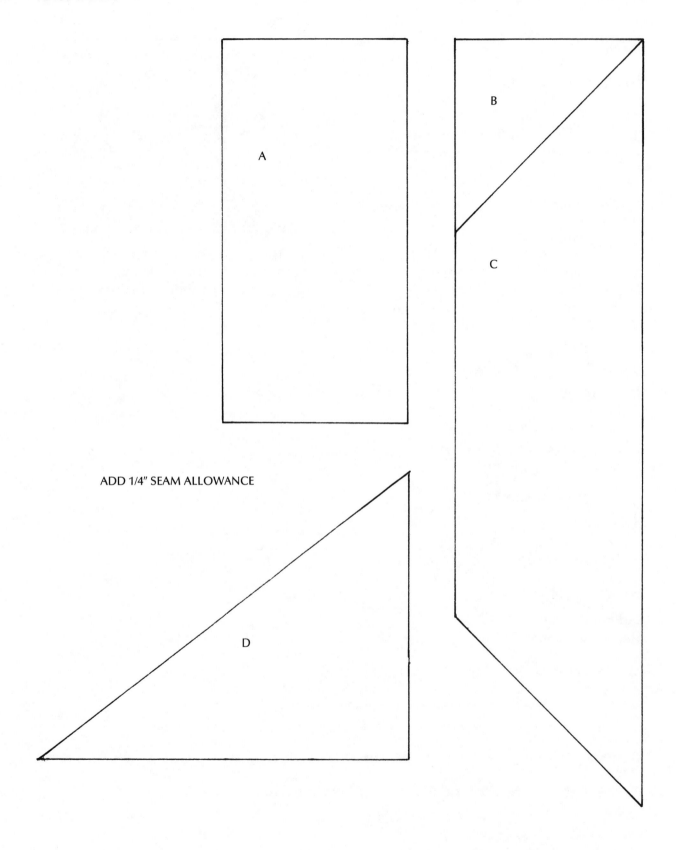

ADD 1/4″ SEAM ALLOWANCE

in color p. 16

BLOCK SIZE: *7″*

QUILT SIZE: *70″ × 84″*

NO. OF BLOCKS: **120**

PIECES PER BLOCK:			PER QUILT:
A	1	White	120
B	8	Print	960
C	4	White	480
D	4	Dark	480
E	4	White	480

FABRIC REQUIREMENTS:

White—4 1/3 yards
Print—1 1/3 yards
Blue—3 1/4 yards

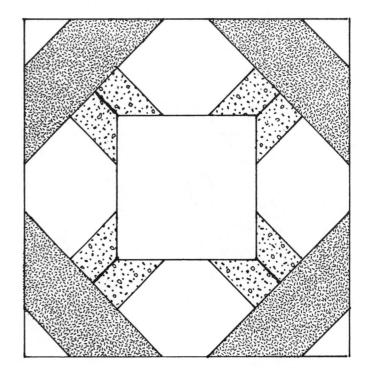

Although the blocks are small, the piecing is easy and this quilt will work up pretty quickly.

When cutting the fabric, reverse 1/2 of the parts for Part B.

Piece two Part B's to each side of Part C. Make four. Sew these completed units to A. Add Parts D and E to finish the block.

A border can be added if desired, but it is not necessary.

ADD 1/4″
SEAM ALLOWANCE

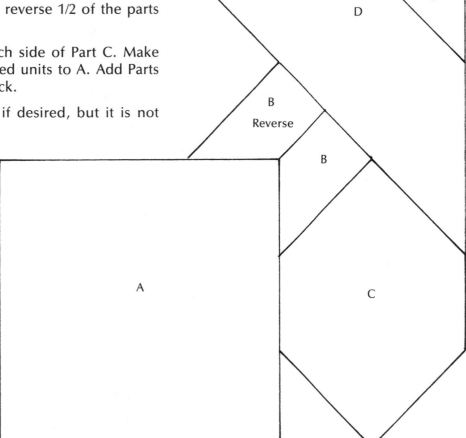

35. Flower Garden

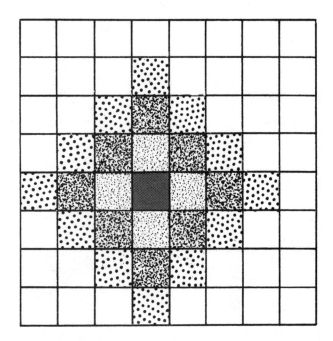

in color p. 10

BLOCK SIZE: 16"

QUILT SIZE: 80" × 80"

NO. OF BLOCKS: 25

PIECES PER BLOCK: **PER QUILT:**
A 39 White   975

FABRIC REQUIREMENTS:

White—4 yards

This is a scrap quilt and is very easy to sew. Each block is done in fabrics of harmonizing print and plain. The solid row of white squares at the top and right side of the block serves as a dividing strip between the blocks, setting off the design of each block.

For each block you will need four fabrics, preferably alternating print and plain. Cut out the 2 1/2" squares and piece them in rows following the above diagram.

On the left side and at the bottom you will have to add a 2 1/2" wide white strip to complete the quilt. This solid strip around the outside serves as a border.

Outline quilt along each seam line.

in color p. 16

BLOCK SIZE: 14″

QUILT SIZE: 70″ × 84″

NO. OF BLOCKS: 30

PIECES PER BLOCK:			PER QUILT:
A	4	Dark	120
B	5	White	150
C	8	Print	240
D	8	White	240

FABRIC REQUIREMENTS:

Dark—1 1/3 yards
White—3 yards
Print—2 3/4 yards

This is a Nancy Cabot design and another easy pattern to piece. Pattern pieces are on p. 80.

Sew together four units of Part C print. Add Part D to each side. Set in Part B. This forms the four corner units. Set two of these together with Part A as shown. For the center strip, sew ABA, add to assembled top row, then add bottom row.

A border is not necessary, but if desired you could add a 2″ wide strip the same color as the central pieces, A.

Outline quilt along each seam.

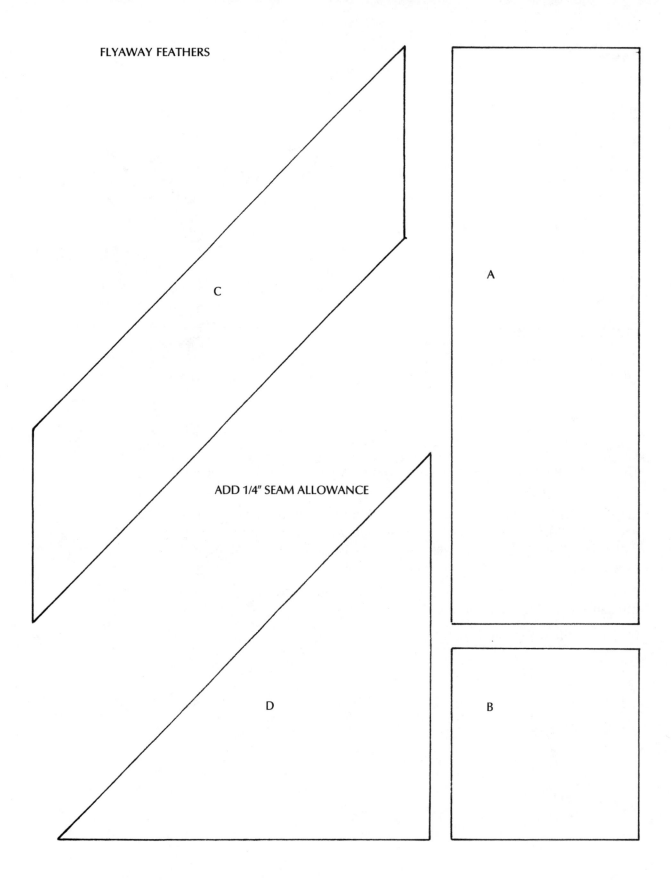

FLYAWAY FEATHERS

C

ADD 1/4" SEAM ALLOWANCE

D

A

B

in color p. 8

BLOCK SIZE: 12″

QUILT SIZE: 84″ × 84″

NO. OF BLOCKS: 49

PIECES PER BLOCK:			PER QUILT:
A	1	Print	49
B	4	White	196
C	8	Print	392
	8	White	392

FABRIC REQUIREMENTS:

White—5 3/4 yards
Print—4 1/4 yards

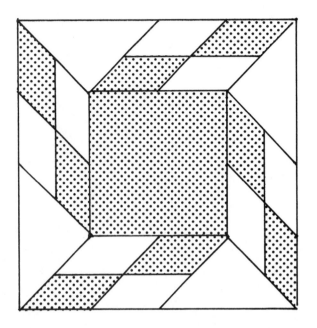

A Ladies Art Company pattern. Pattern pieces on p. 82.

Stitch together the light and dark Part C's to form four large diamond shapes. Sew these diamonds to the four sides of Part A. Set in Part B to complete the block.

An overall quilting design can be used, such as diamonds, or you can follow the seamlines and then use different motifs in the 6″ center squares.

No border is necessary.

FLYING BATS

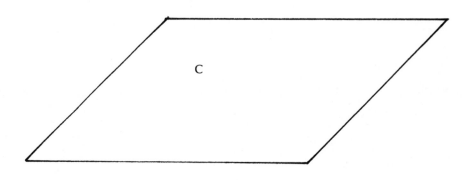

ADD 1/4″ SEAM ALLOWANCE

A

Complete Square

B

in color p. 10

BLOCK SIZE: 12″

QUILT SIZE: 72″ × 84″

NO. OF BLOCKS: 42

PIECES PER BLOCK:			PER QUILT:
A	8	Dark	336
B	8	Light	336
	8	Dark	336

FABRIC REQUIREMENTS:

Dark—5 1/2 yards
Light—2 2/3 yards

A Ladies Art Company pattern.

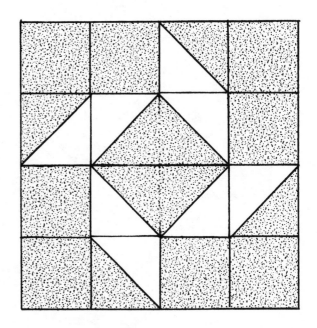

This is an easy pattern to piece. Sew eight light and dark Part B's. Set in rows with A to complete the block. Blocks are set six across and seven down.

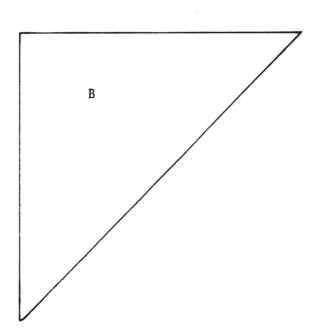

ADD 1/4″ SEAM ALLOWANCE

39. Folded Star

in color p. 16

BLOCK SIZE: 14″

PIECES PER BLOCK:

A	4	Color #1
	8	Color #2
	8	Color #3
	16	Color #4
	16	Color #5
	16	Color #6

A picture of a quilt in *American Quilts & Coverlets* by Carleton L. Safford and Robert Bishop identifies this pattern as Sunburst. The quilt was made in 1850.

This block has been enjoying a popular revival as a decorative wall hanging or as a decoration on utilitarian items, such as pillows. It makes a very beautiful quilt, but is extremely heavy when completed. Each block is the equivalent of over 20 layers of fabric. If a quilt is desired, it is basically a scrap quilt, so I have not given yardage requirements. Including backing fabric, it takes about 28 yards of fabric to complete.

The block can be finished as a circle, its more popular form, a square or an octagon.

PATTERN FOR STAR: Cut a foundation circle from muslin or similar fabric to measure 14 1/2″ in diameter.

Cut a template 5″ square. This makes the points of the star.

Fold the circle in half horizontally and vertically and press in a sharp crease. Press in creases to mark diagonal lines across the circle. You now have eight lines to help place the points of the star.

Using the 5″ template, cut out the required squares of each color needed for the block. A strong contrast in light and dark will show up best.

Take the four squares of Color #1 and fold in half. Press. Fold each resulting corner to the center so they meet and press again.

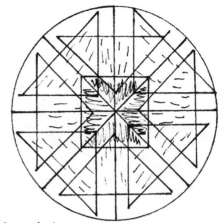

Lay these four squares on the foundation block, lining up the middle of the point with the vertical and horizontal lines of the foundation. Make sure that the points meet in the center with no foundation showing. Tack down each point at the center, then tack down the outer edges.

From the exact center, measure along each crease in the foundation block and mark at the 5/8" point. Fold and crease the eight squares of Color #2 as before. Position four squares over the ones you have tacked down and pin in place, matching the point with the 5/8" mark. Lay the other four squares over these, lining up the point with the diagonal lines on the foundation. Stitch.

Mark out 5/8" from center and position Row #3. Beginning with Row #4, mark out 7/8", and position the folded squares in the same manner. Continue for seven rows.

The size of the completed star can be varied by altering the number of rows used and the spacing between the rows.

For a square block, start with a foundation square measuring 1/2" larger than the completed star. Using this template, lay it over the completed star and cut off the excess fabric.

TO MAKE A WINDOW FOR THE CIRCULAR STAR: Cut two pieces of fabric 2" larger than the completed star. One piece is for the facing. On the facing, draw a circle the size of the finished star. Lay the two pieces of fabric together, right sides facing with the marked circle toward you. Stitch around the circle, then cut it out leaving a 1/4" seam allowance. Clip the seam allowance.

Draw the facing through the hole to the back of the piece. Press. Lay the star behind the window and pin very close to the edge. Lift the top fabric and stitch through the facing and the star. Press.

For a quilt, make the blocks square and set together with lattice strips. As I mentioned, an octagon shape can also be made by following the fabric and cutting it evenly. Add corner blocks to make a square.

40. Friendship Star

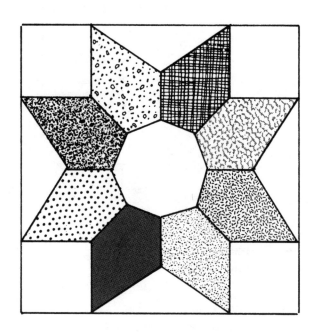

Kansas City Star, 1933.

MODERATE

in color p. 5

BLOCK SIZE: 12″

QUILT SIZE: 84″ × 84″

NO. OF BLOCKS: 49

PIECES PER BLOCK:			**PER QUILT:**
A	1	White	49
B	8	Assorted fabrics	
	4	reversed	392
C	4	White	198
D	4	White	198

FABRIC REQUIREMENTS:

White—5 yards
Assorted scraps

This is a moderately difficult quilt to piece because the outer pieces have to be set in, which means you have several corners to pivot. These corners must lie flat.

Piece the Part B's to A, keeping the longer edges to the middle. Set in Parts C and D to complete the block.

Traditionally the center of this block is for friends to sign and date.

Where the blocks join you have a 6″ square for a floral motif. The central design could be shadow quilted, starting 1/8″ from each seam, then working rows of quilting 1/2″ apart for three rows.

Additional pattern pieces p. 87.

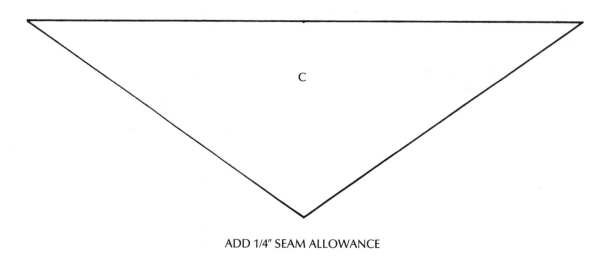

C

ADD 1/4″ SEAM ALLOWANCE

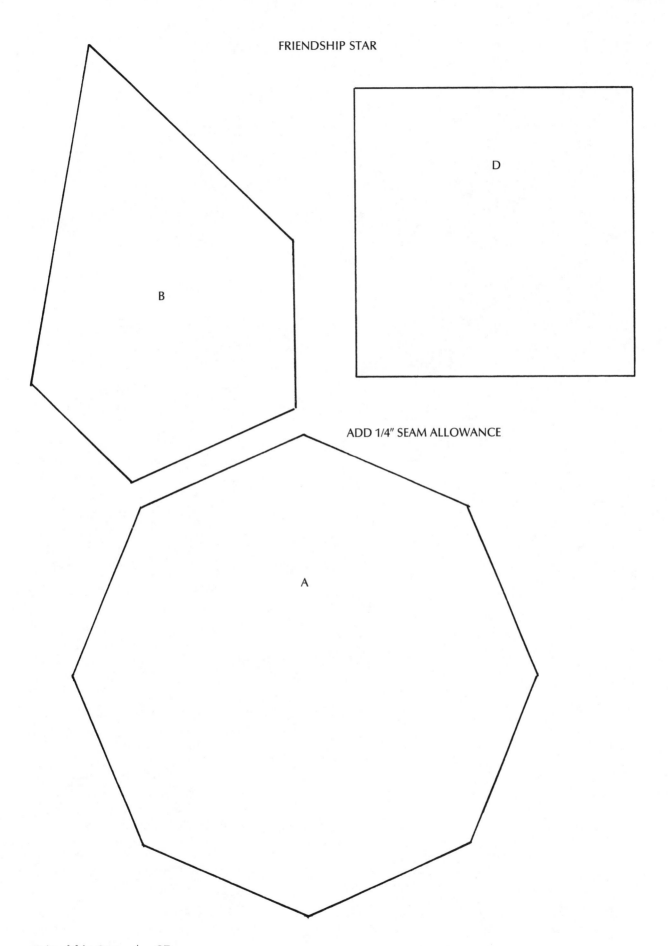

D

ADD 1/4" SEAM ALLOWANCE

B

A

41. Geometry

EASY

in color p. 10

BLOCK SIZE: 8″

QUILT SIZE: 72″ × 80″

NO. OF BLOCKS: 90

PIECES PER BLOCK:			PER QUILT:
A	8	Dark	720
	8	Light	720
B	2	Dark	180
	2	Light	180

FABRIC REQUIREMENTS:

Assorted scraps

This is a scrap quilt that will use up a lot of odds and ends in your fabric cache. It is best if you limit the colors to no more than three. You can use various shades of the three colors, but it is more harmonious if there is some continuity in the color scheme. For a simple pattern, the finished quilt is quite restless, constantly changing pattern and shifting into new designs.

To piece the block, divide it on the diagonal and piece each half separately. Piece two dark and light Part B's, forming half of the center square. Piece four units of light and dark Part A's, and set on the two square sides of the center square. Sew the diagonal seam to finish the block.

On the original quilt, the quilting design consisted of a series of circles where four blocks meet with the rest of the block outline quilted.

No border is necessary.

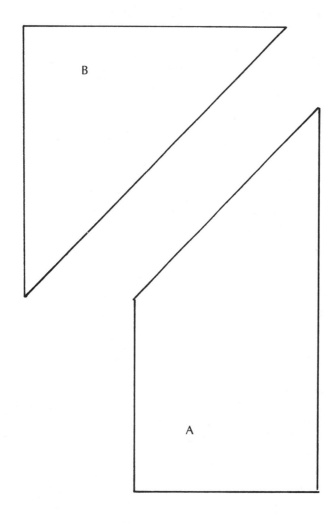

in color p. 10

BLOCK SIZE: 16″

QUILT SIZE: 90″ × 90″

NO. OF BLOCKS: 25 with a 6″ border

PIECES PER BLOCK:			**PER QUILT:**
A	4	White	100
B	8	White	200
C	8	White	200
	12	Light	300
	4	Dark	100
D	16	Dark	400
	4	Light	100

FABRIC REQUIREMENTS:

White—2 2/3 yards
Light—2 yards
Dark—3 1/4 yards

FOR BORDER:

Light—1 yard
Dark—1 yard

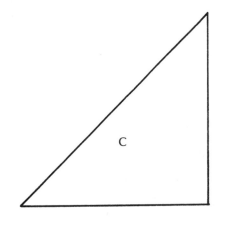

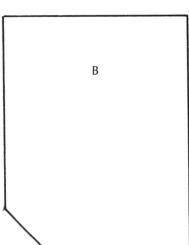

God's Eye is a truly stunning quilt when made up in bright, primary colors such as red and yellow, red and blue, blue and yellow, or orange and brown. It has a strong masculine feel which makes it ideal for the man in your life.

To assemble the block, follow the diagram on p. 90.

BORDER: Cut the fabric into 3 1/2″ wide strips, then piece the strips together to the proper length. You will need two strips (light) 3 1/2″ by 80″, four strips (2 dark and 2 light) 3 1/2″ by 86″, two strips 3 1/2″ by 92″.

Sew the 80″ strips to each side of the completed top, and the 86″ strips to the top and bottom. The other 86″ strips to form the next border are sewn to each side, then the 92″ strip goes at the top and bottom.

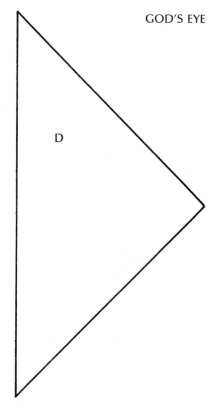

ADD 1/4" SEAM ALLOWANCE

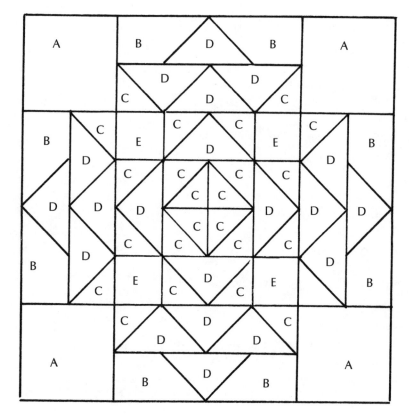

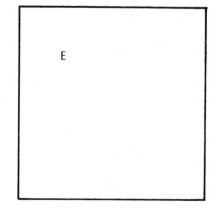

in color p. 12

BLOCK SIZE: 18″

QUILT SIZE: 90″ × 90″

NO. OF BLOCKS: 25

PIECES PER BLOCK:			PER QUILT:
A	12	Dark Yellow	300
B	32	Light Yellow	800
	48	Blue	1200
C	16	Medium Yellow	400
D	1	Dark Yellow	25

FABRIC REQUIREMENTS:

Dark Yellow—2 yards
Light Yellow—1 3/4 yards
Medium Yellow—4 1/4 yards
Blue—2 1/2 yards

Each block of this pattern has a lot of pieces, but it is easy to make up. Pattern pieces are on p. 92.

Break the design down into the four inner squares and the 12 outer ones.

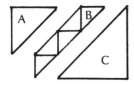
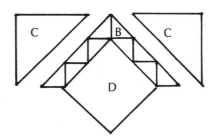

Sew the completed squares in rows to complete the block.

A cable pattern could be used to quilt the center C areas, with outline quilting along the seamlines of the other pieces.

No border is necessary.

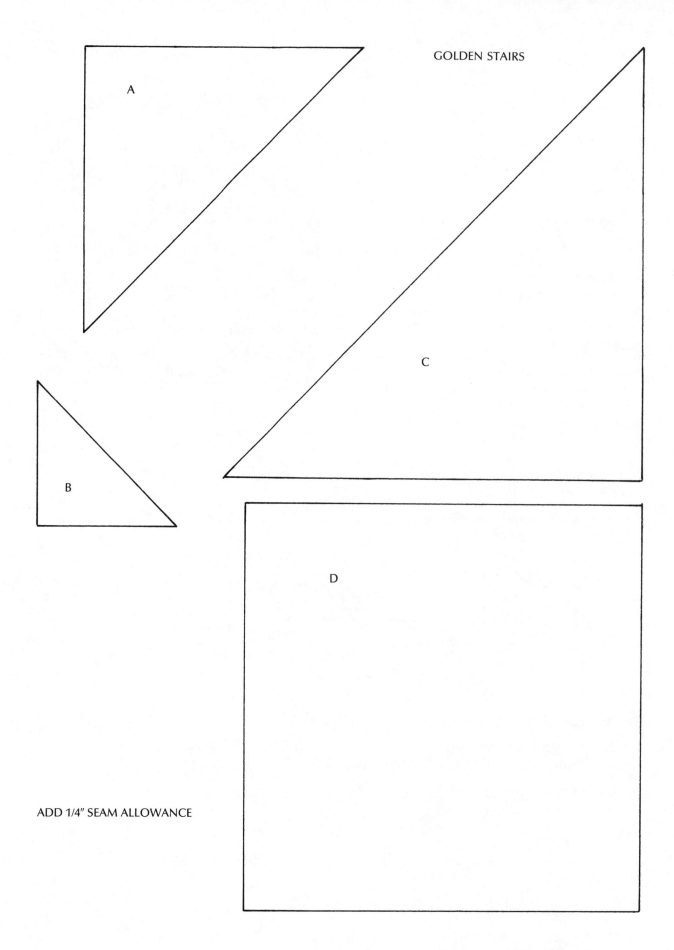

GOLDEN STAIRS

A

C

B

D

ADD 1/4″ SEAM ALLOWANCE

DIFFICULT

in color p. 10

BLOCK SIZE: 12″

QUILT SIZE: 84″ × 84″

NO. OF BLOCKS: 36 plus 6″ border

PIECES PER BLOCK:			PER QUILT:
A	4	Dark	144
B	8	Assorted scraps	288

FABRIC REQUIREMENTS:

Dark—6 yards (includes border)
Assorted scraps measuring 4″ × 4″

Because of the curves, this is a difficult pattern to piece. You may find it easier to treat the scrap pieces as an appliqué onto the dark piece.

Break the block down into four squares and piece each square. Then join them together to form the finished block.

For the border, cut the fabric into 6 1/2″ wide strips and piece together to form strips of the following length: two 72 1/2″ and two 84 1/2″.

Other pattern pieces on p. 94.

ADD 1/4″ SEAM ALLOWANCE

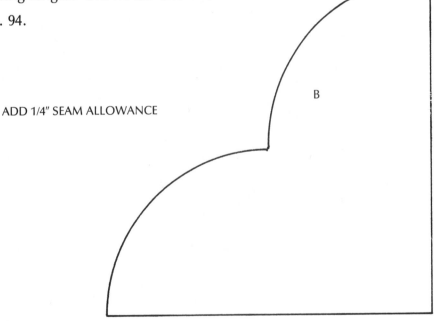

B

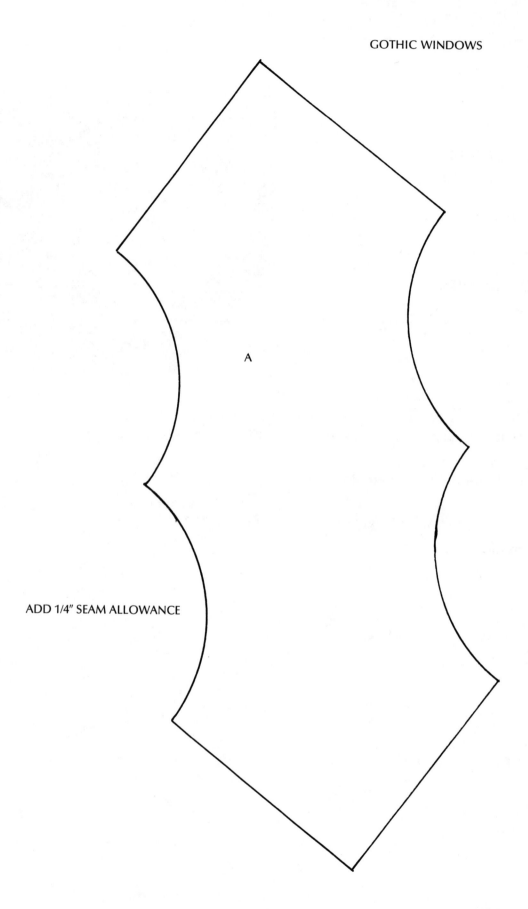

A

ADD 1/4″ SEAM ALLOWANCE

in color p. 12

BLOCK SIZE: 12″

QUILT SIZE: 80″ × 92″

NO. OF BLOCKS: 30

PIECES PER BLOCK:			PER QUILT:
A	2	Red	60
	2	Blue	60
	2	White	60
B	10	White	300
	6	Red	180
	8	Blue	240

FABRIC REQUIREMENTS:

White—4 yards
Red—2 3/4 yards
Blue—2 2/3 yards

FOR BORDER:

Red—3 yards

This pattern appeared some time during the late 20's or early 30's in the *Kansas City Star.*

Cut out pattern pieces on p. 96, adding 1/4″ seam allowance. This pattern is most easily pieced on the diagonal following the diagram below:

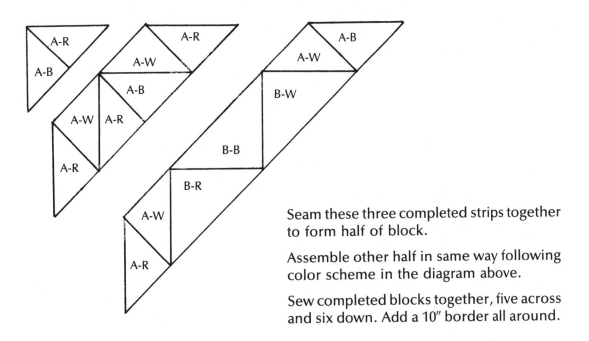

Seam these three completed strips together to form half of block.

Assemble other half in same way following color scheme in the diagram above.

Sew completed blocks together, five across and six down. Add a 10″ border all around.

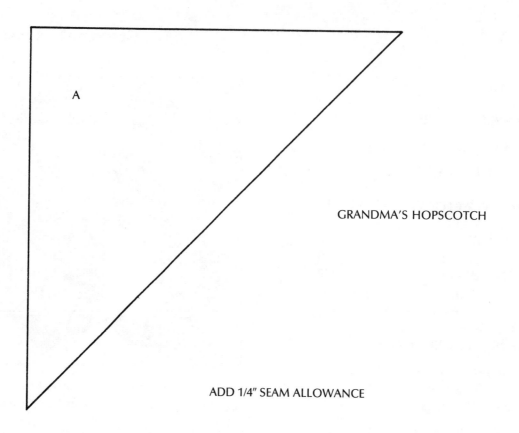

GRANDMA'S HOPSCOTCH

ADD 1/4" SEAM ALLOWANCE

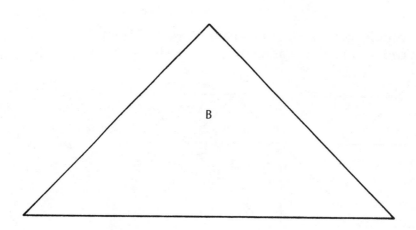

in color p. 8

BLOCK SIZE: 14″

QUILT SIZE: 84″ × 84″

NO. OF BLOCKS: 36

PIECES PER BLOCK:			PER QUILT:
A	4	Print	144
B	8	White	288
	5	Dark	180
C	10	White	360
	16	Dark	576
D	6	White	216

FABRIC REQUIREMENTS:

White—5 1/2 yards
Print—2 1/3 yards
Dark—3 1/4 yards

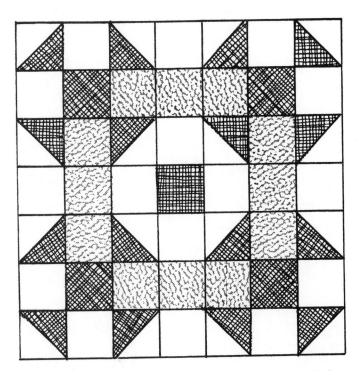

This pattern appears in the book, *Romance of the Patchwork Quilt in America*, which dates it as pre-1933.

The flag of Greece is blue and white and this quilt would make up very nicely in a dark blue with a blue print and white. Pattern pieces are on p. 98.

ROW 1: Dark and light C unit; add white B and a dark C. Add white D, dark C, B, and end with another dark and light C.

ROW 2: White B, dark B, print A, dark B, white B. Sew two of these strips together for the top and bottom of the block.

Now work the three center rows going down. Part D set with two dark Part C's. Need four. Seam one of these units to each side of a Part A. Piece white B, to dark B, to white B. Set the completed units together in a row across the block. Now seam all the units, two rows, three rows and two rows to form the completed block.

GREEK CROSS

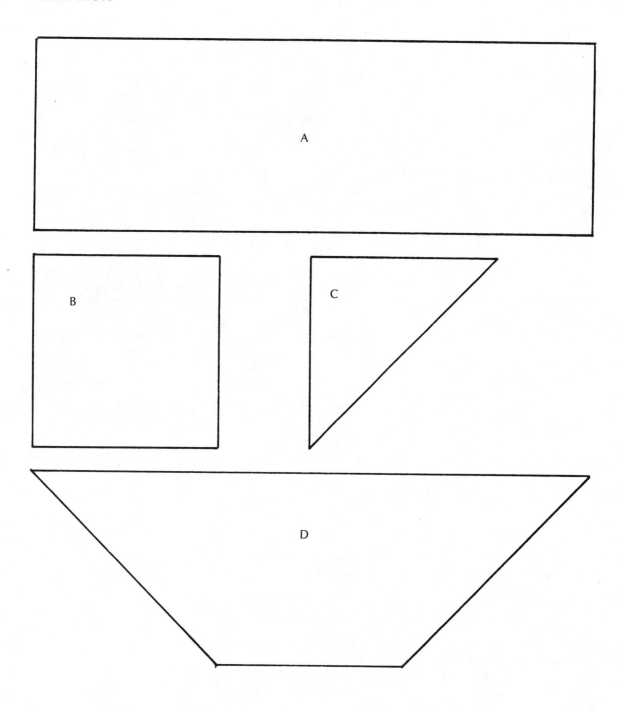

ADD 1/4" SEAM ALLOWANCE

in color p. 11

BLOCK SIZE: 16″

QUILT SIZE: 80″ × 80″

NO. OF BLOCKS: 25

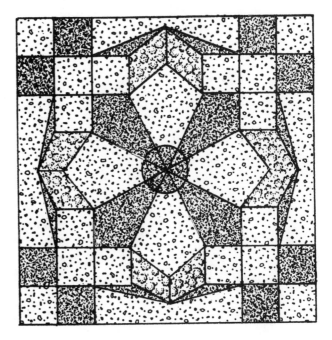

PIECES PER BLOCK:

			PER QUILT:
A	16	Light	400
	8	Red	200
B	8	Light	200
C	8	Red	200
D	8	Dark	200
E	4	Light	100
F	4	Red	100
G	1	Red	25

FABRIC REQUIREMENTS:

Light (red on white print)—4 1/2 yards
Red Plain—2 3/4 yards
Dark (white on red print)—1 1/2 yards

This design is a very slight variation of Little Giant, a pattern which honored Stephen Douglas. He was well-known for his skill as an orator and debater and defeated Abraham Lincoln in the 1858 race for the Senate. The Little Giant pattern dates from around this time, while this variation appeared in the *Kansas City Star* in 1932.

This is a moderately difficult pattern to piece, but if you break it down as shown on pattern p. 100, you shouldn't have too much difficulty. The drawing shows how the center section goes together. The square A pieces are added to the corners to complete the block.

Outline quilting would be appropriate along each seam, with the line repeated for two or three rows on the larger pieces. No border is necessary but may be added if desired.

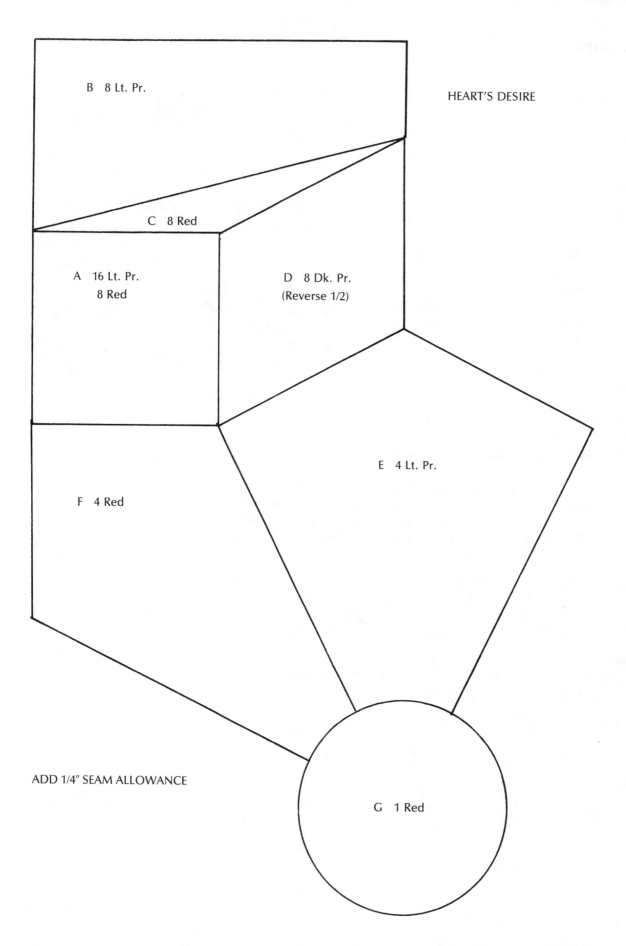

B   8 Lt. Pr.

HEART'S DESIRE

C   8 Red

A   16 Lt. Pr.
8 Red

D   8 Dk. Pr.
(Reverse 1/2)

E   4 Lt. Pr.

F   4 Red

ADD 1/4" SEAM ALLOWANCE

G   1 Red

DIFFICULT

in color p. 7

BLOCK SIZE: 23″ from point to point

QUILT SIZE: 92″ × 92″

NO. OF BLOCKS: 16

PIECES PER BLOCK: PER QUILT:

A	12	Dark Blue	192
	6	Light Blue	96
	6	Red	96
B	6	Red	96
C	6	White	96

FABRIC REQUIREMENTS:

Dark Blue—2 1/3 yards
Light Blue—1 1/4 yards
Red—2 yards
White—6 1/2 yards

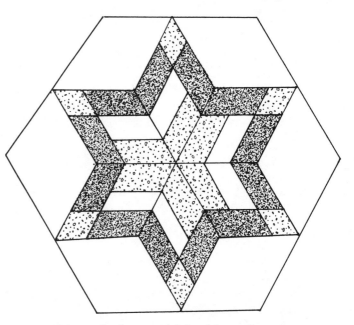

The quilt from which this pattern was taken was made during the late 1800's. The design is quite versatile because of the many variations in color. The wide expanses of white help it to blend in to any decor.

The large white diamonds set the quilt together. Along the edges you must cut the quilt square.

To piece the central star, break it down into six sections. Each one contains a center strip beginning with red, then light blue, and dark blue. Along the other edge add a second dark blue Part A. Set the red diamond into the point.

To assemble a six-point diamond, seam two together and press. Add another point and again press, fanning out the seams as you progress, continuing to add points.

Set the white C diamond between the points. Assemble the next star and sew to the diamonds of the first star, filling in any empty areas between points. Continue adding stars and diamonds. When quilt is proper size, cut edges off even.

Other pattern pieces on p. 102.

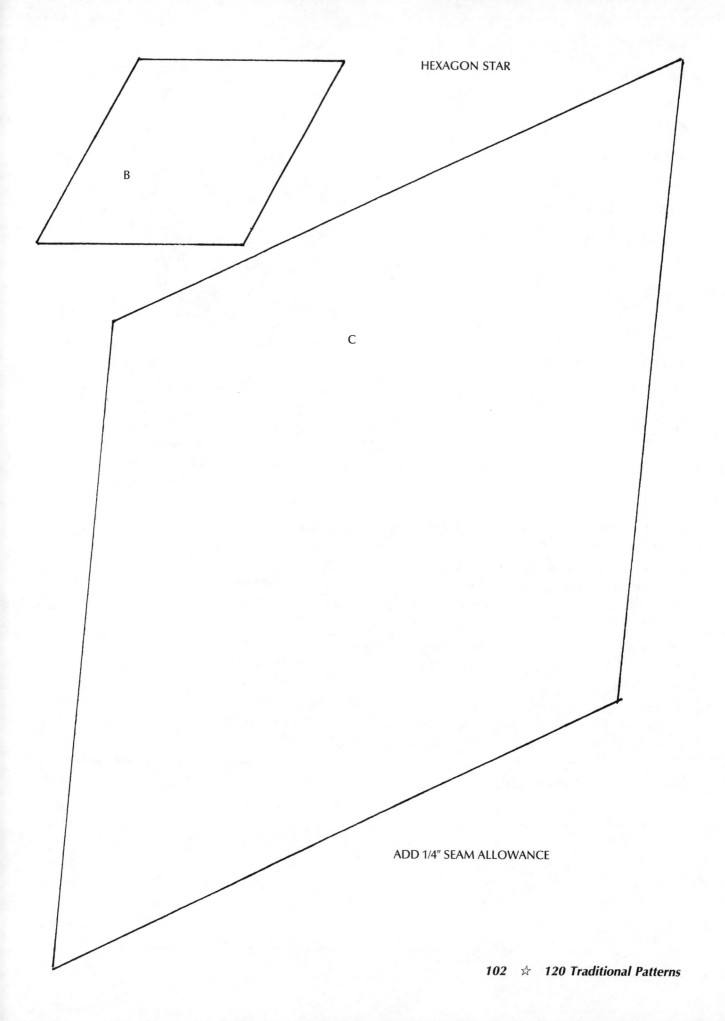

HEXAGON STAR

B

C

ADD 1/4" SEAM ALLOWANCE

in color p. 12

BLOCK SIZE: 12″

QUILT SIZE: 84″ × 96″

NO. OF BLOCKS: 56

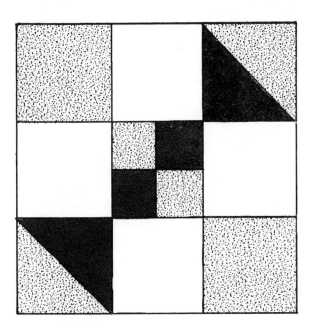

PIECES PER BLOCK:			**PER QUILT:**
A	2	Print	112
	4	Plain	224
B	2	Print	112
	2	Dark Plain	112
C	2	Print	112
	2	Dark Plain	112

FABRIC REQUIREMENTS:

Print—3 1/2 yards
White or light solid—3 3/4 yards
Dark solid—1 1/2 yards

This is probably one of the earliest patterns devised by quiltmakers. Its simple shape goes together quickly and easily. It makes an excellent scrap pattern, or you can follow the suggested colors. If made up as a scrap pattern, set it together with lattice strips and add a matching border to finish the edges.

Cut out pattern pieces, on p. 104, adding 1/4″ seam allowance. To assemble the block, stitch together Parts B, print and plain, to form a square. Then stitch together the center square, using Part C, 2 print and 2 plain. Now assemble the block following the diagram.

When the blocks are set together you will have an 8″ square for a small quilting motif, if desired. You could also use an overall design of diamonds.

If you use the suggested color scheme, no border is necessary. Just bind the edges.

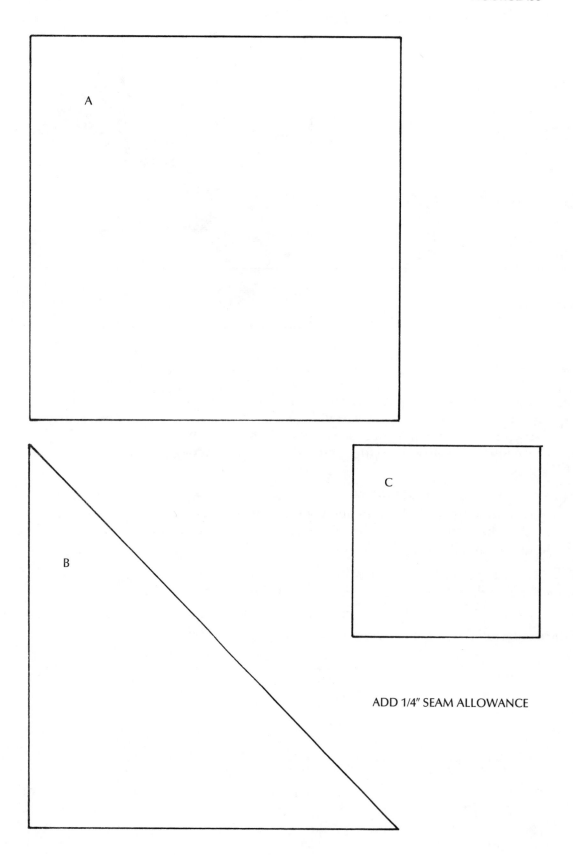

A

B

C

ADD 1/4" SEAM ALLOWANCE

MODERATE

in color p. 5

BLOCK SIZE: 12″

QUILT SIZE: 84″ × 84″

NO. OF BLOCKS: 49

PIECES PER BLOCK:			**PER QUILT:**
A	4	Dark Green	196
	4	Green or White Print	196
B	8	Dark Green	392
	8	Green or White Print	392
C	4	Dark Green	196
	4	Green or White Print	196

FABRIC REQUIREMENTS:

Dark Green—5 3/4 yards
Green or White Print—5 3/4 yards

This is one of the patterns included in *The Romance of the Patchwork Quilt in America*, so it is pre-1933.

The template pattern on p. 106 shows 1/4 of the block and how I've broken it down. By following this diagram you will be sewing all straight seams rather than piecing a star. As each completed block is set with its neighbor, another star appears at the intersection of four blocks.

Shadow quilting from the seams would most effectively accentuate the star design.

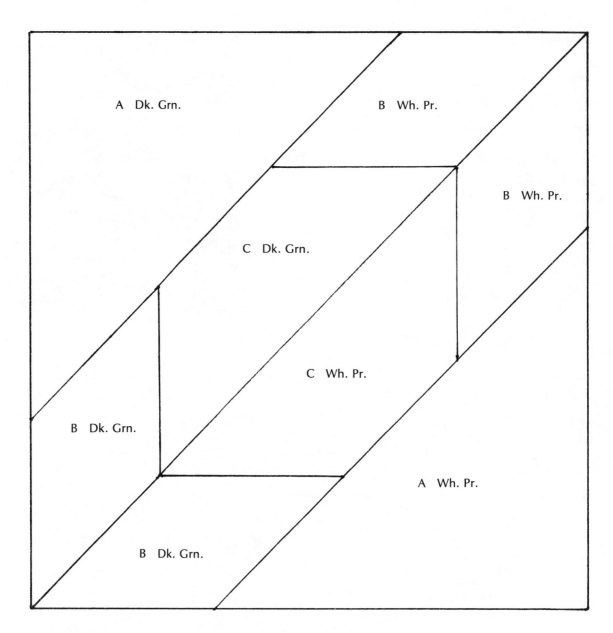

A   Dk. Grn.

B   Wh. Pr.

B   Wh. Pr.

C   Dk. Grn.

C   Wh. Pr.

B   Dk. Grn.

A   Wh. Pr.

B   Dk. Grn.

1/4 of the block (this shows the lower left corner)

ADD 1/4″ SEAM ALLOWANCE

in color p. 4

PIECES PER BLOCK:
A	4	All the same or 2 print 2 plain
C	2	Print or Plain
D	4	Dark
	4	Light

The Improved 4-Patch design dates from at latest 1860. The Jewel Box is a more recent variation of this design.

Both are made entirely from scrap fabrics set with a harmonizing color border and lattice strips.

The corner square A for Improved 4-Patch can be all the same color, or you can use two different fabrics, alternating corners.

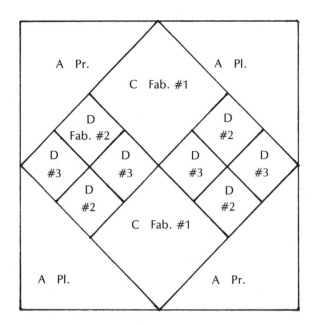

EASY

BLOCK SIZE: 12″

QUILT SIZE: 88″ × 88″

NO. OF BLOCKS: 36

PIECES PER BLOCK:
A	4	Print or Solid
B	4	Dark Print or Solid
	4	Light Print or Solid

3 yards of fabric required for lattice strips and border

LATTICE STRIPS: Cut
30 13 1/2″ ×   2 1/2″ strips
 5   2 1/2″ × 82 1/2″ strips

BORDER:
3 1/2″ × 82 1/2″ need 2
3 1/2″ × 88 1/2″ need 2

54.   Jewel Box

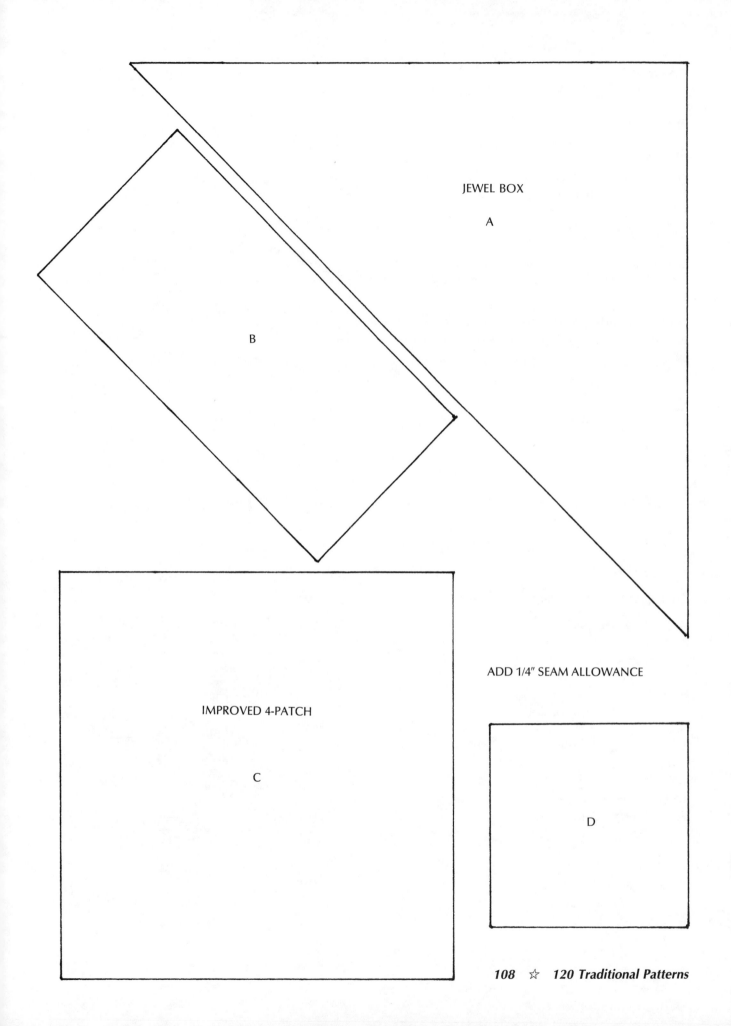

JEWEL BOX

A

B

IMPROVED 4-PATCH

C

ADD 1/4" SEAM ALLOWANCE

D

in color p. 13

BLOCK SIZE: 15″

QUILT SIZE: 75″ × 90″

NO. OF BLOCKS: 30

PIECES PER BLOCK:			PER QUILT:
A	8	White	240
	8	Dark	240
B	28	White	840
	32	Dark	960
C	8	White	240
D	8	White	240
	8	Dark	240
E	1	Dark	30

FABRIC REQUIREMENTS:

White—8 yards
Dark—4 2/3 yards

This block is beautiful worked up in the bright strong colors of Indian blankets. Yellow and black, yellow and blue, orange and brown; you might even experiment with three colors, such as red, black and white.

The diagrams below show how the block is broken down into units and assembled. Pattern pieces are on p. 110.

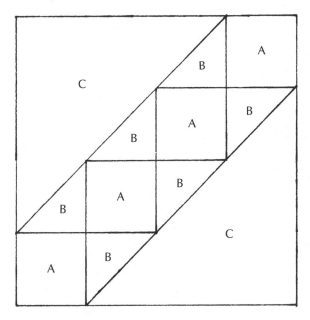

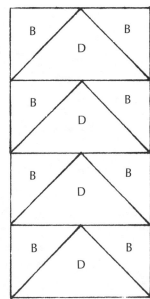

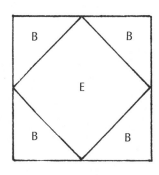

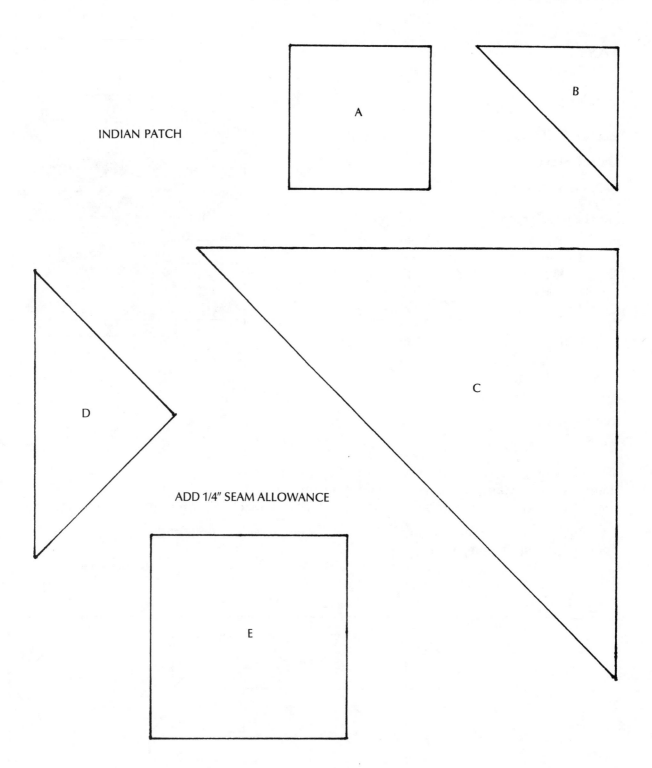

INDIAN PATCH

A

B

D

C

ADD 1/4" SEAM ALLOWANCE

E

in color p. 14

BLOCK SIZE: 16″

QUILT SIZE: 80″ × 80″

NO. OF BLOCKS: 25

PIECES PER BLOCK:			PER QUILT:
A	1	White	25
B	20	Medium	500
	20	Dark	500
	8	White	200
C	16	White	400
D	4	White	100
E	4	White	100

FABRIC REQUIREMENTS:

White—5 1/2 yards
Medium—2 yards
Dark—2 yards

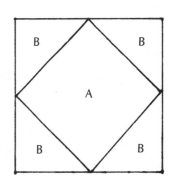

The pattern appears complex, but if you follow the diagram below you shouldn't have any trouble. The block has been broken down into three separate units: the four corner units, the four middle units and the center. Assemble each of the units then set them together to form the block. Pattern pieces are on p. 112.

Outline quilting along each seam would be most appropriate to accent the lines of the quilt. Fill in the larger areas with shadow quilting.

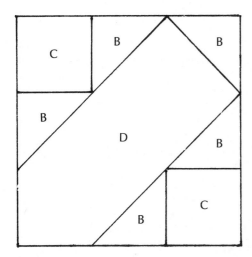
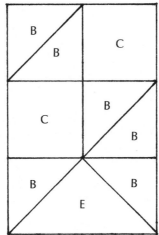

54. Jewel Box is to be found on p. 107.

INTERWOVEN PUZZLE

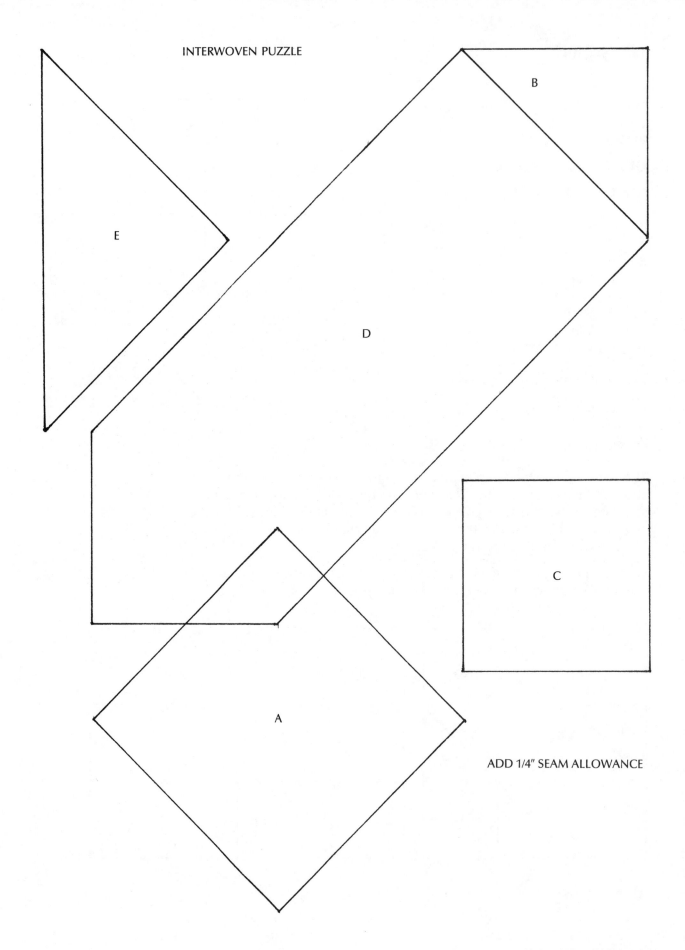

ADD 1/4″ SEAM ALLOWANCE

in color p. 10

BLOCK SIZE: 16″

QUILT SIZE: 80″ × 80″

NO. OF BLOCKS: 25

PIECES PER BLOCK:			PER QUILT:
A	8	Dark	200
B	8	White	200
	8	Dark	200
C	8	Print	200
D	16	Print	400
	16	White	400

FABRIC REQUIREMENTS:

White—4 1/4 yards
Dark—1 2/3 yards
Print—5 1/2 yards

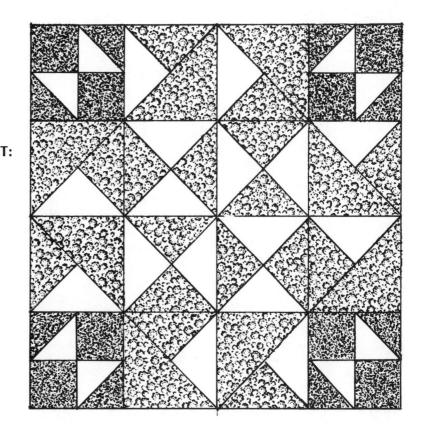

This is a *Kansas City Star* pattern and another easy one to piece. Pattern pieces on p. 114.

Just follow the diagram to sew each square of the block. This pattern works up very fast on the sewing machine. Starting with the corner block, feed through the machine all the dark and light B pieces. Cut apart and press. Sew an A square to the completed B unit. Cut apart and press. Sew two of these units together to form the corner square. Work in the same manner for each of the squares.

When all squares are completed, sew them together to form the block, or you can work in rows across the entire width of the quilt top.

A border can be added if desired, but is not necessary.

The original pattern suggested that this be worked in two colors, light and dark. If you follow my color scheme, where the blocks join, you will have a secondary star pattern.

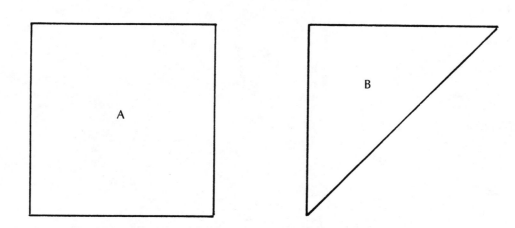

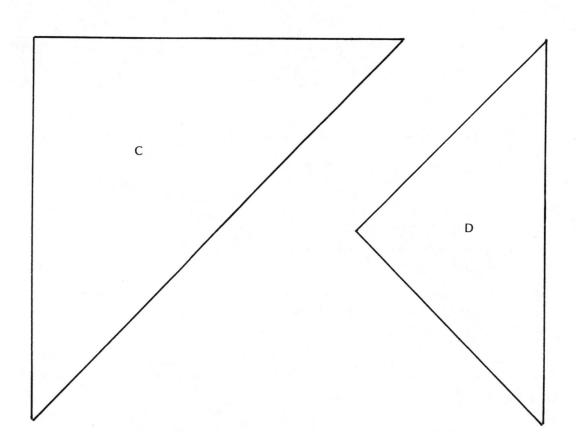

in color p. 13

BLOCK SIZE: 9″

QUILT SIZE: 90″ × 90″

NO. OF BLOCKS: 100

PIECES PER BLOCK:			PER QUILT:
BLOCK A: 50			
A	4	Dark	200
B	4	Light	200
C	4	White	200
BLOCK B: 50			
A	4	Light	200
B	4	Dark	200
C	4	White	200

FABRIC REQUIREMENTS:

White—3 1/3 yards
Dark—5 1/2 yards
Light—5 1/2 yards

(This can be made as a scrap quilt.)

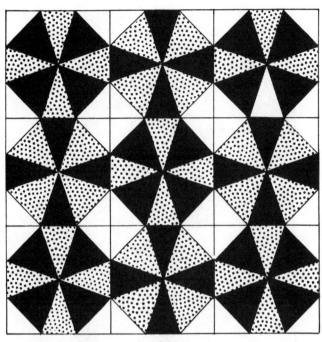

This a very easy pattern to piece and one of the most versatile in any collection. A muted monochromatic color scheme will produce a subtle, elegant quilt, while at the other end a scrap quilt will give you a constantly shifting design, full of movement and excitement.

To carry out the design, the dark and light is alternated from block to block.

Outline quilting is most effective for this pattern since you will want to accentuate the shifting forms of the quilt top.

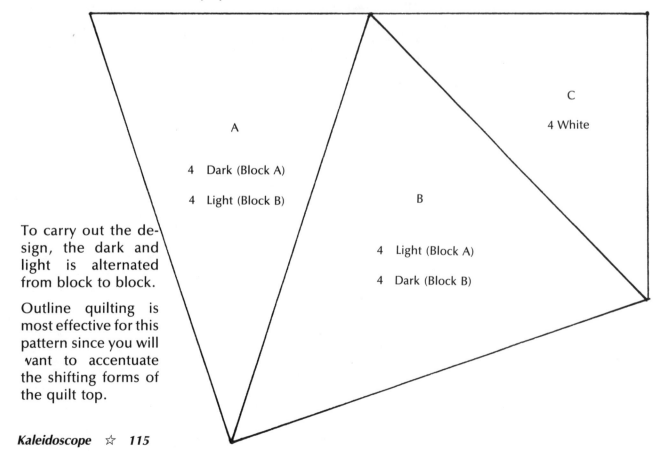

A

4   Dark (Block A)

4   Light (Block B)

B

4   Light (Block A)

4   Dark (Block B)

C

4 White

57. Kansas Dust Storm

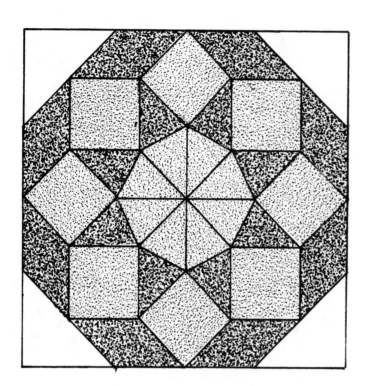

in color p. 15

BLOCK SIZE: 12″

QUILT SIZE: 72″ × 72″

NO. OF BLOCKS: 36

PIECES PER BLOCK:			**PER QUILT:**
A	4	White	144
B	8	Light Print	288
C	8	Dark	288
D	8	Dark Print	288
	8	Light Print	288

FABRIC REQUIREMENTS:

White—1 yard
Dark—2 2/3 yards
Light Print—4 yards
Dark Print—2 1/4 yards

This design appeared in the *Kansas City Star* in 1935. Pattern pieces are on p. 117.

TO ASSEMBLE: Piece light D to dark print D to form eight diamond shapes. Sew these together to form center of block. Set in B pieces between the points of each star. Set in C diamond shapes. To finish block, add A triangles to each corner.

Outline quilt along each seam. Where four blocks join you will have an 8″ square for a fancy motif.

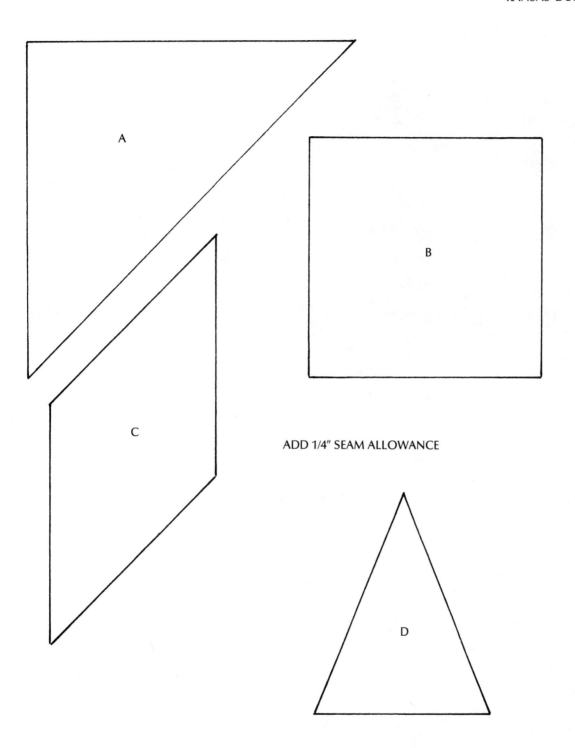

A

B

C

ADD 1/4″ SEAM ALLOWANCE

D

58. King's Crown

in color p. 13

BLOCK SIZE: 15″

QUILT SIZE: 75″ × 90″

NO. OF BLOCKS: 30

PIECES PER BLOCK:			PER QUILT:
A	1	White	30
B	4	Dark Plain	120
C	4	Medium Print	120
	8	White	240
D	12	Light Print	360
E	4	Light Print	120

FABRIC REQUIREMENTS:

White—2 yards
Dark Plain—2 2/3 yards
Medium Print—2/3 yard
Light Print—2 2/3 yards

This appears to be a complex pattern, but if you follow the diagram below you should have no trouble assembling the block. It's all straight-seam sewing. Pattern pieces are on p. 119.

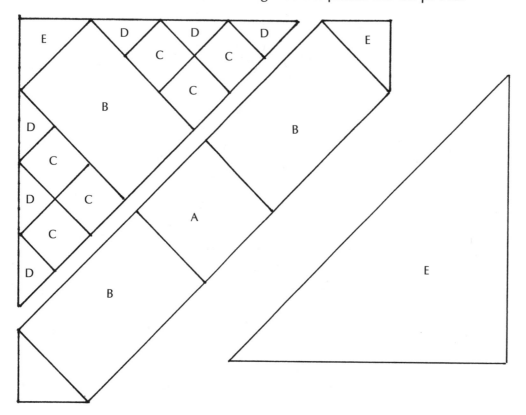

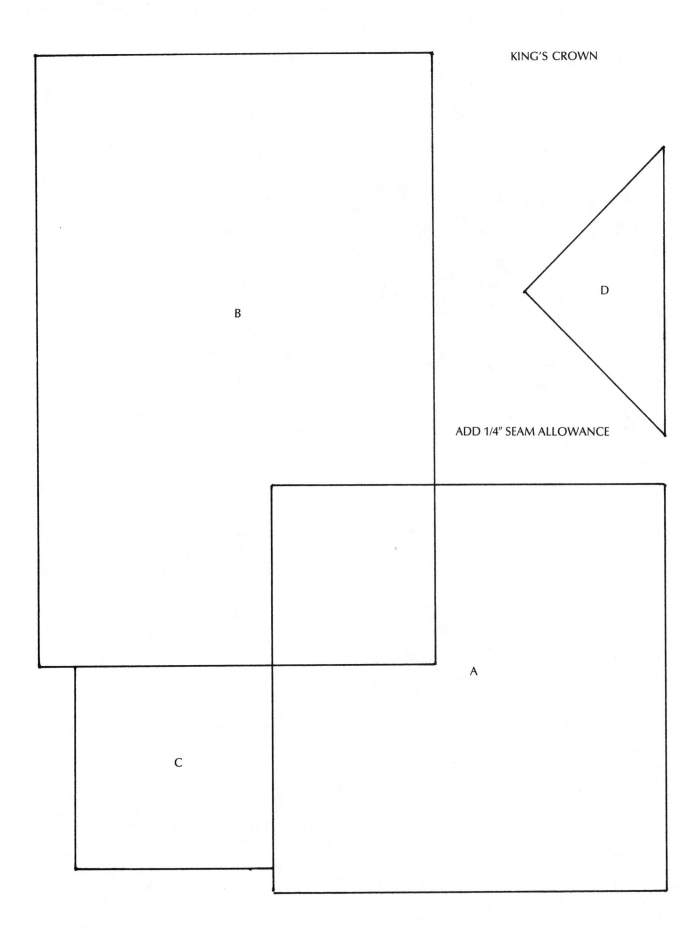

KING'S CROWN

D

ADD 1/4" SEAM ALLOWANCE

B

A

C

59. Kitchen Woodbox   EASY

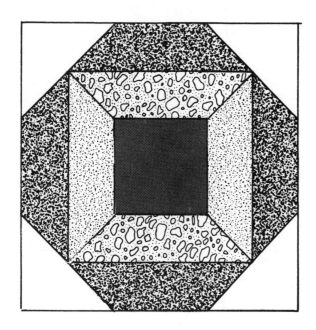

in color p. 12

BLOCK SIZE: 12″

QUILT SIZE: 84″ × 84″

NO. OF BLOCKS: 49

PIECES PER BLOCK:			PER QUILT:
A	4	White	196
B	4	Dark	196
	2	Medium	98
	2	Light	98
C	1	Solid color	49

FABRIC REQUIREMENTS:

White—2 1/3 yards
Dark—3 1/3 yards
Medium—1 2/3 yards
Light—1 2/3 yards
Solid—1 1/4 yards

Cut pattern pieces as indicated, adding seam allowance.

SEWING INSTRUCTIONS: Stitch together two dark B and two medium B; two dark B and two light B. Stitch these completed sections to the center solid square. Add white corner pieces, Part A. Pattern pieces on p. 121.

A border is optional, but you might want to add the following to finish the quilt:

Yardage is not included for border.

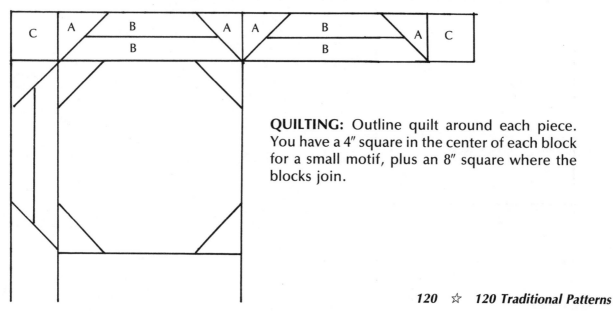

QUILTING: Outline quilt around each piece. You have a 4″ square in the center of each block for a small motif, plus an 8″ square where the blocks join.

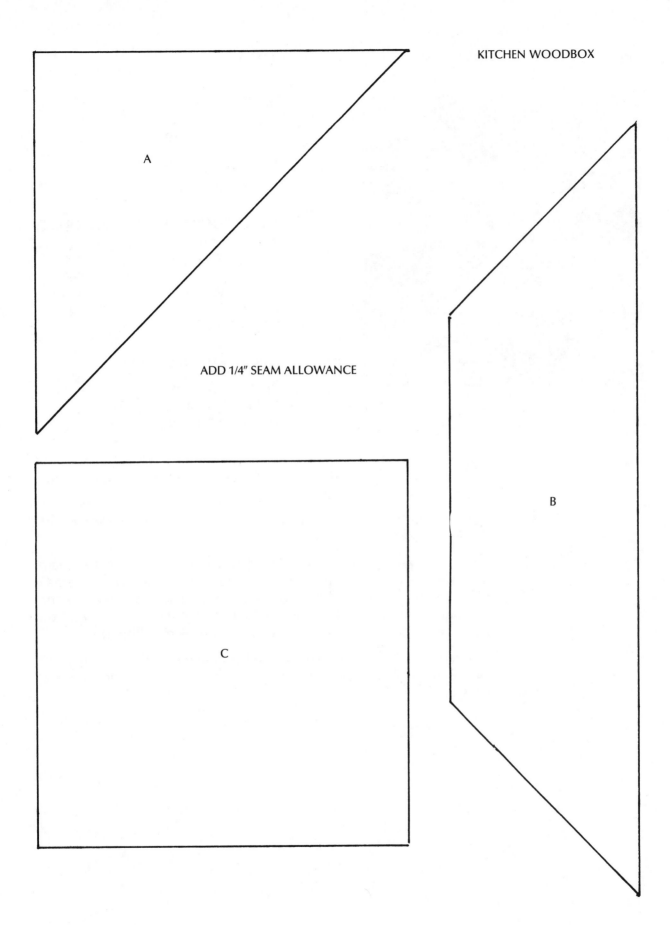

A

ADD 1/4″ SEAM ALLOWANCE

B

C

60. Lady of the White House

EASY

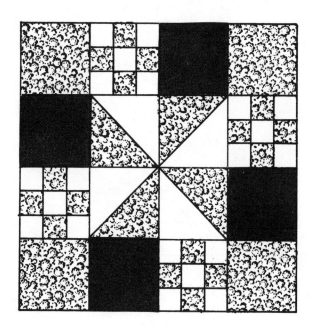

in color p. 12

BLOCK SIZE: 18″

QUILT SIZE: 90″ × 90″

NO. OF BLOCKS: 25

PIECES PER BLOCK:			PER QUILT:
A	4	Print	100
	4	Plain	100
B	4	Print	100
	4	White	100
C	20	White	500
	16	Print	400

FABRIC REQUIREMENTS:

Print—3 3/4 yards
Plain—1 1/4 yards
White—2 3/4 yards

This is an easy pattern and will work up quickly on the sewing machine. Pattern pieces are on p. 123.

Following the diagram, work up each square, then assemble the squares in rows to complete the block.

You have several options for quilting this design. Each of the plain squares is 4 1/2″ and could be used as a sampler for a variety of small quilting motifs. You could also follow the nine-patch design along the outer squares and quilt the inside square following the seamlines. You might also try an overall pattern, ignoring the seams altogether.

If desired, you could cut down the number of blocks in this quilt and add a border to finish the edges. If you make it the full 90 × 90, no border is necessary.

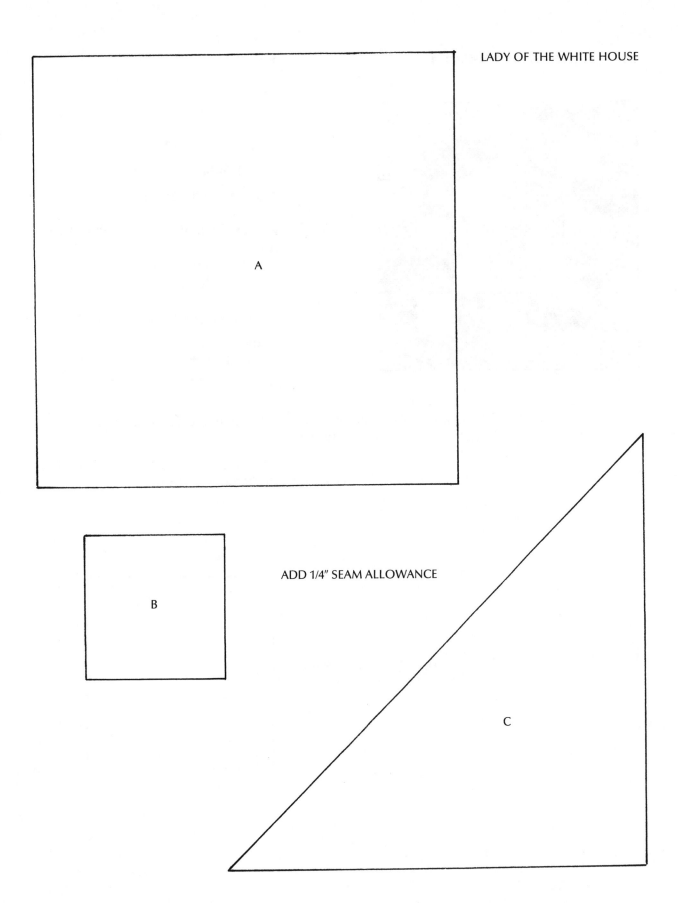

LADY OF THE WHITE HOUSE

A

ADD 1/4″ SEAM ALLOWANCE

B

C

61.   Leavenworth 9-Patch

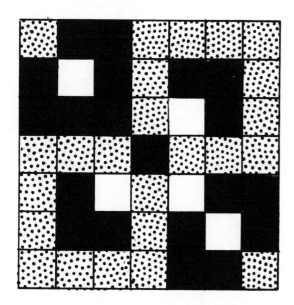

EASY

in color p. 9

BLOCK SIZE: 14″

QUILT SIZE: 84″ × 84″

NO. OF BLOCKS: 36

PIECES PER BLOCK:			PER QUILT:
A	24	Print	846
	19	Plain	684
	5	White	180

FABRIC REQUIREMENTS:

Print—5 yards
Plain—4 yards
White—1 yard

This is a very easy pattern. The design is made up of 2″ squares sewn together in the pattern shown.

Quilting can be done along each seamline, or around each block of color. You might also try an overall diamond pattern.

No border is required.

ADD 1/4″ SEAM ALLOWANCE

in color p. 16

BLOCK SIZE: 8″

QUILT SIZE: 80″ × 80″

NO. OF BLOCKS: 100

PIECES PER BLOCK: **PER QUILT:**
BLOCK A: 50

A	4	Light	200
B	4	Dark	200

BLOCK B: 50

A	4	Dark	200
B	4	Light	200

FABRIC REQUIREMENTS:

Light—5 yards
Dark—5 yards

This originally appeared in *Godey's Lady's Book* in 1859.

This is a very easy pattern and lends itself to any color combinations of strongly contrasting light and dark, print or plain fabrics. The pattern is achieved by alternating the color placement from block to block.

A border is not required and simple outline quilting can be used. You could also choose an overall design, ignoring the seams completely.

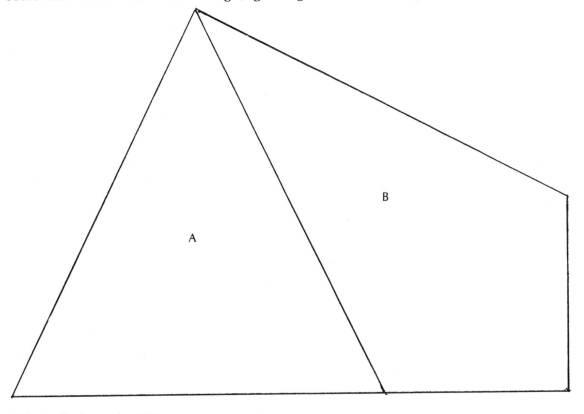

63. Lightning

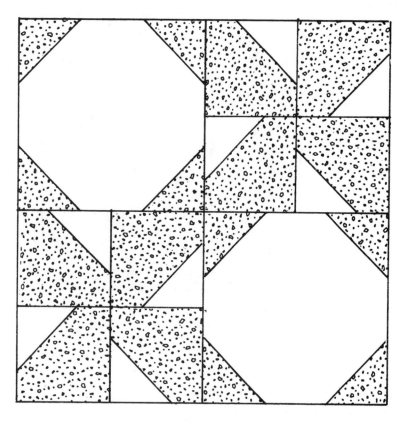

in color p. 7

BLOCK SIZE: 12″

QUILT SIZE: 84″ × 84″

NO. OF BLOCKS: 49

PIECES PER BLOCK:		PER QUILT:
BLOCK A: 25		
A	4 Print	100
BLOCK B: 24		
A	4 Plain	96
B	4 Print	96

FABRIC REQUIREMENTS:

Print—4 yards
Plain—5 1/4 yards

This quilt combines two blocks set alternately to form a new pattern. Pieces are on p. 127.

Block A is fairly simple being a hexagon with the corners filled to form a square. You will note on the pattern page that Block A and B use the same pattern pieces. However, for A, this is only 1/4 of the pattern. Fold a piece of paper into quarters and lay the dashed lines along the folds. Using carbon paper, draw the solid lines, then cut along the drawn lines to form the whole hexagon. Sew four A triangles to form the corners of the block.

Block B uses Parts A and B. B is used as given, ignoring the dash lines. Sew a plain A to a print B to form the four squares making up this block. When sewing them together note that each one is given a quarter turn.

Outline quilt along each seam and use an elaborate floral or geometric in the center of Part A.

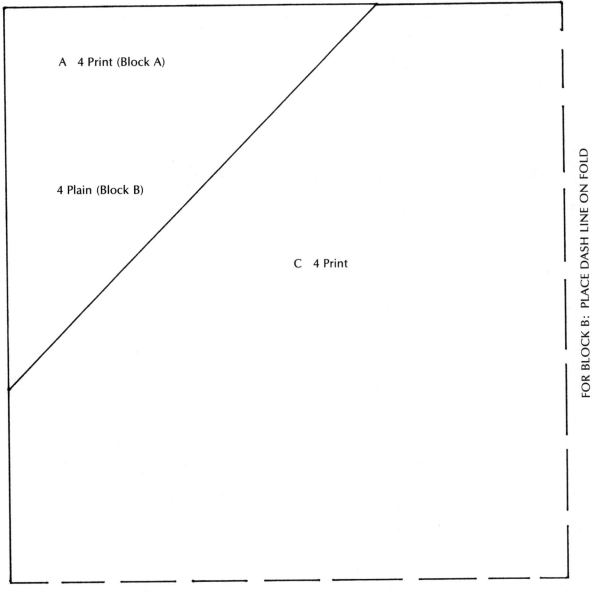

A   4 Print (Block A)

4 Plain (Block B)

C   4 Print

FOR BLOCK B: PLACE DASH LINE ON FOLD

FOR BLOCK B: 1/4 PATTERN—PLACE DASH LINE ON FOLD

BLOCK A: B   1 Plain

64. Lily of the Valley

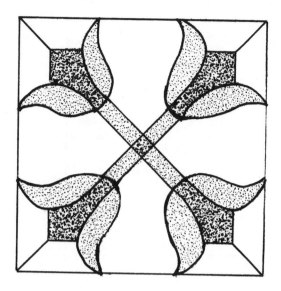

A Ladies Art Company pattern.

in color p. 3

BLOCK SIZE: 18″

QUILT SIZE: 87″ × 87″

NO. OF BLOCKS: 16
Set with 3″ lattice strips and 3″ border

PIECES PER BLOCK:			PER QUILT:
A	4	Red	64
B	8	White	128
C	8	Green	128
D	8	White	128
E	4	Green	64

FABRIC REQUIREMENTS:

Red—2 1/4 yards
Green—2 yards
White—6 yards

This is a difficult pattern to piece, but well worth the effort. The pattern pieces are drawn in their proper order, with D fitting into the curve of C and E being the stem. Pieces are on pp. 131 and 132.

The completed blocks are set together with lattice strips made up of three 1″ strips alternating white, red, white. At the intersection of each block there is a 9-patch square made up of 1″ squares.

For the lattice strips and border you will need: 40 1 1/2″ × 18 1/2″ red strips
80 1 1/2″ × 18 1/2″ white strips

For the intersecting squares, each one requires:

4 green or 100
4 white or 100
1 red or 25

Outline quilt along each seam, then shadow quilt around the lily design.

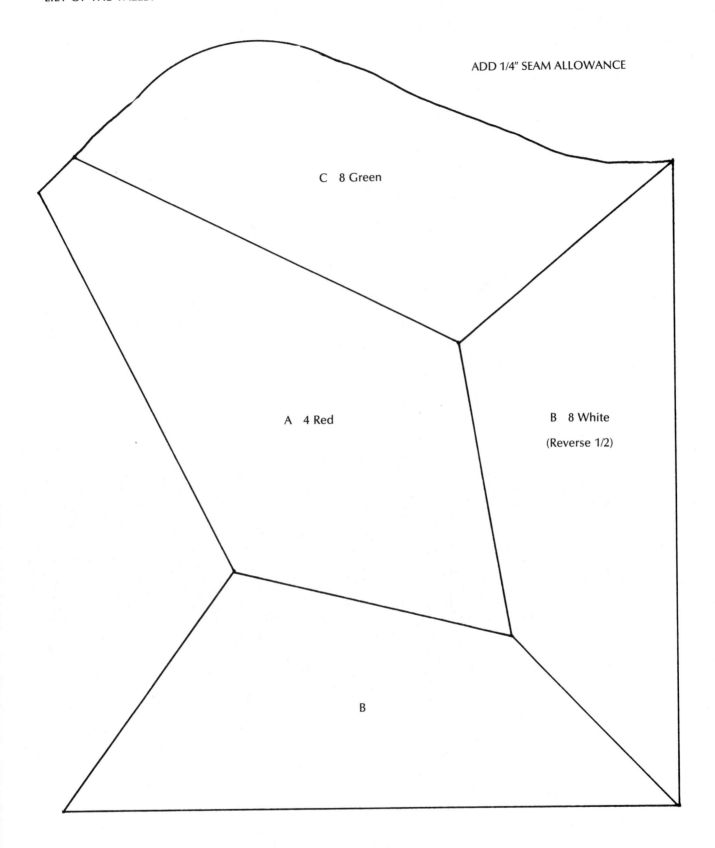

ADD 1/4″ SEAM ALLOWANCE

C   8 Green

A   4 Red

B   8 White

(Reverse 1/2)

B

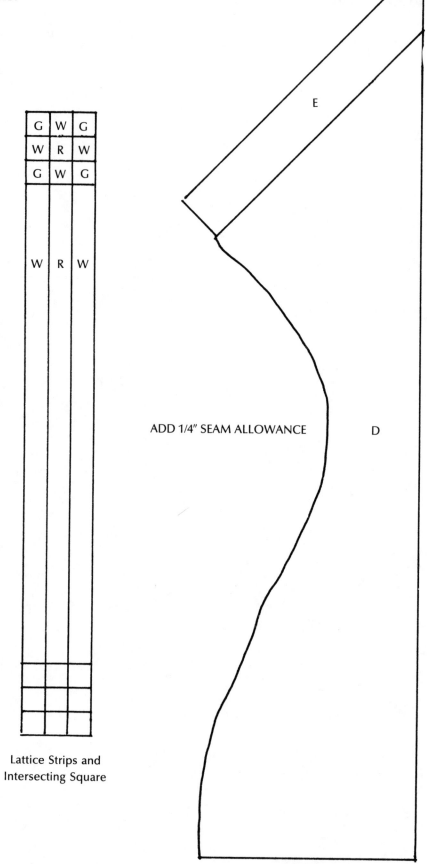

G	W	G
W	R	W
G	W	G

W	R	W

Lattice Strips and
Intersecting Square

E

ADD 1/4″ SEAM ALLOWANCE

D

in color p. 3

BLOCK SIZE: 26″

QUILT SIZE: 82″ × 102″
2 blocks across × 3 blocks down
15″ border on each side
12″ border at top and bottom

NO. OF BLOCKS: 6

PIECES PER BLOCK:			PER QUILT:
A	4	White	24
B	48	White	288
	32	Yellow	192
	21	Green	126
	12	Yellow Print	72
	8	Light Blue	48
C	8	Yellow	48
	22	White	132

FABRIC REQUIREMENTS:

White—4 yards
Yellow—1 1/4 yards
Yellow Print—1/3 yard
Green—1/2 yard
Light Blue—1/4 yard

BORDER: 3 1/2 yards White

Lily Pool was published in *Needlecraft Magazine* in 1934.

This is an easy pattern to piece. For the main body of the pattern, you piece the squares and triangles following the above diagram. Add the corner A pieces and the block is completed. Pattern pieces are on p. 132.

For the border, cut two strips of white fabric 16″ × 79″. Stitch to each side of completed top. Cut two strips 13″ × 83″ and sew to top and bottom.

Quilt around each block of color in the design to emphasize each element. The border provides a large space for a fancy cable or floral motif.

LILY POOL

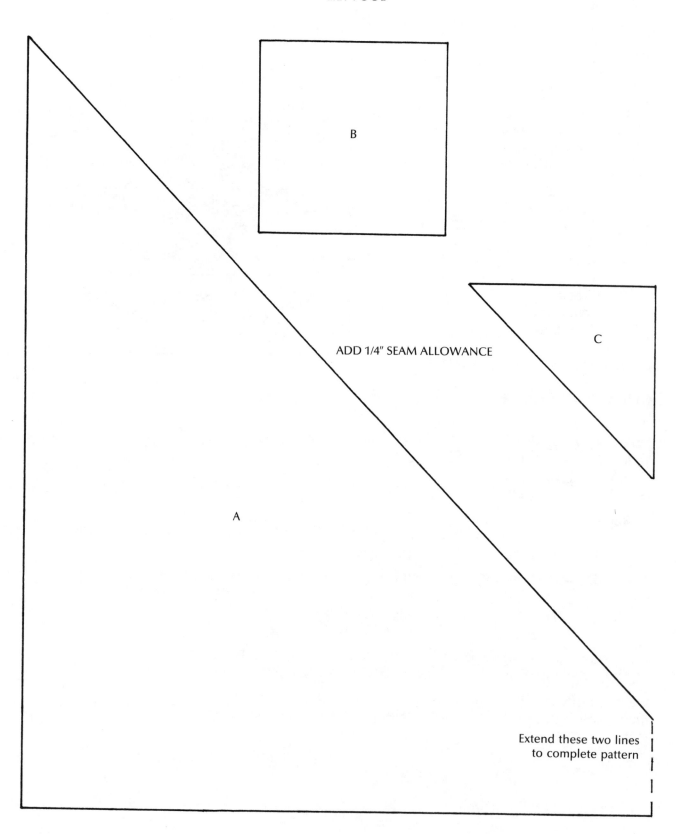

B

ADD 1/4″ SEAM ALLOWANCE

C

A

Extend these two lines
to complete pattern

in color p. 8

BLOCK SIZE: 8″

QUILT SIZE: 80″ × 80″

NO. OF BLOCKS: 100

PIECES PER BLOCK: PER QUILT:
A   4   Print   400
B   4   White   400
C   8   White   800
D   4   Print   400

FABRIC REQUIREMENTS:

White—7 yards
Print—3 3/4 yards

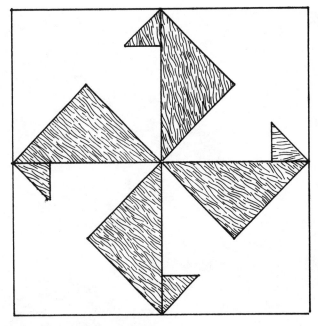

This pattern is obviously to honor Charles A. Lindbergh and his famous exploits. It's a very easy pattern and would be most suitable for the small boy in your life. The size given is for a full-size bed, but it can be scaled down for a twin bed if needed.

The pattern drawing below is full size for 1/4 of the block, showing how the pieces fit together.

For quilting, outline quilt the print sections, then shadow quilt the corners following the diagonal line of the outer edge.

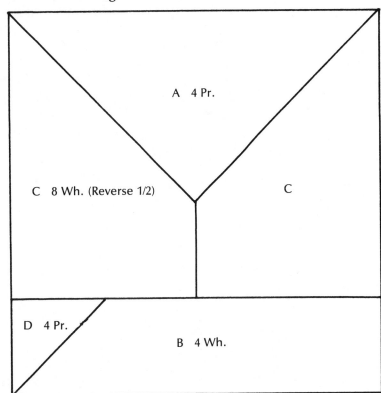

A   4 Pr.

C   8 Wh. (Reverse 1/2)   C

ADD 1/4″ SEAM ALLOWANCE

D   4 Pr.

B   4 Wh.

67. Little Star

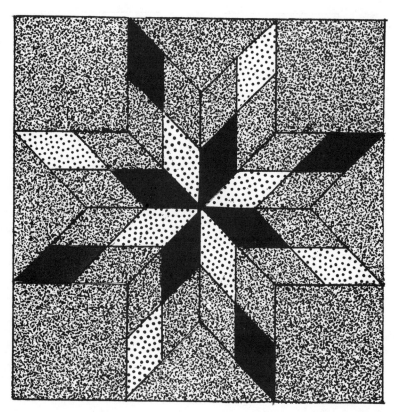

in color p. 13

BLOCK SIZE: 13 1/2"

QUILT SIZE: 81" × 81"

NO. OF BLOCKS: 36

PIECES PER BLOCK:			PER QUILT:
A	8	Light	288
	8	Medium	288
	16	Dark Print	576
B	4	Dark Print	144
C	4	Dark Print	144

FABRIC REQUIREMENTS:

Light Print or Plain—1 1/4 yards
Medium Print or Plain—1 1/4 yards
Dark Print—6 1/2 yards

There are numerous eight-point star designs, and the main difference is color placement. This variation is quite striking. When the block is completed, you see only the center star with its radiating diamond tips. The second row of diamonds becomes part of the background. Any color combination would work up beautifully ranging from strongly contrasting colors to monochromatic to scraps.

TO PIECE AN EIGHT-POINT STAR: Piece each point separately. Sew the appropriately colored diamond pieces for each point. Sew two completed units together and press. Repeat for other six. You now have four units of two diamonds. Sew two of these together to form half of the star. Press, then sew the other half to complete the star.

Set in the corner squares and the triangle.

Pattern pieces are on p. 135.

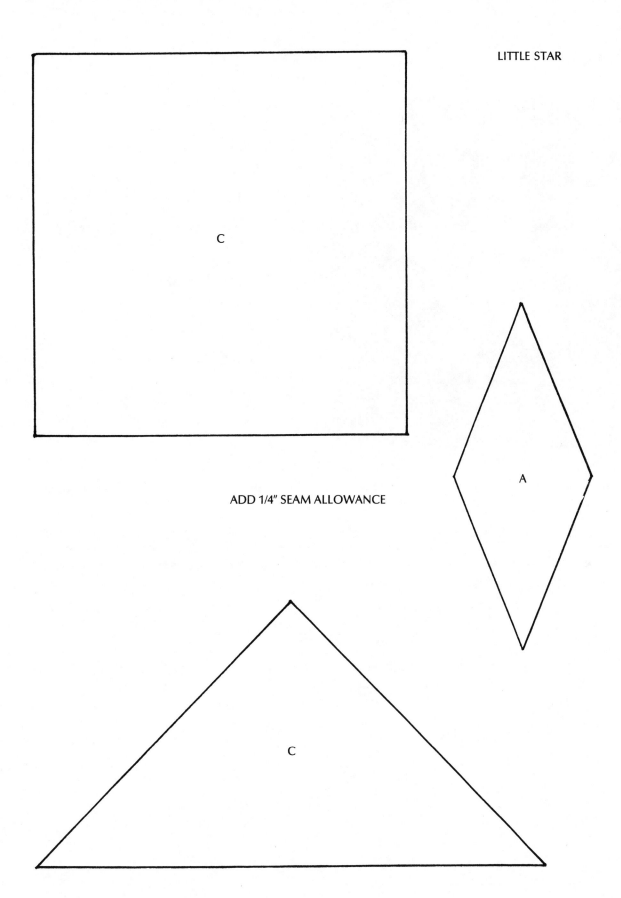

C

ADD 1/4" SEAM ALLOWANCE

A

C

68. Lone Star

DIFFICULT

in color p. 7

BLOCK SIZE: 11″

QUILT SIZE: 77″ × 88″

NO. OF BLOCKS: 56

PIECES PER BLOCK:				PER QUILT:
A	1	Yellow		56
B	5	Blue		280
C	1	11 1/2″ square		56
		Red		

FABRIC REQUIREMENTS:

Yellow—3 1/2 yards
Blue—4 yards
Red—6 1/4 yards

A Ladies Art Company pattern. It's also known as Union Star or Texas Star. Pattern pieces are on p. 137.

This is a combination of piecing and appliqué. Using a lightweight paper, make a pattern of the complete star, matching the dash lines. Now make a template for cutting. Set the Part B pieces between the points of the star.

Cut 56 squares measuring 11 1/2″ (includes seam allowance). Appliqué the star with its circle of blue in the center of the red square. Set the completed squares seven across and eight down.

Shadow quilting to emphasize the three elements of the design would work best for this pattern.

ADD 1/4" SEAM ALLOWANCE

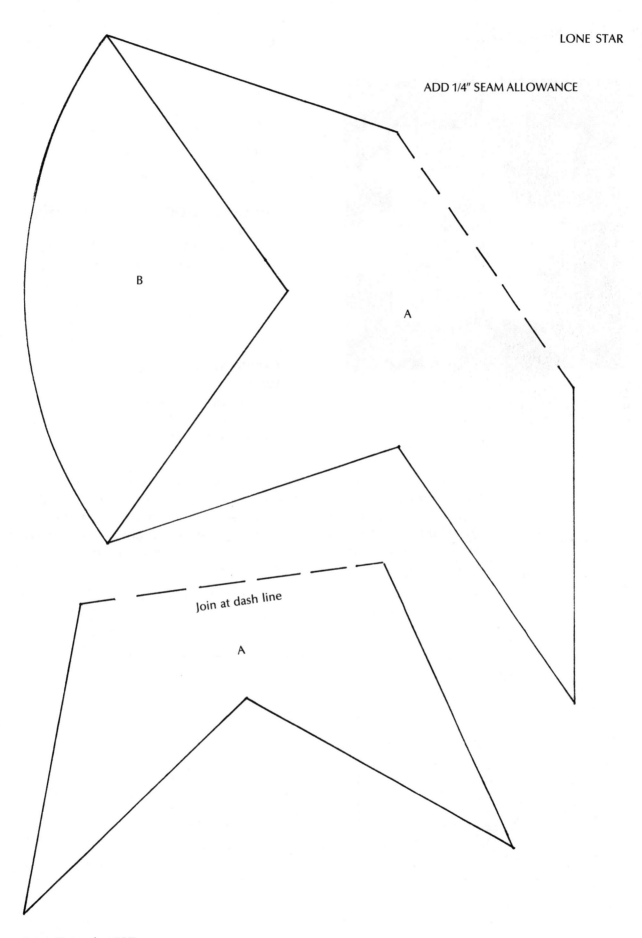

B

A

Join at dash line

A

69. Loop the Loop

EASY

in color p. 4

BLOCK SIZE: 12″

QUILT SIZE: 84″ × 84″

NO. OF BLOCKS: 49

PIECES PER BLOCK:			PER QUILT:
A	16	Dark	784
	5	Light Print	245
	5	Medium Print	245
	8	White	392
B	1	Light Print	49
	1	Medium Print	49
	2	White	98

FABRIC REQUIREMENTS:
White—2 yards
Dark Plain—3 1/4 yards
Light Print—1 1/4 yard
Medium Print—1 1/4 yard

There are only two pattern pieces for this design, which makes it very easy to sew. The way I've broken the pattern down you wind up with more pieces, but it is all straight-seam sewing. The pattern is made up of 2″ squares, except for the two in the center which are half-square triangles. Follow the diagram in rows, keeping in mind that there are six rows per block.

When quilting, follow the pattern design rather than the squares that make up the block.

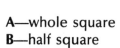

A—whole square
B—half square

ADD 1/4″ SEAM ALLOWANCE

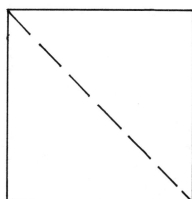

in color p. 11

BLOCK SIZE: 14″

QUILT SIZE: 84″ × 84″

NO. OF BLOCKS: 36

PIECES PER BLOCK:			PER QUILT:
A	82	White	2952
	38	Dark	1368
	40	Light Print	1440
	36	Medium Print	1296

FABRIC REQUIREMENTS:

White—4 1/8 yards
Dark—2 yards
Light Print—2 yards
Medium Print—2 yards

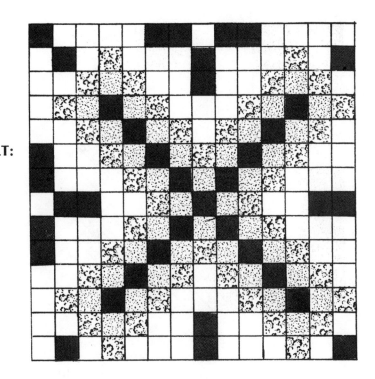

This pattern appeared in *Romance of the Patchwork Quilt in America* so it dates to pre-1933.

This is a very easy though time-consuming pattern to piece since each square is only 1″. To speed it up a bit you could try the following method: Cut the white fabric into strips 1 1/2″ wide. You could also cut a few dark strips 1 1/2″ wide. Starting with the top row, you use a 1 1/2″ square of dark, then you have four squares of white, which would equal 4″ plus 1/2″ for seams. Cut a strip of white 4 1/2″ long. Sew to the dark square. Next you have two squares of dark, one white, and two more dark. Adding seam allowance, cut a 2 1/2″ strip of dark, 1 1/2″ square of white and 2 1/2″ strip of dark and add to strip already sewn. Continue in this manner for those areas in which two or more squares are the same color.

Outline quilt 1/8″ from each seam when top is completed.

A

71. Maryland Beauty

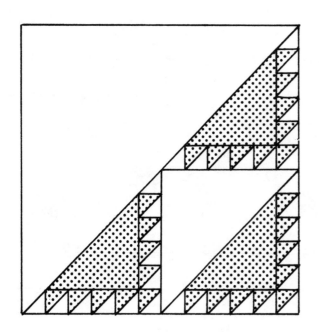

EASY

in color p. 4

BLOCK SIZE: 12"

QUILT SIZE: 72" × 84"

NO. OF BLOCKS: 42

PIECES PER BLOCK:			PER QUILT:
A	27	Print	1134
	33	White	1386
B	3	Print	126
C	1	White	42
D	1	White	42

FABRIC REQUIREMENTS:

Print—3 3/4 yards
White—7 yards

This is a variation of the Sawtooth pattern, which is one of the oldest designs known to quiltmakers. Pattern pieces are on p. 141.

Piece the Part A print and white half-triangles into strips and set with the print Part B. Set one of these units with white Part C to form a square, then add the other two to form a triangle. Finish the square with a triangle made from a 12" square which has been cut in half.

The blocks should be set so that the white side of the triangle always lines up with the pieced triangle of the previous block.

Outline quilt the sawtooth strips. Carry the quilting lines onto the B and C pieces. The design can be repeated on the white portion of the block or you can do some fancy quilting on this triangle.

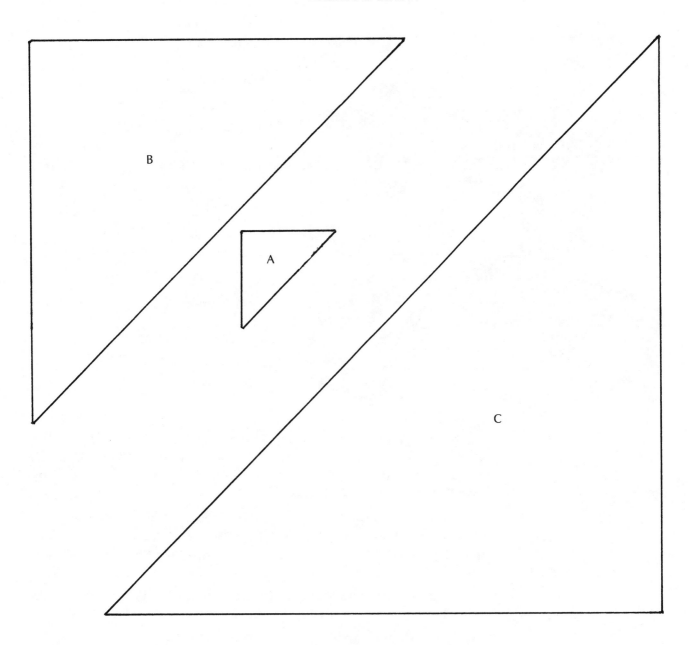

D is a 12″ square cut in half on the diagonal.

ADD 1/4″ SEAM ALLOWANCE

72. Missouri Puzzle

EASY

in color p. 14

BLOCK SIZE: 15″

QUILT SIZE: 75″ × 75″

NO. OF BLOCKS: 25

PIECES PER BLOCK:			PER QUILT:
A	4	White	100
B	4	White	100
	12	Print	300
C	1	White	25
D	20	White	500
	16	Print	400
E	8	Print	200
	4	White	100

FABRIC REQUIREMENTS:

White—4 1/2 yards
Print—4 1/4 yards

This pattern appears in the book *Romance of the Patchwork Quilt in America* by Carrie A. Hall and Rose G. Kretsinger. These patterns all date prior to 1933 and many are from before the turn of the century. Pattern pieces are on p. 143.

This is an easy pattern for piecing in that it is all straight-seam piecing. Break the block into the following units: four dark and light B's corner squares. Four BAB center strips. Four nine-patch D units; four dark and light E units.

Outline quilt along the seams of the center square. Where the blocks join, you have a larger space for a quilting motif.

No border is necessary.

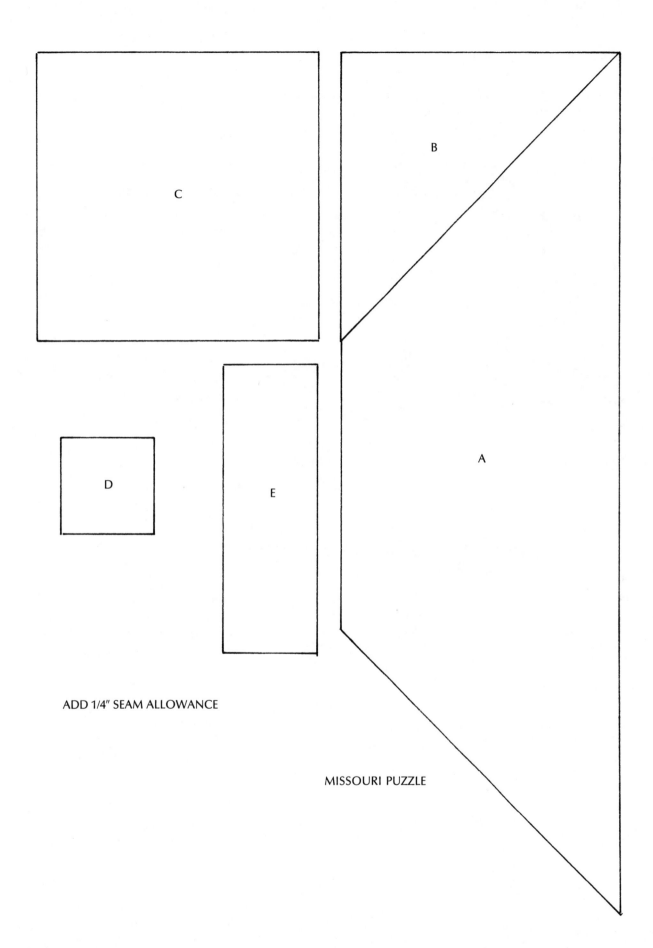

C

B

D

E

A

ADD 1/4" SEAM ALLOWANCE

MISSOURI PUZZLE

Missouri Puzzle ☆ *143*

73. Mollie's Choice

in color p. 15

BLOCK SIZE: 18″

QUILT SIZE: 90″ × 90″

NO. OF BLOCKS: 25

PIECES PER BLOCK:			PER QUILT:
A	4	Print	100
	12	White	300
B	4	Print	100
C	4	White	100
D	4	Print	100
E	16	Print	400
F	8	White	200
G	1	White	25

FABRIC REQUIREMENTS:

Print—5 1/4 yards
White—6 3/4 yards

A Ladies Art Company pattern. Pattern pieces are on p. 145.

This is basically a nine-patch design, which makes it easy to sew. Stitch each square of the nine, following the above drawing, then set the completed squares together to form the block.

Set the completed blocks five across and five down.

This is a large block and simple outline quilting would not be enough to keep the top from shifting. A design following the diagonal lines of the quilt would be interesting. By using polyester batting, you can space the lines 1 1/2″ apart to match the width of the corner strip and carry it in to the center of each block.

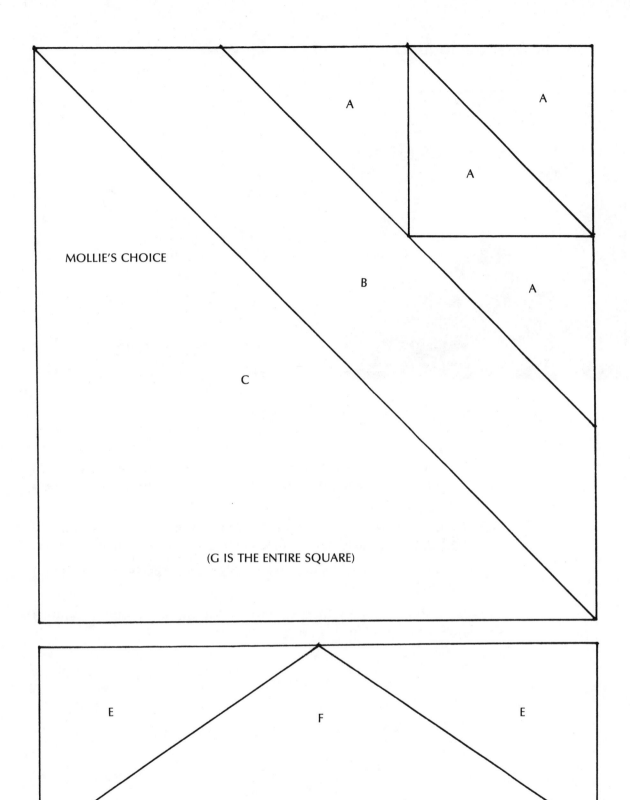

MOLLIE'S CHOICE

A

A

A

A

B

C

(G IS THE ENTIRE SQUARE)

E

F

E

(D IS THE ENTIRE RECTANGLE)

ADD 1/4" SEAM ALLOWANCE

74. Moon Over the Mountain

EASY

in color p. 3

BLOCK SIZE: 10"

QUILT SIZE: 70" × 90"

NO. OF BLOCKS: 32 Pieced
32 Plain

PIECES PER BLOCK:			PER QUILT:
A	1	Dark Blue	32
B	1	Yellow	32

64 Blue and White print squares for
background 10 1/2"

FABRIC REQUIREMENTS:

Blue and White Print—5 1/3 yards
Dark Blue—1 3/4 yards
Yellow—1 1/3 yards

This is a very simple appliqué design. It seems to be of fairly recent origin since I can't trace it back much further than the 1940's. Pattern pieces are on p. 147.

Cut background blocks 10 1/2" square. Position the moon and mountain on the background and sew in place with a small whipstitch.

The pieced blocks are set alternately with plain blocks, seven across and nine down.

Quilting should follow the design and the moon-mountain pattern should be repeated in the plain blocks.

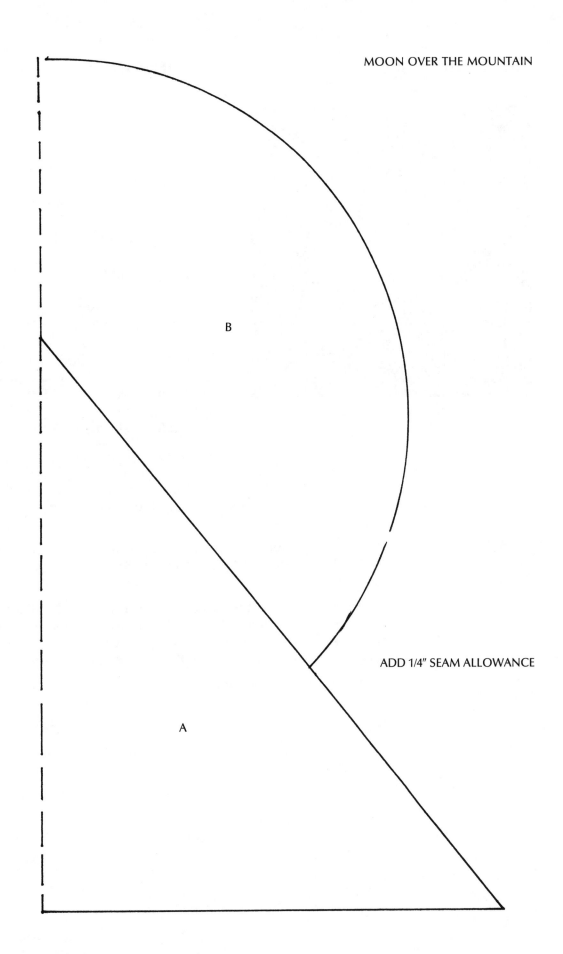

MOON OVER THE MOUNTAIN

B

ADD 1/4" SEAM ALLOWANCE

A

75. Morning Glory

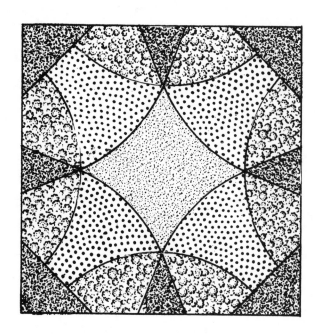

in color p. 5

BLOCK SIZE: 12"

QUILT SIZE: 72" × 84"

NO. OF BLOCKS: 42

PIECES PER BLOCK:			PER QUILT:
A	1	Yellow	42
B	4	Light Blue	168
C	8	Medium Blue	336
D	4	Dark Blue	168
E	4	Dark Blue	168

(Fabrics can be all print, all plain or a combination of both. This also makes a good scrap quilt if you repeat the same color for Parts D and E throughout.)

FABRIC REQUIREMENTS:

Yellow—1 3/4 yards
Medium Blue—3 1/4 yards
Light Blue—3 1/4 yards
Dark Blue—2 1/4 yards

This is a fairly new pattern dating from the turn of the century. It is complex and difficult to piece though, so the novice is advised to pass it by for a while.

Pattern p. 149 shows the pieces in their proper order. Part A shows 1/4 of the center so a full-sized template must be made first. Fold a piece of paper into quarters and lay the Part A pattern with the dash lines along the folds. Using it, draw the curved line. Cut on the curve.

A border can be added if desired.

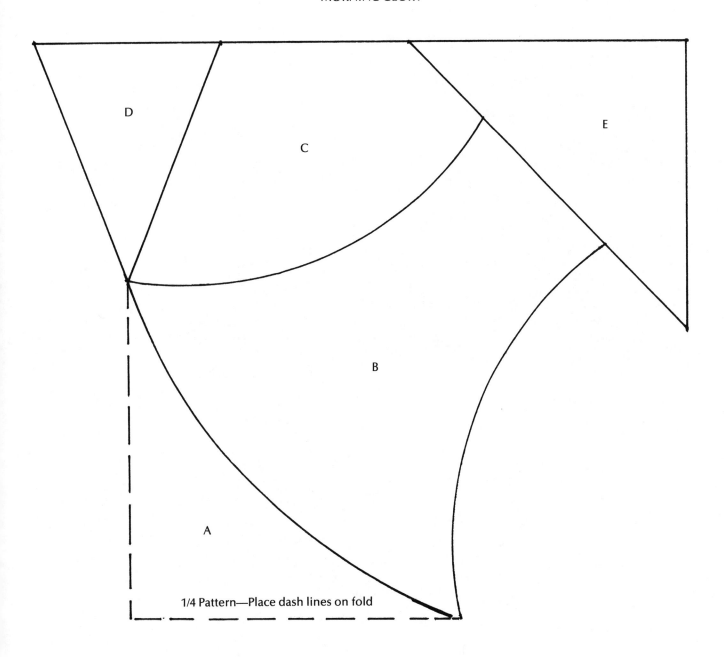

1/4 Pattern—Place dash lines on fold

ADD 1/4″ SEAM ALLOWANCE

76. Nebraska

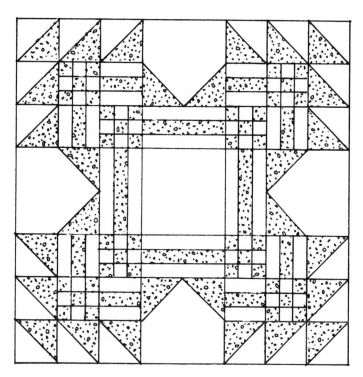

A Nancy Cabot design.

EASY

in color p. 7

BLOCK SIZE: 24″

QUILT SIZE: 96″ × 96″

NO. OF BLOCKS: 16

PIECES PER BLOCK:

			PER QUILT:
A	28	Print	448
	20	White	320
B	16	White	256
	8	Print	128
C	40	Print	640
	32	White	512
D	4	White	64
E	8	White	128
	4	Print	64
F	1	6 1/2″ square	16

FABRIC REQUIREMENTS:

Print—5 3/4 yards
White—8 1/4 yards

Each block of this pattern contains 161 pieces, but it is all straight-seam sewing and only 16 blocks make a good-sized quilt. You could also use this pattern as a medallion for the center of a quilt, or use four or six and fill it out with a border.

The following diagrams, pp. 151 and 152, show the pattern pieces set in the order in which they will go together. Break the block down into the four corner squares, then piece the center sections and set it all together with the F 6″ square in the center.

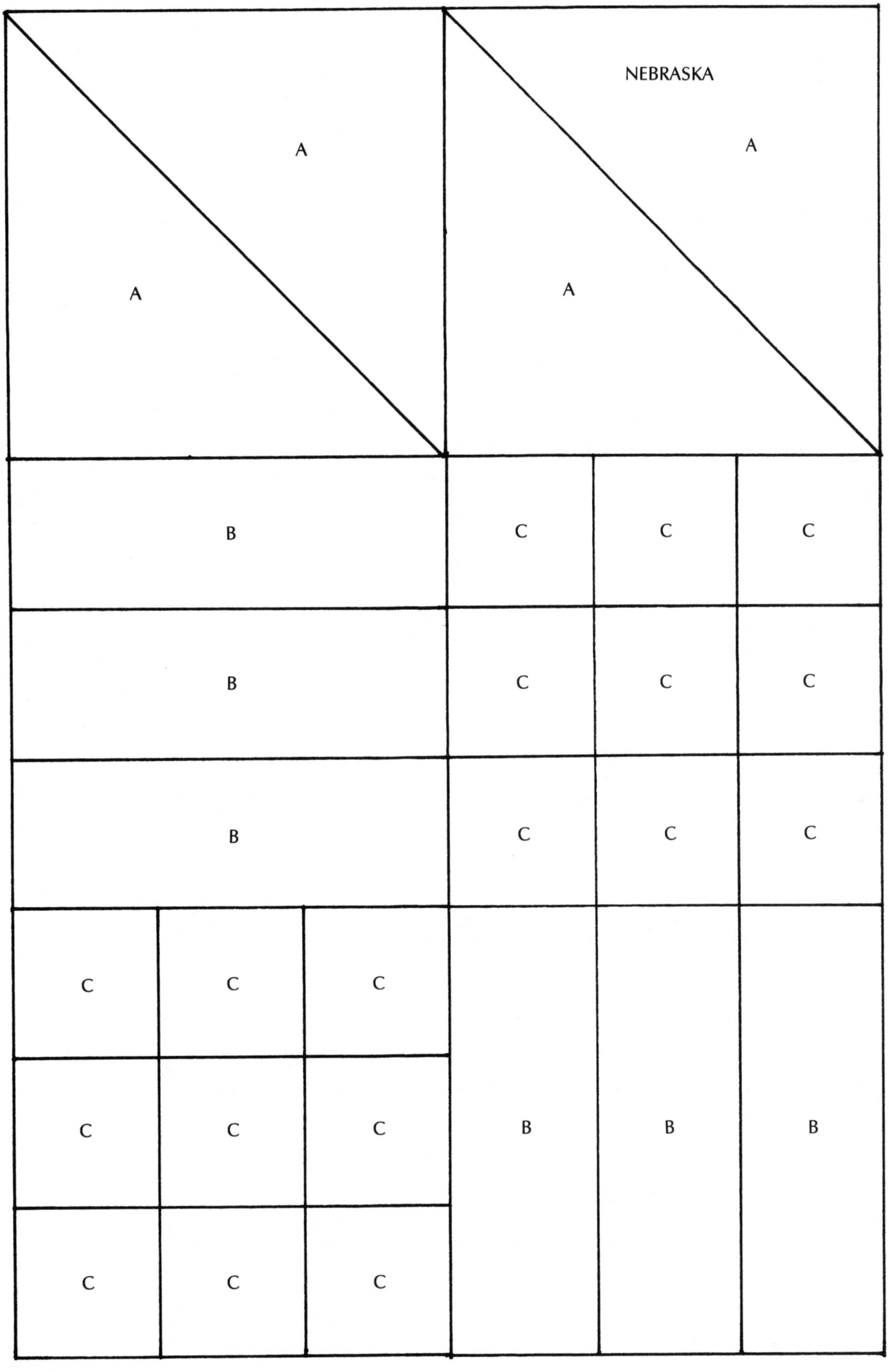
NEBRASKA
A
A
A
A
B
C
C
C
B
C
C
C
B
C
C
C
C
C
C
C
C
C
B
B
B
C
C
C

CORNER SECTION—ADD 3 PART A SQUARES TO OUTER EDGE

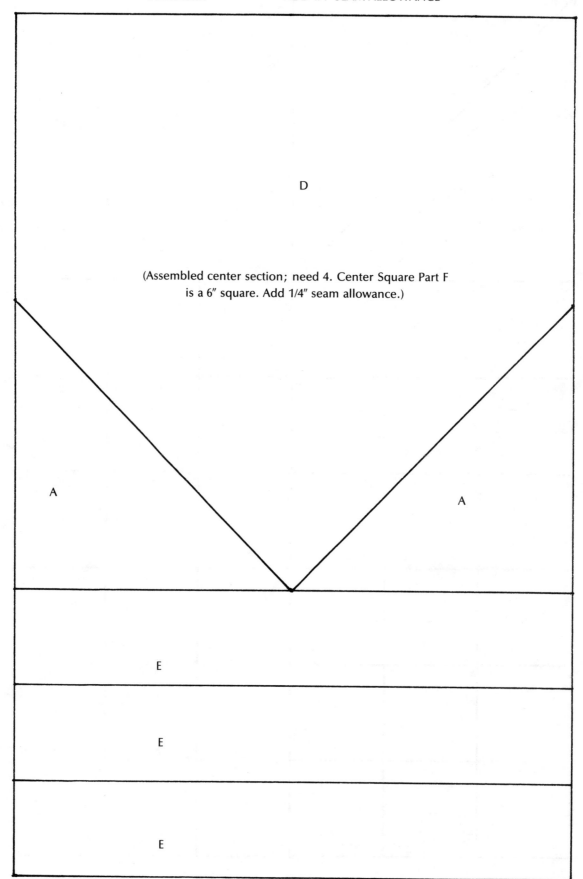

D

(Assembled center section; need 4. Center Square Part F
is a 6″ square. Add 1/4″ seam allowance.)

A

A

E

E

E

in color p. 9

BLOCK SIZE: 14″

QUILT SIZE: 84″ × 84″

NO. OF BLOCKS: 56

PIECES PER BLOCK:			PER QUILT:
A	4	Medium Print	224
B	5	White	280
	4	Medium Print	224
C	8	Dark	448
D	4	White	224

FABRIC REQUIREMENTS:

White—5 2/3 yards
Medium Print—3 yards
Dark—3 yards

This pattern was published by *Hearth & Home Magazine* in 1928. I've taken a small liberty with the design by changing the four corner blocks to a different color. In the original these four squares are the same color as the points of the star but I felt that this slight change made a more interesting block. Pattern pieces are on p. 154.

TO ASSEMBLE: Divide the blocks visually into three rows: top, middle and bottom. Top and bottom are the same. Piece two dark C's to one white D. Add medium A to each end. For the center row, piece the nine-patch center, then add assembled units CDC to each side. Sew the three rows together to complete the block.

A border isn't necessary but may be added if desired.

The star could be quilted along each seam. Where the blocks meet you will have an 8″ square and the center white piece will be 6″ × 8″. These spaces can be treated with a fancy floral motif, or you could just use an overall design for the entire top.

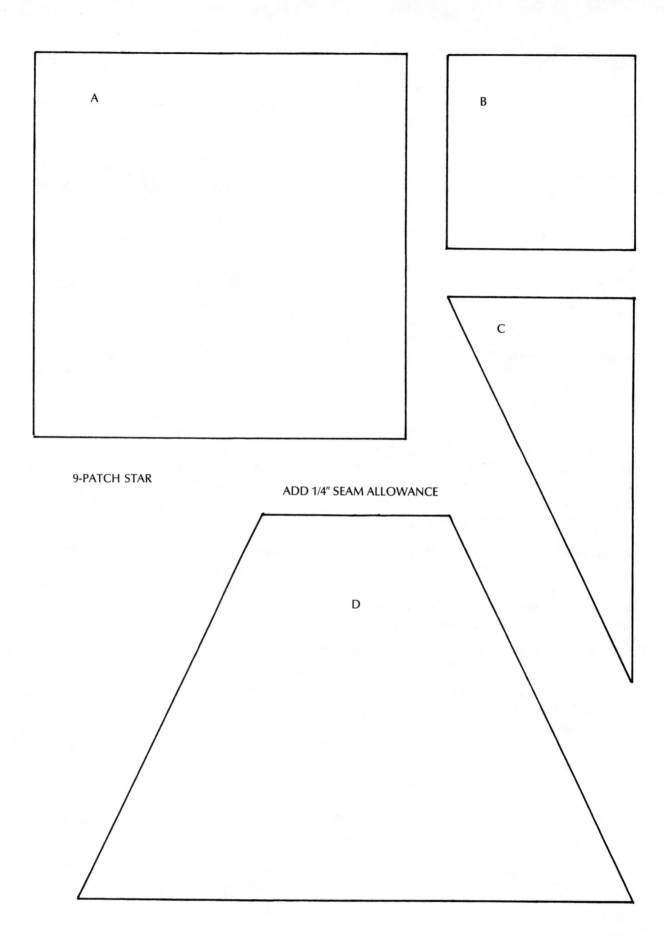

A

B

C

9-PATCH STAR

ADD 1/4" SEAM ALLOWANCE

D

MODERATE

in color p. 10

BLOCK SIZE: 12″

QUILT SIZE: 84″ × 84″

NO. OF BLOCKS: 49

PIECES PER BLOCK:			PER QUILT:
A	1	Print	49
B	8	Plain	392
C	4	Print	196
D	4	Plain	196
	12	White	588
E	4	White	196

FABRIC REQUIREMENTS:

Print—2 3/4 yards
Plain—4 yards
White—3 3/4 yards

This is a fairly easy pattern to assemble. Pieces are on p. 156.

The pattern is drawn to show how the pieces go together. Sew four BCB units; add E to each unit. Sew two of these units to Part A, a 4 1/4″ square. Set aside and sew the D pieces to form the center edge triangle. Sew one of these triangles to each side of the other two BCB units. Sew all assembled units together to form the block.

Outline quilt 1/8″ from each seam, then shadow quilt a few rows into each piece.

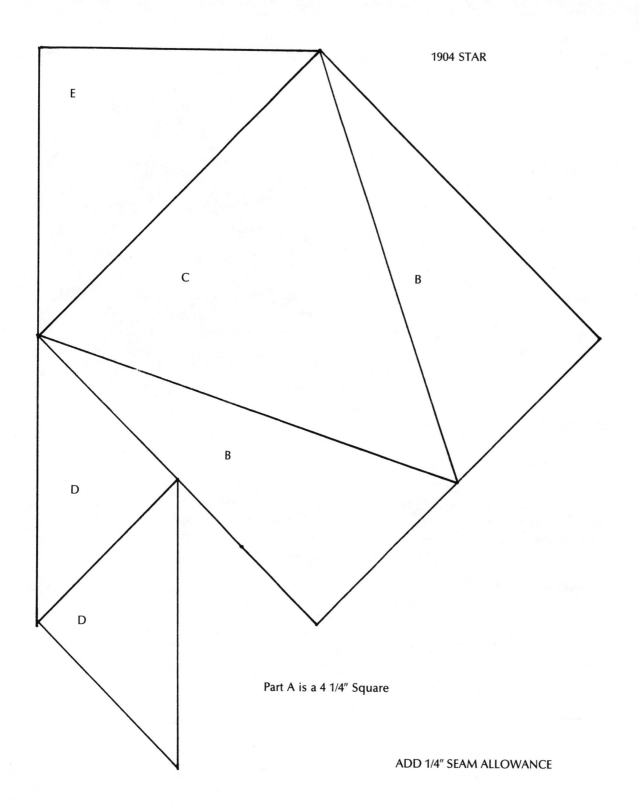

E

C

B

B

D

D

Part A is a 4 1/4″ Square

ADD 1/4″ SEAM ALLOWANCE

in color p. 9

BLOCK SIZE: 14″

QUILT SIZE: 84″ × 84″

NO. OF BLOCKS: 36

PIECES PER BLOCK:			PER QUILT:
A	1	Dark	36
	20	Print	720
	16	White	576
B	4	Dark	144
C	8	White	288

FABRIC REQUIREMENTS:

Dark—1 1/2 yards
Print—3 yards
White—4 1/3 yards

This is a nine-patch variation and is fairly easy to piece.

Make templates adding 1/4″ seam allowance. Cut out fabric.

Stitch together four CBC's. Set aside. Sew together the nine-patch corners, then assemble these with the CBC pieces as shown in the diagram.

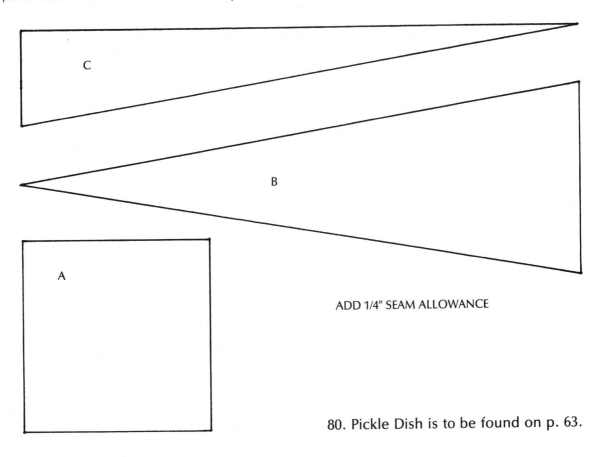

ADD 1/4″ SEAM ALLOWANCE

80. Pickle Dish is to be found on p. 63.

81. Pigeon Toes

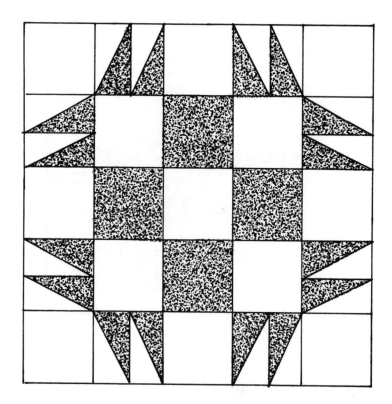

in color p. 16

BLOCK SIZE: 15″

QUILT SIZE: 75″ × 90″

NO. OF BLOCKS: 30

PIECES PER BLOCK:			PER QUILT:
A	13	White	390
	4	Dark	120
B	16	White	480
	16	Dark	480

FABRIC REQUIREMENTS:

White—5 1/2 yards
Dark—3 1/4 yards

A fast, easy pattern for piecing.

When cutting the fabric, be sure to reverse half the pieces for Part B.

You could use strip piecing for the center squares. Cut strips of white and dark fabric 3 1/2″ wide. Sew a white, dark, white strip. Press, then cut into 3 1/2″ lengths. Sew a second strip using dark, white, dark. Press and again cut into 3 1/2″ lengths. Repeat a second white, dark, white and sew these three strips together to form the center of the block.

Sew the light and dark B squares, and add to the outer edges of the center block along with the white A squares to complete the block.

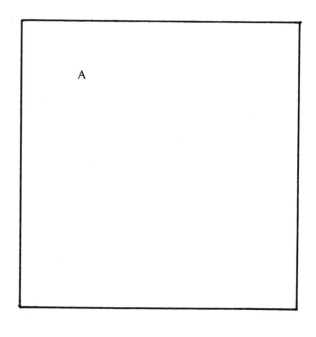

A

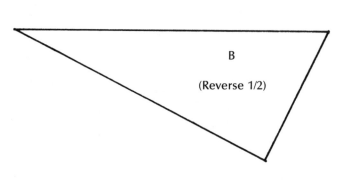

B

(Reverse 1/2)

DIFFICULT

in color p. 16

BLOCK SIZE: 12″

QUILT SIZE: 72″ × 84″

NO. OF BLOCKS: 42

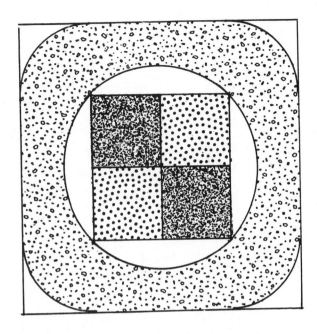

PIECES PER BLOCK:		PER QUILT:
A	2 Print #1	84
	2 Print #2	84
B	4 White	168
C	4 Print #3	168
D	4 White	168

FABRIC REQUIREMENTS:

Print #1—3/4 yard
Print #2—3/4 yard
Print #3—5 2/3 yards
White—2 1/4 yards

Because of the curves, this is a more difficult pattern to piece. I've given yardages for an overall design, but the quilt could be made up as a scrap quilt set with lattice strips or alternate plain blocks.

The pattern pieces on p. 160, as drawn, show the placement of each unit. Begin in the center with the four squares, add the Part B's, then C and D.

An allover circular quilting design would work well on this pattern to accent the curves.

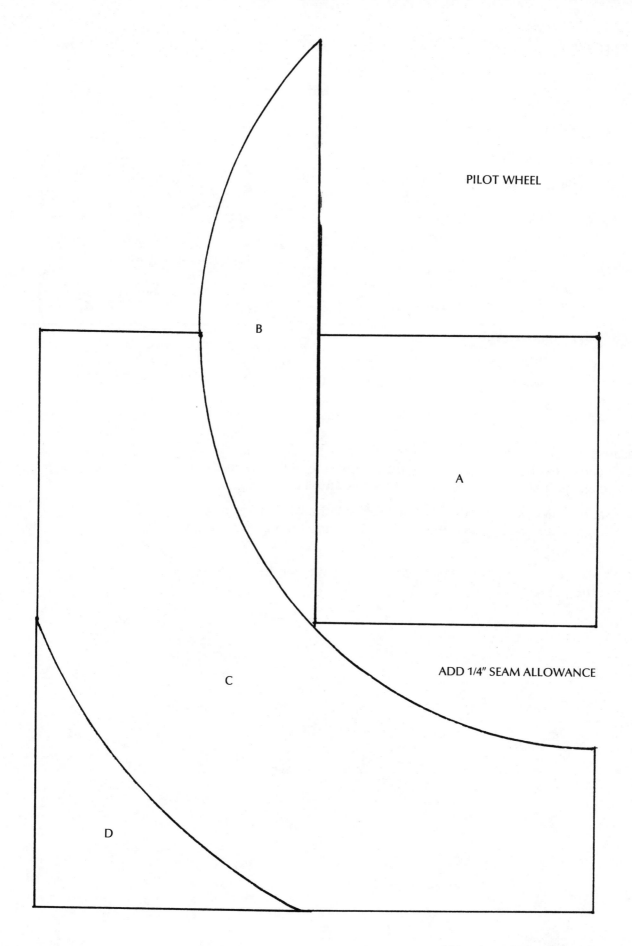

PILOT WHEEL

B

A

ADD 1/4″ SEAM ALLOWANCE

C

D

in color p. 5

BLOCK SIZE: 18″

QUILT SIZE: 76 1/2″ × 102″

NO. OF BLOCKS: 12 Pieced

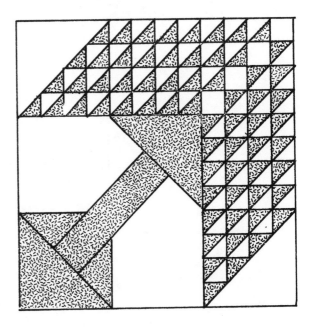

PIECES PER BLOCK:			PER QUILT:
A	1	Dark	12
B	2	Dark	24
C	1	Dark	12
D	1	Dark	12
	2	White	24
E	4	White	48
F	46	White	672
	64	Dark	768
G	2	White	24

FABRIC REQUIRED: The usual color for this pattern is blue, but you could use any dark colored fabric, such as green or brown.
Dark—3 1/2 yards
White—7 2/3 yards

The pine tree was and is a favorite for quiltmakers and this pattern is only one of dozens available. There are a lot of pieces per block, but since it is a large block set on the diagonal, it only takes 12 to make a quilt. Pattern pieces are on pp. 162 and 163.

In addition to the pieces for the pieced blocks you will need:

 6 Plain White blocks cut 18 1/2″ square
10 Plain White half-blocks (cut a paper pattern 18″ square, then cut it in half on the diagonal. Add seam allowance before cutting fabric.)
 4 Plain White quarter-blocks (using the other half of the 18″ paper square, cut it in half from the corner to the center of the diagonal cut. Add seam allowance.)

Once the pieced blocks are completed, lay them on the diagonal so the tree is pointing up. Lay the plain white blocks between them, then the half-blocks along the edges. Pin the blocks in diagonal rows, then stitch the rows together. Add the four corner blocks to finish the top. The plain blocks are perfect for your elaborate quilting patterns. Outline quilt the pieced blocks.

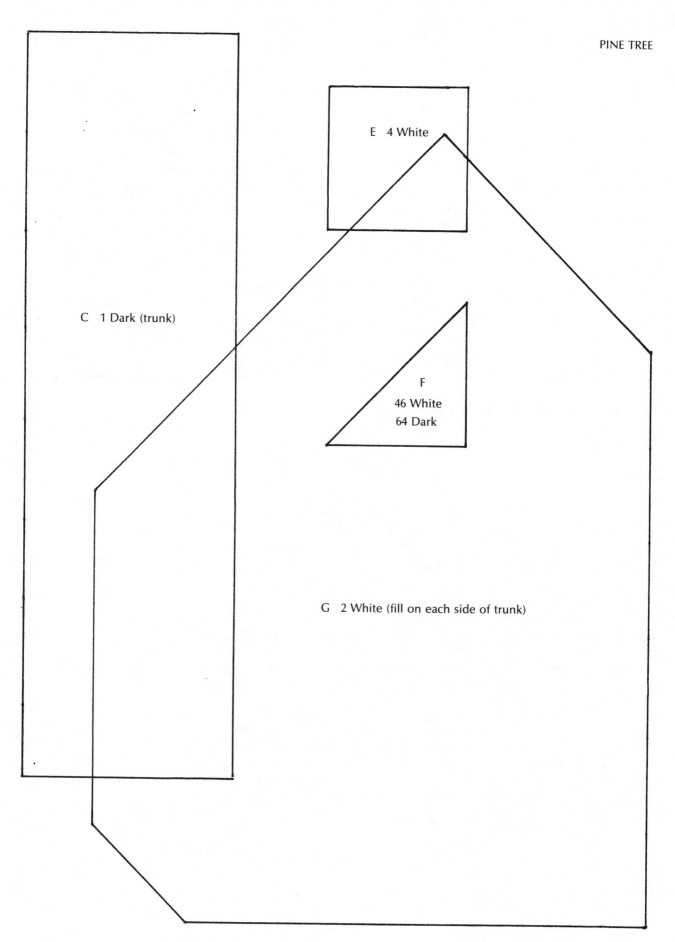

C   1 Dark (trunk)

E   4 White

F
46 White
64 Dark

G   2 White (fill on each side of trunk)

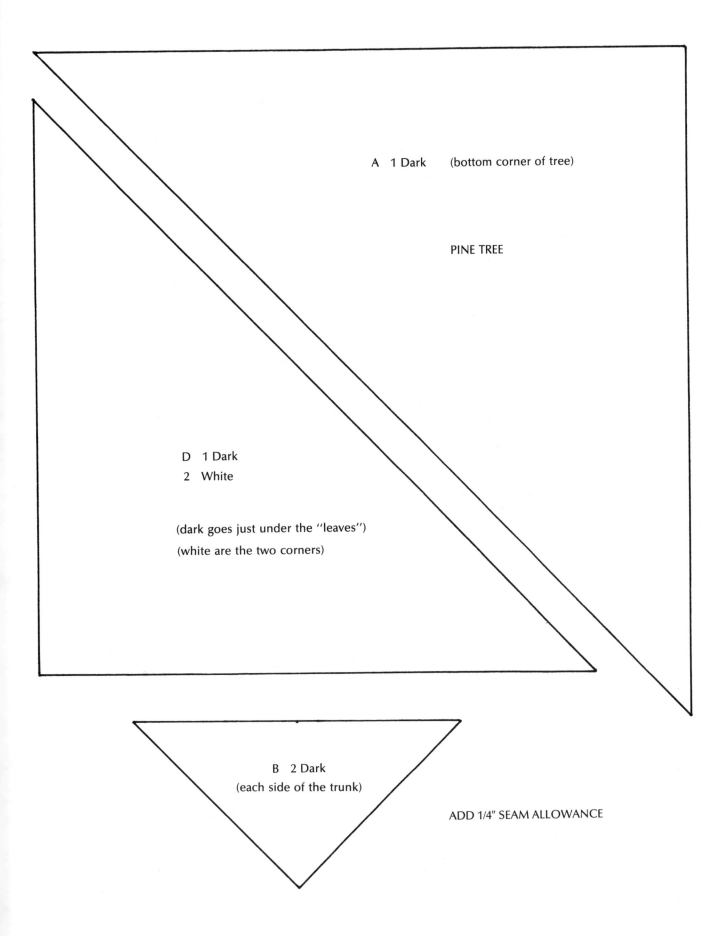

A   1 Dark   (bottom corner of tree)

PINE TREE

D   1 Dark
2   White

(dark goes just under the "leaves")
(white are the two corners)

B   2 Dark
(each side of the trunk)

ADD 1/4" SEAM ALLOWANCE

84. Pinwheel Square

in color p. 6

BLOCK SIZE: 15″

QUILT SIZE: 90″ × 90″

NO. OF BLOCKS: 36

PIECES PER BLOCK:			PER QUILT:
A	5	Print	180
B	4	White	144
C	4	Print	144
D	4	White	144
E	4	Print	144
	4	White	144

FABRIC REQUIREMENTS:

Print—5 1/3 yards
White or Plain—4 1/2 yards

A Ladies Art Company pattern. Pattern pieces are on p. 165.

This is another easy pattern to piece. Break the block down into the four corner squares consisting of A, B, C, and D, and the center pieces consisting of two F's making one unit. Make four of these set with a center Part A.

Since each part of the block is fairly large, an overall quilting design of diamonds, circles or squares would be best for quilting.

No border is necessary, but one may be added if desired.

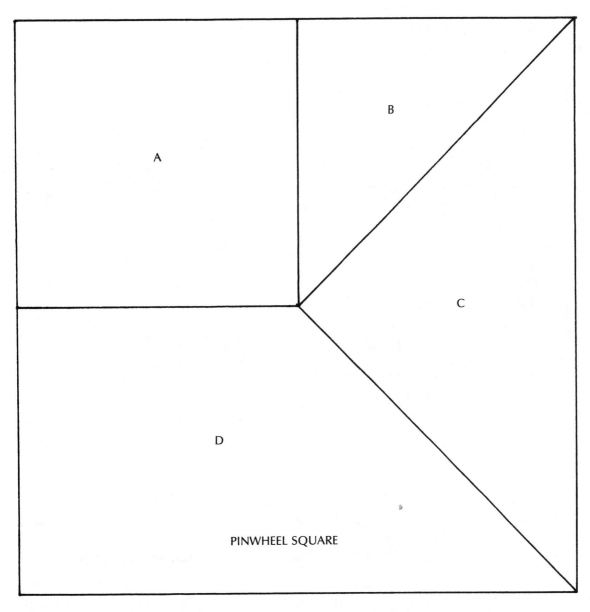

A

B

C

D

PINWHEEL SQUARE

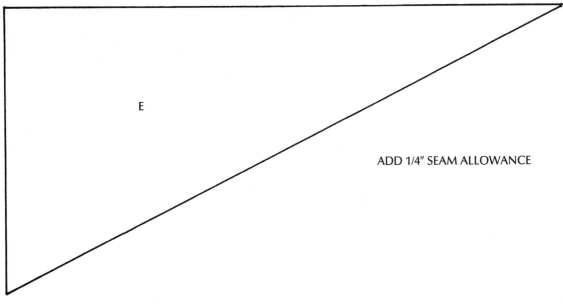

E

ADD 1/4″ SEAM ALLOWANCE

Pinwheel Square ☆ *165*

85. Postage Stamp Baskets

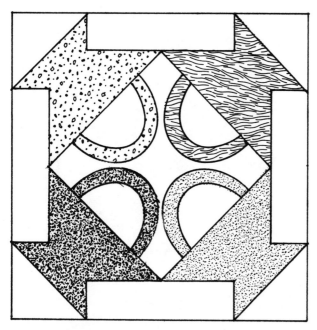

This pattern was designed as a commemorative United States stamp in 1978.

EASY

in color p. 16

BLOCK SIZE: 16″

QUILT SIZE: 80″ × 96″

NO. OF BLOCKS: 30

PIECES PER BLOCK:			PER QUILT:
A	1	White	30
B	4	Print	120
C	4	Print	120
D	4	Print	120
E	4	White	120
F	4	White	120

FABRIC REQUIREMENTS:

White—5 1/4 yards
9″ × 12″ Scrap for each basket

It is a very easy pattern, and will use up a lot of scraps. Pattern pieces are on pp. 167 and 168.

To make the template for Part A, fold a piece of paper into quarters and line up the dash lines along the folds. Draw the diagonal line and cut along it. The unfolded paper will form your square template.

Cut out 30 such squares of fabric for the center of the block. Add a different color Part B to each diagonal edge; then stitch Part C, to form bottom of basket. Add Part F for corner and set in Part E to finish square. The handles are appliquéd in place.

Outline quilting 1/8″ from each seam will best display the pattern of this quilt.

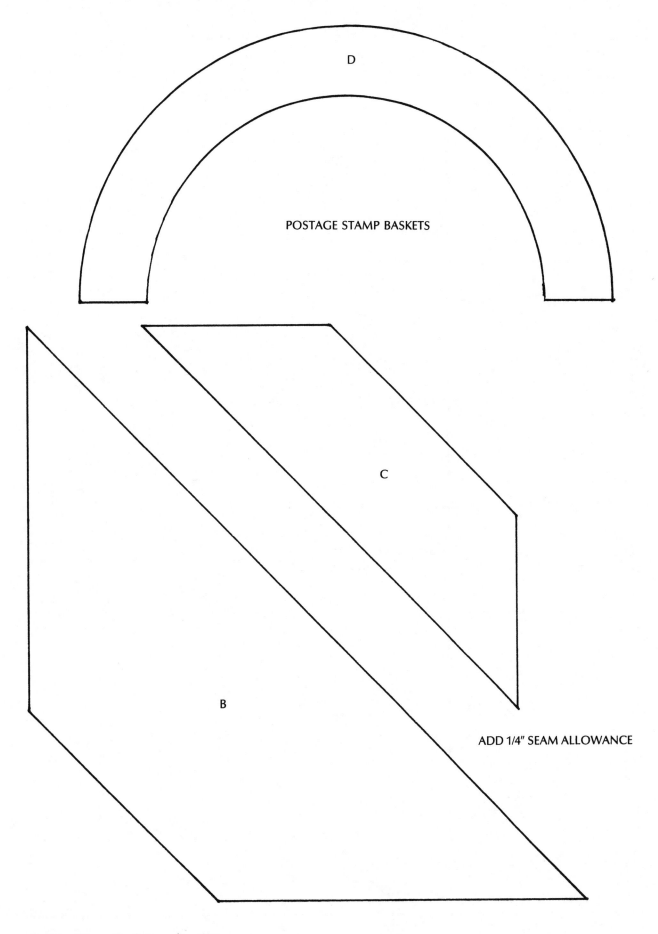

POSTAGE STAMP BASKETS

ADD 1/4" SEAM ALLOWANCE

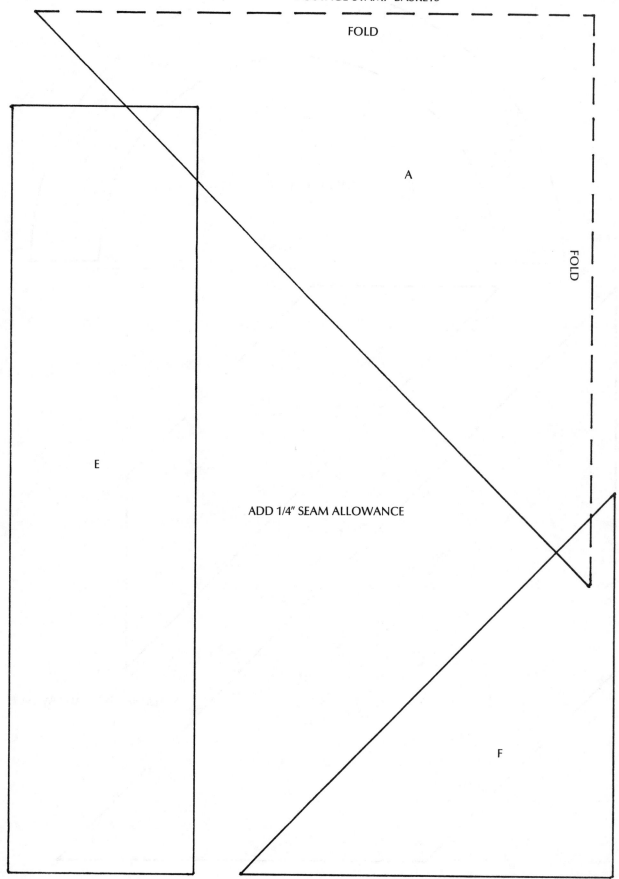

FOLD

A

FOLD

E

ADD 1/4" SEAM ALLOWANCE

F

in color p. 6

BLOCK SIZE: 13 1/2"

QUILT SIZE: 81" × 94 1/2"

NO. OF BLOCKS: 42

PIECES PER BLOCK:			PER QUILT:
A	4	Medium	168
B	4	Light	168
C	8	Dark	336
D	4	Light	168
E	4	Medium	168
F	4	Medium	168
G	1	Light	42

FABRIC REQUIREMENTS:

Dark—3 yards
Medium—3 3/4 yards
Light—4 1/2 yards

I can't pinpoint the exact time that this pattern first appeared, but it was published in the *Quilt Pattern Book, Patchwork and Appliqué,* issued by The Ladies Art Company of St. Louis, Missouri, in 1922, under the title Miss Jackson. Nancy Cabot published it in the 1930's as Prosperity Block. It is also known as Empty Spools.

SEWING INSTRUCTIONS: Cut out pattern pieces, on pp. 170 and 171, adding seam allowance. When cutting fabric for Part C, cut half the pieces needed, then reverse the pattern for the other half.

Sew together Parts A, B, and F. This is the corner and you will need four. Then sew together four units of Parts C, D, and E. Sew the completed units together and then to Part G.

This pattern is somewhat difficult because of the points that must be pivoted when sewing the block together. With a slight change in the pattern, you can make this all straight-line sewing even though you will have more parts.

For the simplified method, you will need to cut the following pieces per block: **A**—4, **B**—4, **H**—16 medium, 8 light, 16 dark, **E**—4, **I**—4 light, 8 dark.

CORNER SQUARE: Assemble A, B and medium H. Center Square: Row 1 and 3. Assemble medium H to dark H and dark H to light H. Sew to form strip with dark I in the middle. Center strip is formed by E and light I. Sew the three strips to form the center square. Sew the four medium H parts to the corners of G. You now have nine squares to be assembled, following the diagram.

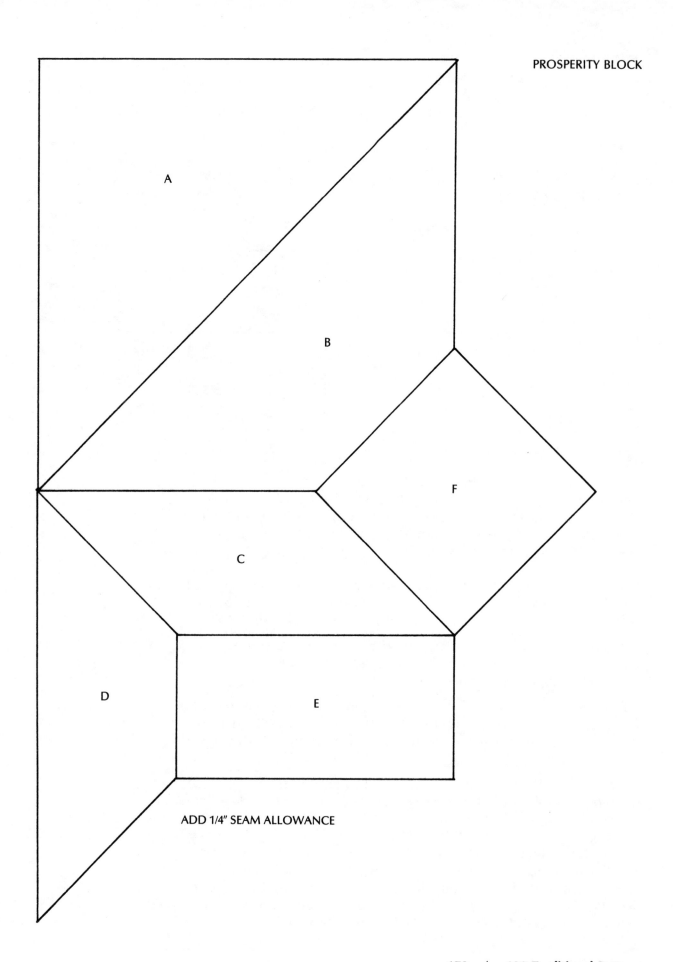

A

B

F

C

F

D

E

ADD 1/4" SEAM ALLOWANCE

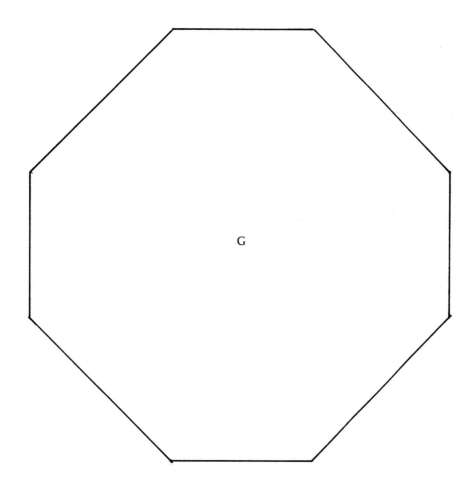

ADD 1/4" SEAM ALLOWANCE

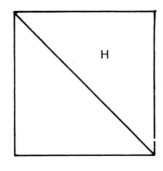

PART I is the whole square
which measures 1 1/2" plus
seam allowance.)

87. Pyramids

in color p. 14

BLOCK SIZE: 16″

QUILT SIZE: 80″ × 96″

NO. OF BLOCKS: 30

PIECES PER BLOCK:			PER QUILT:
A	1	Light Print	30
B	20	Medium Print	600
	8	Light Print	240
C	4	Light Print	120
	8	Dark	240
D	4	White	120

FABRIC REQUIREMENTS:

White—1 yard
Light—3 1/2 yards
Medium—4 1/4 yards
Dark—2 1/2 yards

A Nancy Cabot pattern. Pattern pieces on p. 173.

This is an overall design which can be worked in all prints, print and plain or all plain fabrics. Just keep the color values of light, medium and dark so the design will stand out.

To assemble the block, follow the diagrams below:

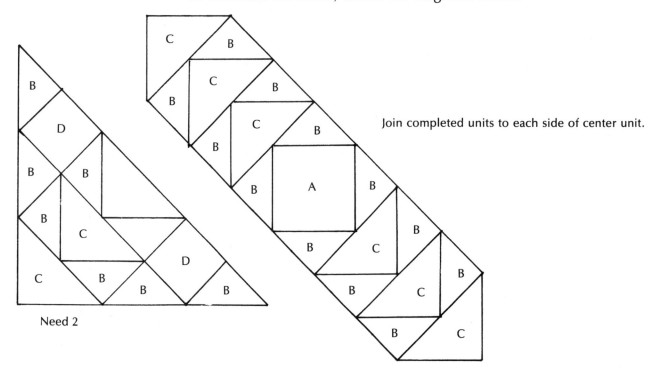

Join completed units to each side of center unit.

Need 2

PYRAMIDS

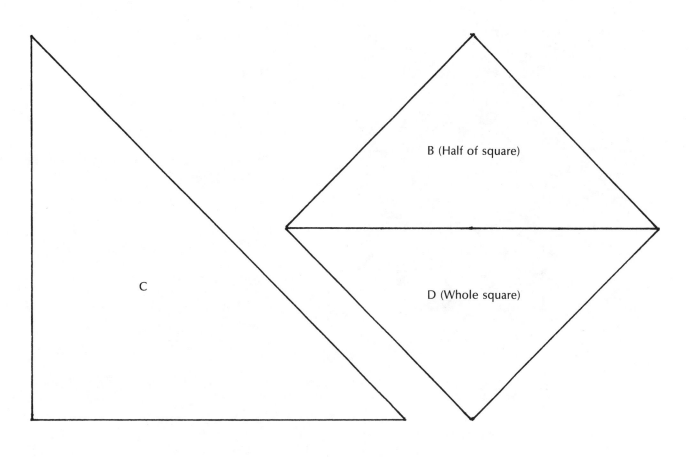

B (Half of square)

D (Whole square)

C

ADD 1/4″ SEAM ALLOWANCE

A

88. Railroad Crossing

EASY

in color p. 5

BLOCK SIZE: 18″

QUILT SIZE: 72″ × 90″

NO. OF BLOCKS: 20

PIECES PER BLOCK:			**PER QUILT:**
A	10	Dark Plain	200
	20	White	400
	10	Print	200
B	32	Dark Plain	640
	32	White	640

FABRIC REQUIREMENTS:

Dark Plain—3 yards
White—4 1/4 yards
Print—1 1/4 yards

An easy pattern using only two pieces. Square A uses Part A and Square B uses Part B. For Square B you could use strip piecing to speed up the process. Cut strips of dark and white fabric into widths of 2″. Sew these strips together, alternating light, dark, light, dark so you have four strips. Press. Measure down from the top 2″ and cut apart. You have your first strip of the block. Again measure down 2″, turn the strip so that the dark is on the left side and sew to the previous light, dark, light, dark strip. Continue until you have the four rows that make up the block.

A border can be added if desired, but is not necessary. Outline quilt 1/8″ from all seams.

ADD 1/4″ SEAM ALLOWANCE

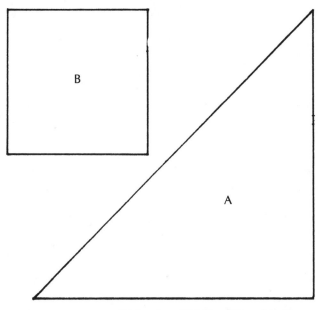

MODERATE

in color p. 3

BLOCK SIZE: 12″

QUILT SIZE: 72″ × 80″

NO. OF BLOCKS: 42

PIECES PER BLOCK:			PER QUILT:
A	4	Print	168
B	4	Pieced	168
C	8	Plain (white or color)	336

FABRIC REQUIREMENTS:

Scraps
White or Plain—5 2/3 yards

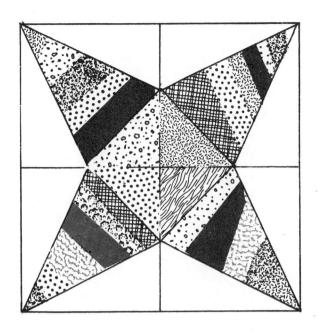

This basic pattern is known by many names. Job's Tears, Job's Troubles, World Without End, Kaleidoscope, Crossed Canoes and Arkansas Traveller are only a few. Each one becomes unique because of the color placement of each unit. This design carries it a step further by being made entirely of scrap fabrics. You must first make the fabric for the block, then cut the separate units. Pattern pieces are on p. 176.

Lay out your scrap fabrics on a large, flat surface and arrange them to form a pleasing pattern. For this design, the strips look best if they are going across the points of the star. Once you have a pleasing arrangement, cut the fabric into strips ranging from 3/4″ wide up to 2″ wide and sew them together to create a large piece of fabric.

Cut the templates for the block and cut A and B from this manufactured fabric. From the plain or white fabric, cut out units C. The template diagram shows 1/4 of the block and if you use it as a sewing guide, you will sew straight seams, then set four such squares together to form the completed block. If desired, you can piece A and B, assemble the star and then, treating C as a half-pattern, cut out a large diamond shape to set in between the points of the star.

An allover quilting design works very well for this pattern.

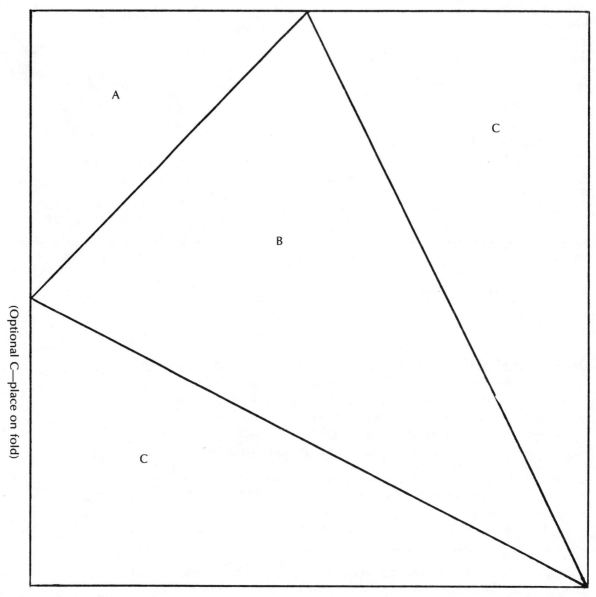

A

C

B

(Optional C—place on fold)

C

(Optional C—1/4 of pattern, place on fold)

in color p. 15

BLOCK SIZE: 18″

QUILT SIZE: 90″ × 90″

NO. OF BLOCKS: 25

PIECES PER BLOCK:			PER QUILT:
A	1	Yellow	25
B	8	White	200
C	8	Scrap	200
D	8	White	200
E	8	Yellow	200

FABRIC REQUIREMENTS:

Yellow—1 2/3 yards
White—6 1/3 yards
Assorted Scraps 4″ × 7″ (preferably
in the same color range)

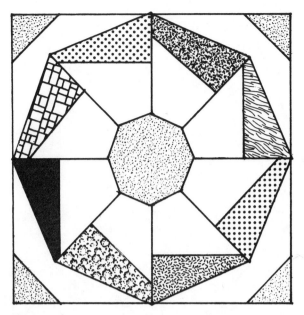

This is a moderately difficult pattern to piece.

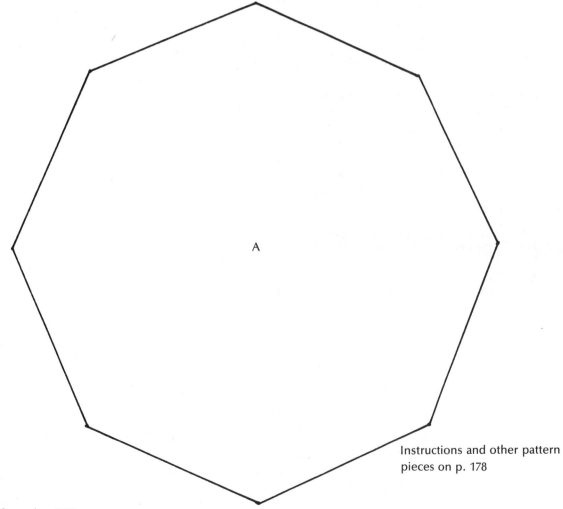

A

Instructions and other pattern
pieces on p. 178

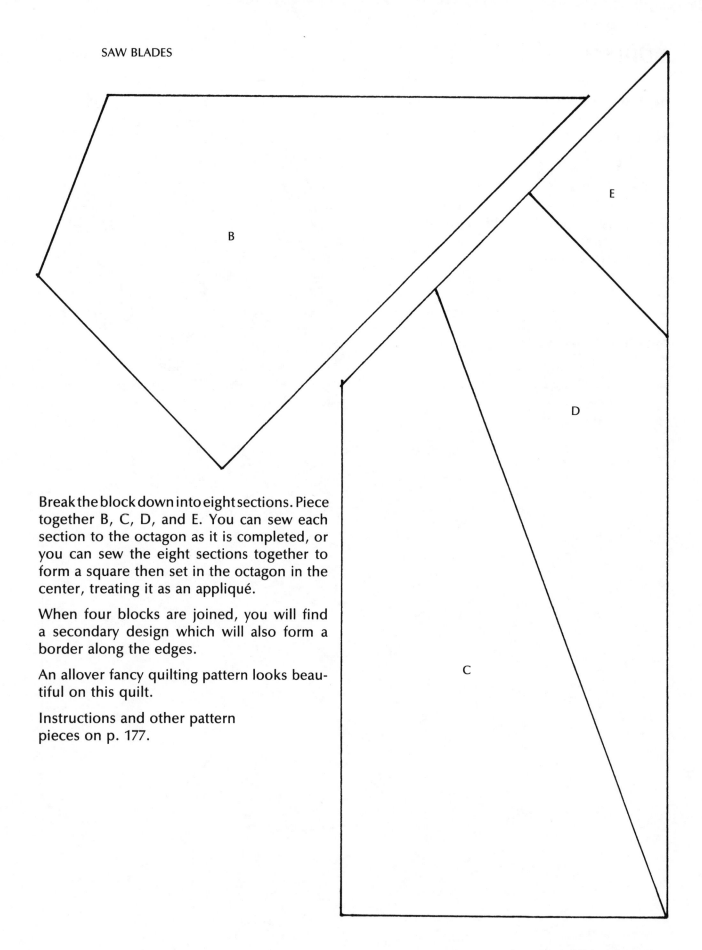

B

E

D

C

Break the block down into eight sections. Piece together B, C, D, and E. You can sew each section to the octagon as it is completed, or you can sew the eight sections together to form a square then set in the octagon in the center, treating it as an appliqué.

When four blocks are joined, you will find a secondary design which will also form a border along the edges.

An allover fancy quilting pattern looks beautiful on this quilt.

Instructions and other pattern pieces on p. 177.

in color p. 12

BLOCK SIZE: 9″

QUILT SIZE: 81″ × 81″

NO. OF BLOCKS: 81

PIECES PER BLOCK:			**PER QUILT:**
A	4	Medium Print	324
	4	White	324
B	2	Dark	162
	2	White	162

FABRIC REQUIREMENTS:

White—4 3/4 yards
Medium Print—2 yards
Dark—2 3/4 yards

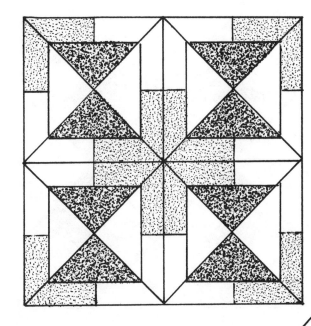

This pattern first appeared in the *Kansas City Star.*

The drawing above shows 4 blocks set together. Cut out templates adding 1/4″ seam allowance. When cutting fabric for Part A, reverse the template for half the pieces.

TO ASSEMBLE: Stitch together four units of Part A, medium print and white. Stitch completed units to each of the part B pieces, 2 white and 2 dark. Sew two completed A, B units together diagonally to form one-half the block. Repeat with second unit. Stitch these two units together to complete the block.

This pattern forms its own border. Quilt along each seamline to emphasize the design.

B

A
Reverse half

92. Secret Drawer

in color p. 7

BLOCK SIZE: 12″

QUILT SIZE: 84″ × 84″

NO. OF BLOCKS: 49

PIECES PER BLOCK:			PER QUILT:
A	1	Print	49
B	8	White	392
C	4	Dark	196
D	4	Print	196
E	4	White	196

FABRIC REQUIREMENTS:

White—5 3/4 yards
Print—2 1/4 yards
Dark—3 1/4 yards

Secret Drawer was published in the *Kansas City Star* in 1930. It is also known as Spools and Arkansas Traveller.

Pattern pieces are on p. 181.

To assemble the block, piece four units of BCBD. Attach two completed units to each side of Part A. Sew Part E to each side of the remaining BCBD units. Seam these three completed units together to finish the block.

Outline quilt 1/8″ from each seam. The four white triangles will form a diagonal square 12″ wide for some fancy quilting.

A border may be added if desired.

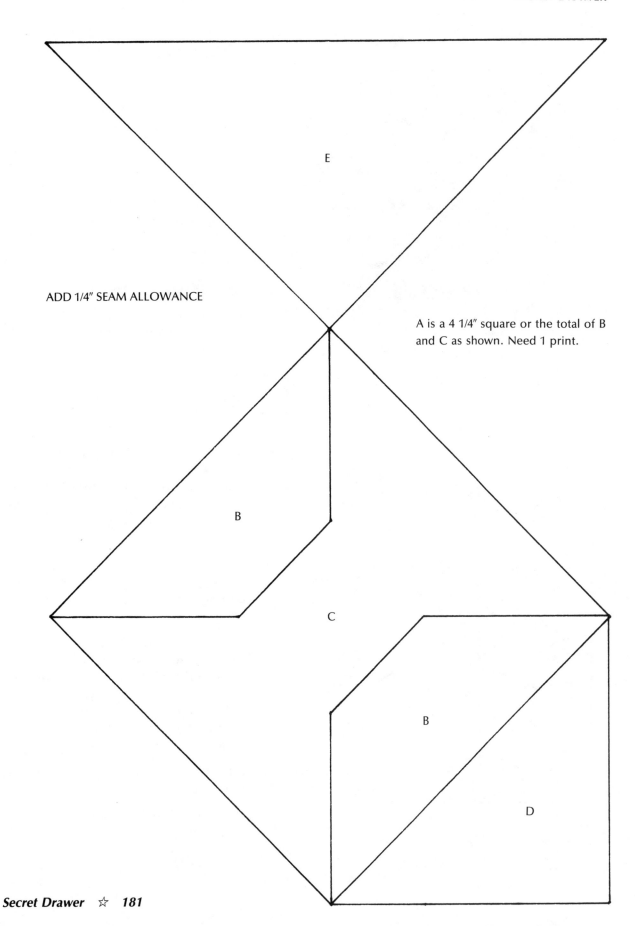

E

ADD 1/4″ SEAM ALLOWANCE

A is a 4 1/4″ square or the total of B and C as shown. Need 1 print.

B

C

B

D

93. Seven Sisters

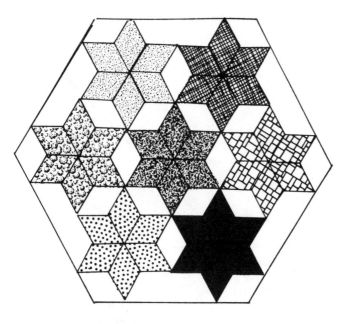

A Ladies Art Company pattern.

Pattern pieces on p. 183.

DIFFICULT

in color p. 6

BLOCK SIZE: 13″ × 15″

QUILT SIZE: 89″ × 99″

NO. OF BLOCKS: 22 with a 12″ border

PIECES PER BLOCK:			PER QUILT:
A	42	(6 each of seven fabrics)	924
	18	White	396
B	6	White	132
C		Setting Unit	42

FABRIC REQUIREMENTS:

1/8 yard scrap for each star
White—5 2/3 yards

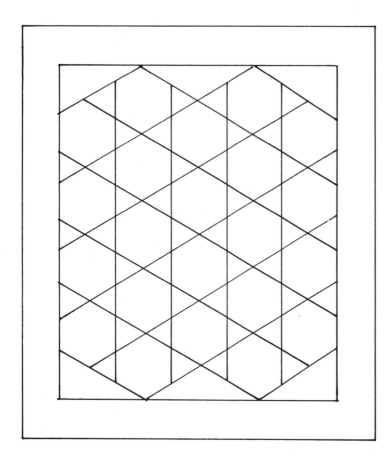

A little extra care is needed to piece this block, but it's not really all that difficult. Piece the seven stars for the block. Set the stars together with the white A, following the diagram above. Set in Part B to complete the block.

To join the blocks, sew Part C to each edge of the first hexagon. As each block is completed, set it into the triangle, adding triangles for the next block to set into.

When all the blocks are completed and set together, you will have to square off the edges. Measure the corner and cut a pattern, then cut white fabric to fill. The middle piece is half a diamond; again measure and cut the fabric to fit.

Cut white fabric into 12 1/2″ wide strips. Sew to each edge to complete quilt.

Outline quilt 1/8″ from each seam, then shadow quilt to fill in any large areas.

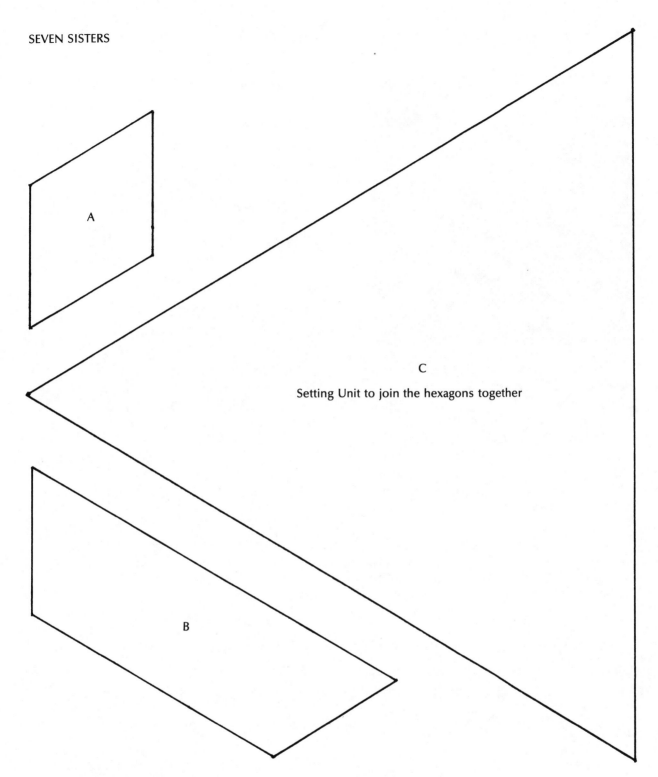

A

C

Setting Unit to join the hexagons together

B

ADD 1/4" SEAM ALLOWANCE

94. Shadows

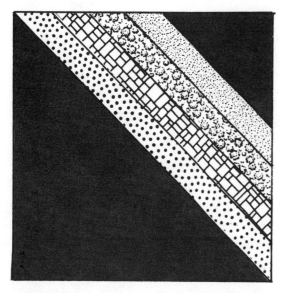

This is an Amish design, also called Rainbow Block, Roman Stripe or Sunlight and Shadows. When choosing colors for this quilt, keep in mind that Amish quilts are very bright. The large corner should be in a dark color, such as navy or even black, with the strips in colors like shocking pink, bright yellow, turquoise, or any bright primary colors.

in color p. 9

BLOCK SIZE: 10″

QUILT SIZE: 88″ × 98″
3″ inner border
6″ outer border

NO. OF BLOCKS: 56

PIECES PER BLOCK: **PER QUILT:**
One of each pattern is   36
needed per block.

FABRIC REQUIREMENTS:

Color 1 for Part A   1 1/2 yards
Color 2 for Part B   1 1/2 yards
Color 3 for Part C   1 1/4 yards
Color 4 for Part D   3/4 yards
Color 5 for Part E   1/2 yard
Color 6 for Part F   6 1/2 yards

BORDER: Inner border—choose one of the colors you've used in the block—1 1/4 yards
Outer Border, Color 6—1 3/4 yards.

TEMPLATES: Pattern pieces for A and B are in two pieces and on pp. 185 and 186. Trace A-1 onto a large sheet of paper, then line up the dash line with that of A-2 and continue drawing the finished pattern. Do the same with B. Use these finished patterns for your templates.

Part F is a 10″ square cut on the diagonal. Add seam allowance.

This is an easy block to sew; start with Part F and add A through E.

BORDER: Inner Border: Cut two strips 4″ × 81″ and 2 strips 4″ × 77″. Sew the 4″ × 81″ strips to each size and the 4″ × 77″ strips to top and bottom.
Outer Border: Two side strips 7″ × 87″; strips for top and bottom are 7″ × 99″.

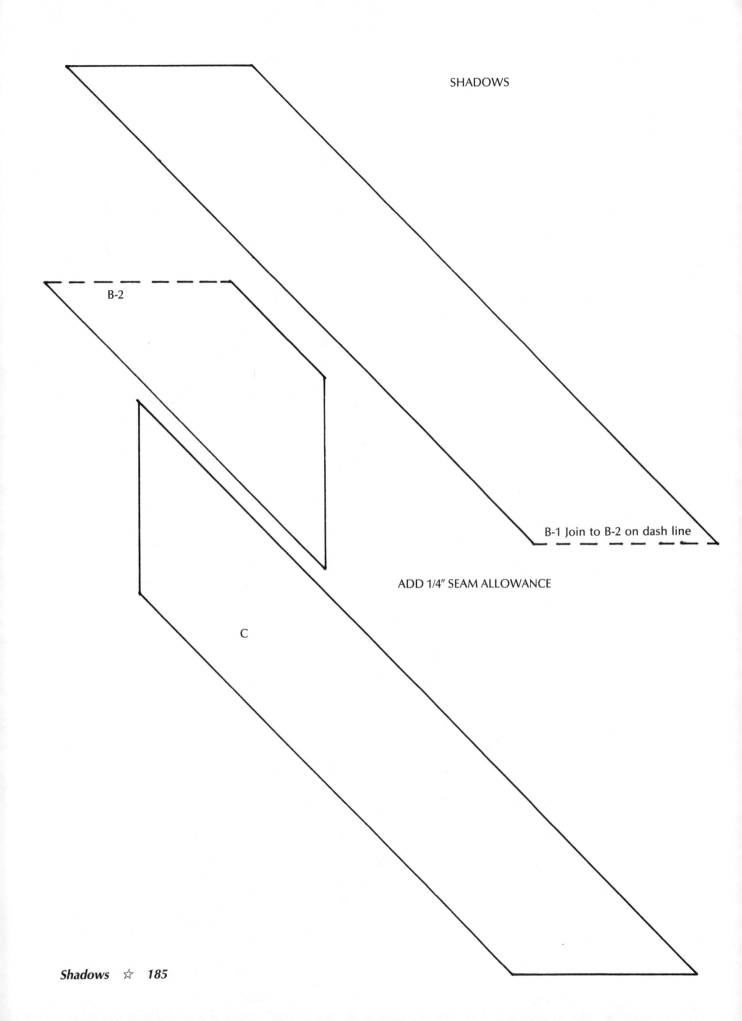

B-2

B-1 Join to B-2 on dash line

ADD 1/4" SEAM ALLOWANCE

C

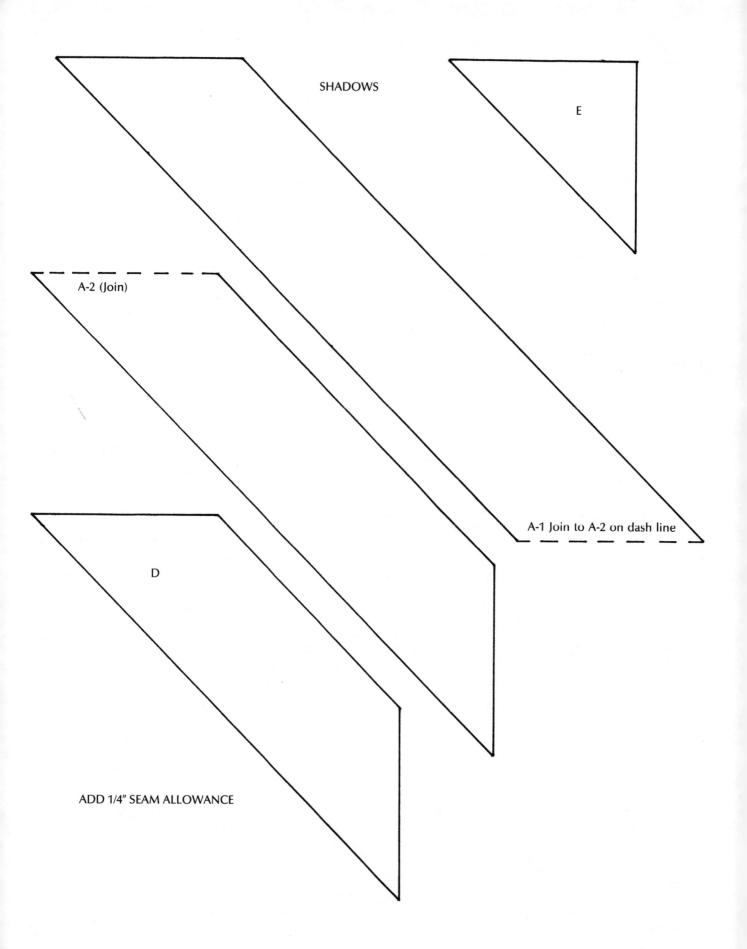

SHADOWS

E

A-2 (Join)

A-1 Join to A-2 on dash line

D

ADD 1/4" SEAM ALLOWANCE

in color p. 13

BLOCK SIZE: 10″

QUILT SIZE: 80″ × 90″

NO. OF BLOCKS: 72

PIECES PER BLOCK:			PER QUILT:
A	4	Red Plain	288
	4	Red Print (Reverse)	288
B	8	Blue Plain	576
	8	White	576
	4	Yellow Plain	288
	4	Yellow Print	288
C	4	White	288

FABRIC REQUIREMENTS:

White—5 yards   Red Plain—1 2/3 yards
Red Print—1 2/3 yards Blue—2 2/3 yards
Yellow Plain—1 1/3 yards Yellow Print—1 1/3 yards

Break the block down into four parts. Follow the diagram on the pattern page for setting each piece in place. Piece the four corners, then set them together to form the completed block. Outline quilt 1/8″ from each seam. A border may be added if desired.

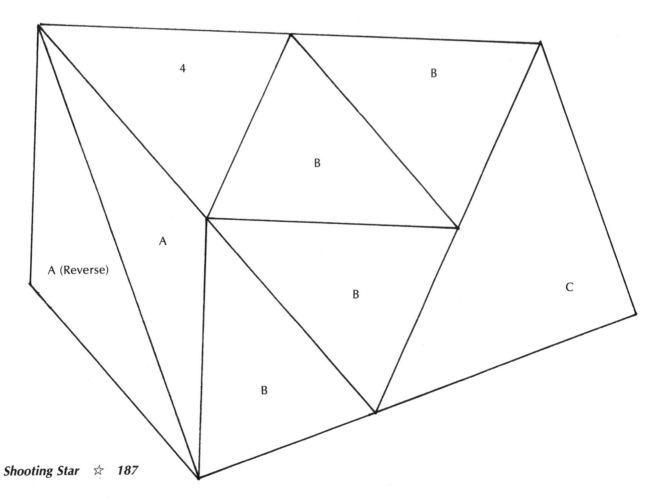

4

B

B

A

A (Reverse)

B

B

C

B

96. Snake's Trail

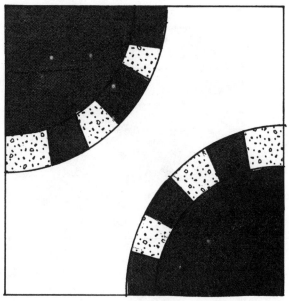

Snake's Trail seems to have originated in the South during the 1800's. It is also known as Snake in the Hollow, and a variation is called Drunkard's Trail.

Other pattern pieces on p. 189.

MODERATE

in color p. 8

BLOCK SIZE: 10″

QUILT SIZE: 80″ × 100″

NO. OF BLOCKS: 80

PIECES PER BLOCK:			PER QUILT:
A	2	Plain	160
B	3	Print	240
	3	Plain	240
C	1	White	80

FABRIC REQUIREMENTS:

Plain—2 3/4 yards
Print—3/4 yard
White—4 1/2 yards

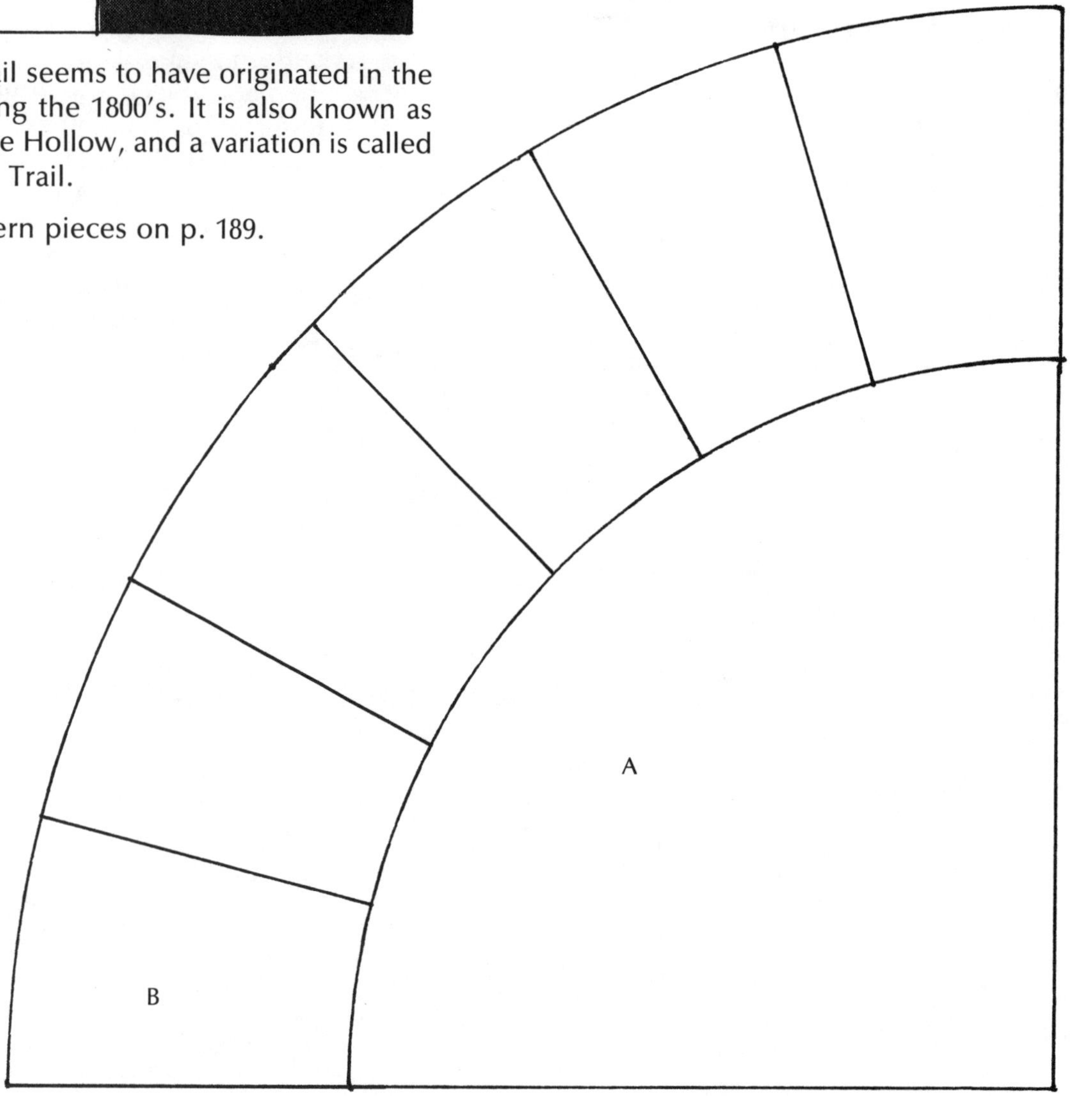

A

B

Piece the curved B strip, alternating print and plain. Sew to A, then set the A pieces into C.

The blocks are set side by side, being sure that the pieced portion is always in the upper left- and lower right-hand corners. This pattern should be set solid to develop the design. Never use plain blocks or lattice strips.

No border is required.

Outline quilt along each seam line, then quilt a few rows into pieces A and C.

The difference between Drunkard's Trail and Snake's Trail is that the curved piece becomes solid rather than pieced. Both designs can also be worked up as scrap quilts, keeping the white center, and for Drunkard's Trail, keep B the same color throughout.

Once the blocks have been completed, follow the setting diagram to assemble the quilt top. It's a little tricky, so be careful that you have the blocks going in the right direction.

1/2-Pattern—Place on Fold

ADD 1/4" SEAM ALLOWANCE

C

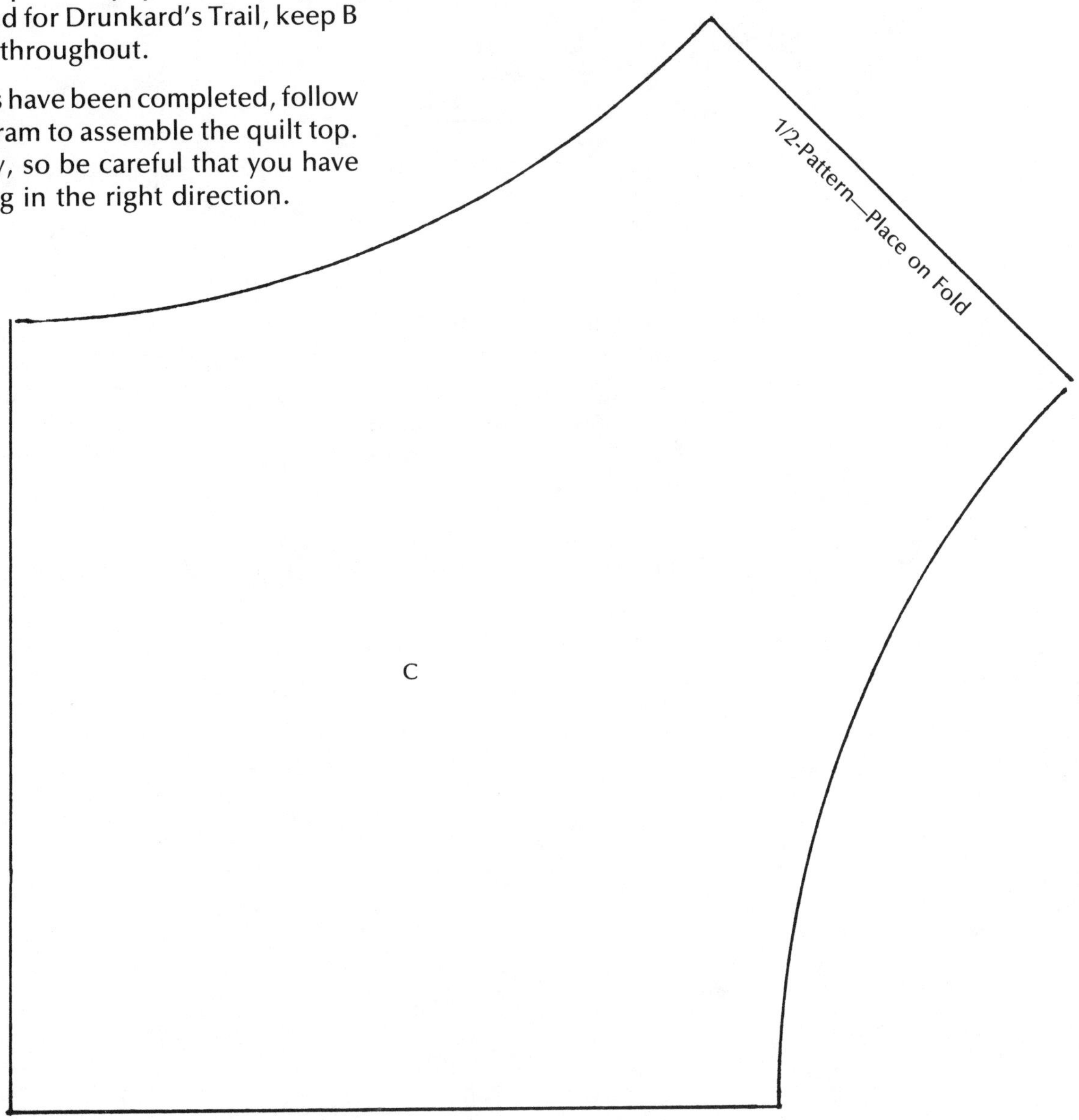

97. Spider's Den

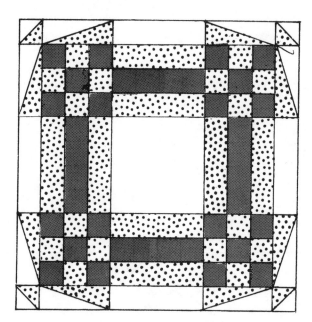

A Ladies Art Company pattern.
Pattern pieces on p. 191.

in color p. 4

BLOCK SIZE: 12"

QUILT SIZE: 84" × 84"

NO. OF BLOCKS: 49

PIECES PER BLOCK:			PER QUILT:
A	1	White	49
B	8	White	392
	8	Dark	392
C	8	White	392
	8	Dark	392
D	4	White	196
	4	Dark	196
E	16	Dark	784
	20	White	980

FABRIC REQUIREMENTS:

White—6 3/4 yards
Dark—6 yards

Following the diagram for color placement, piece the four nine-patch squares; the four center pieces consisting of light and dark Part B's; eight light and dark Part C's and four light and dark Part D's. Sew a C unit to the nine-patch square and sew a C and D unit together. Add this to the nine-patch square. Sew the units together in rows, adding the white Part A to the center row.

Outline quilt 1/8" from all seams. The center square can repeat the nine-patch pattern or you could quilt in a small spiderweb.

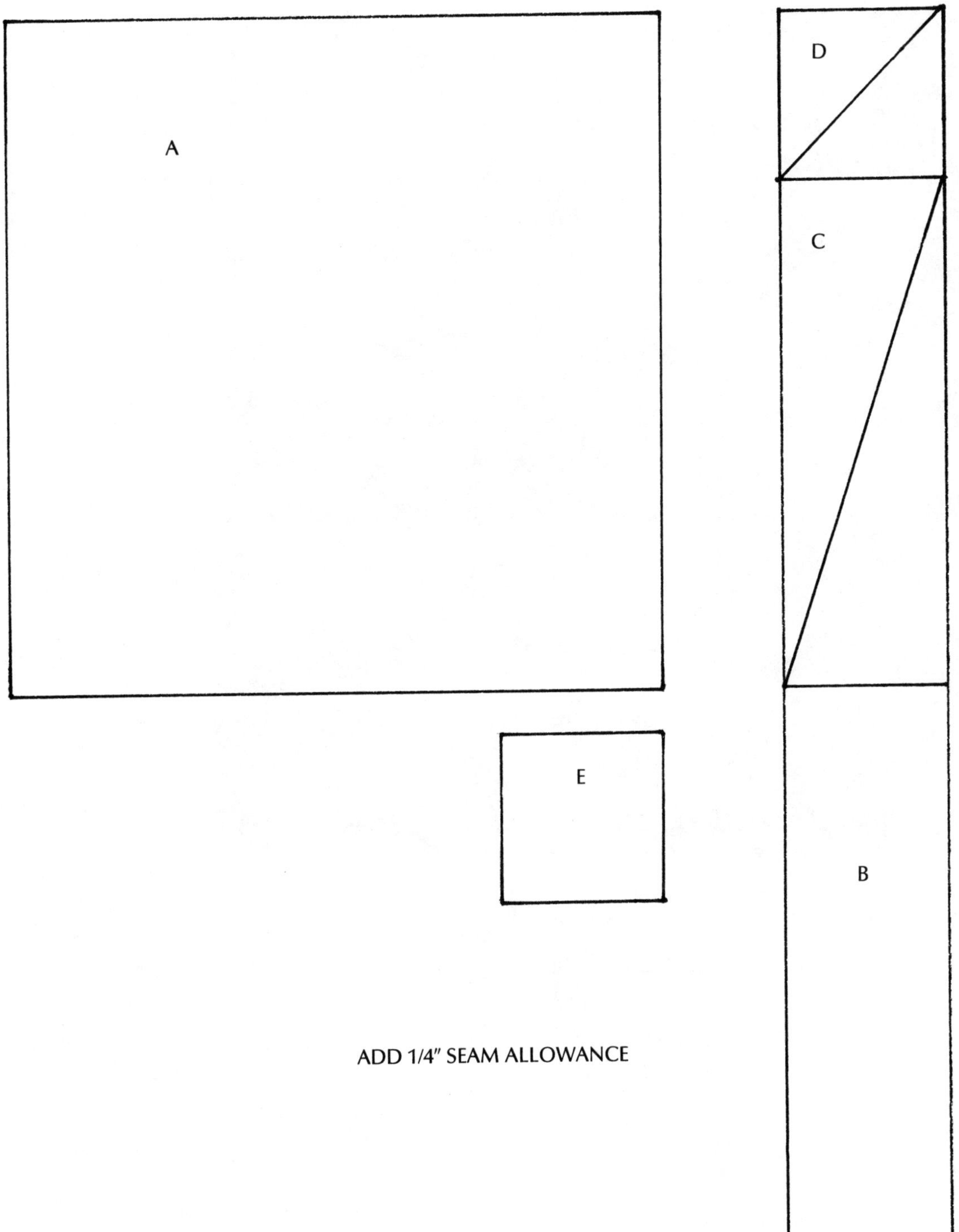

A

D

C

E

B

ADD 1/4" SEAM ALLOWANCE

98. Spider Web

in color p. 4

BLOCK SIZE: 16″

QUILT SIZE: 80″ × 80″

NO. OF BLOCKS: 16
    Half-Blocks 16
    Corner-Blocks 4

PIECES PER QUILT:

A	Yellow	200
B	Red	100
C	Blue	100
D	Red	100
E	Yellow	100
F	Blue	100
G	Red	100
H	Yellow	100
I	Yellow	40
	Red	40
J	Yellow	20
	Red	20

FABRIC REQUIREMENTS:

Yellow—4 yards
Red—4 1/3 yards
Blue—1 2/3 yards

This pattern was taken from a quilt made in Pennsylvania in 1885. The colors given are the same as those used in the original quilt.

Using the diagram above and the layout of the pattern pieces on pp. 193 and 194 you shouldn't have any trouble with this quilt. As you can see, the outer row forms a border for the quilt.

Outline quilt 1/8″ from all seams.

SPIDER WEB

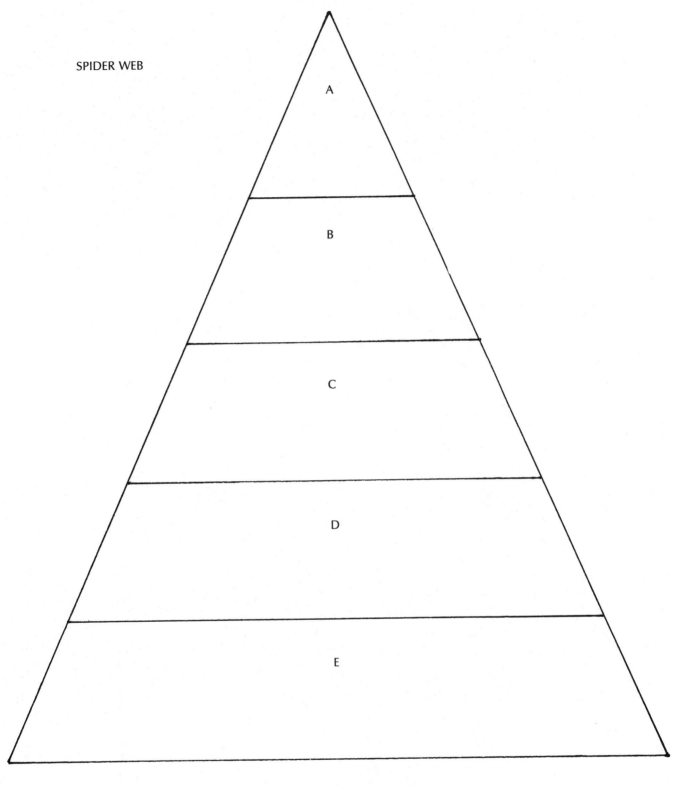

A

B

C

D

E

ADD 1/4″ SEAM ALLOWANCE

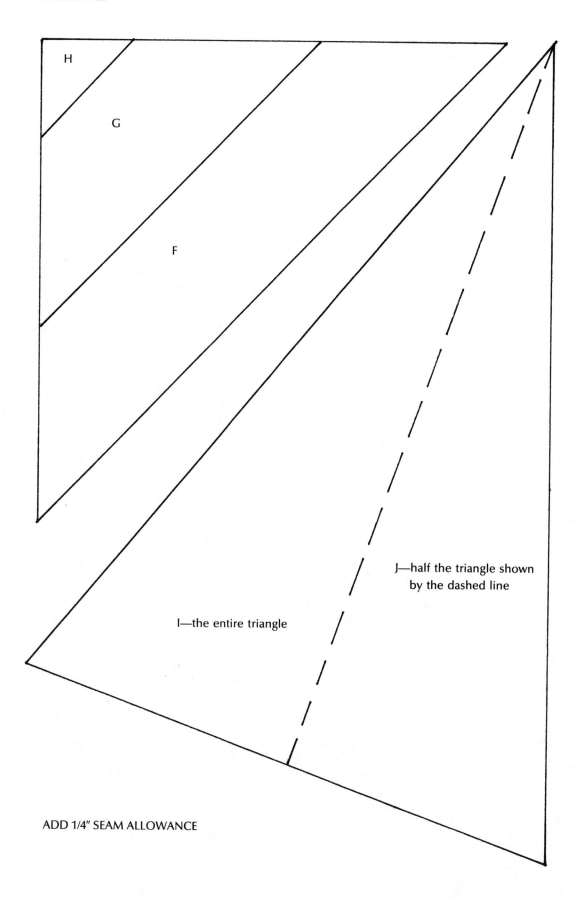

H

G

F

J—half the triangle shown
by the dashed line

I—the entire triangle

ADD 1/4" SEAM ALLOWANCE

DIFFICULT

in color p. 15

BLOCK SIZE: 14″

QUILT SIZE: 92″ × 92″

NO. OF BLOCKS: 36 with a 4″ border

PIECES PER BLOCK:			PER QUILT:
A	8	Medium Blue	288
B	8	White	288
C	4	Light Blue	144
D	4	Medium Blue	144
E	8	White	288
F	2	Light Blue	72
	2	Medium Blue	72

FABRIC REQUIREMENTS:

Medium Blue—4 1/2 yards
White—5 yards
Light Blue—2 yards

This is a difficult pattern to piece because of all the corners that must be turned. It is an extremely beautiful quilt though, and well worth the care required.

Pattern pieces are on p. 196.

Begin in the center and piece the star. Continue outward in rows, setting in the pieces as needed. As much as I try I can't come up with an easier way to piece the block without winding up with enough pieces to make a jigsaw puzzle.

Set the completed blocks six across and six down. Add a 4″ border.

Outline quilt 1/8″ from all seams.

STARLIGHT

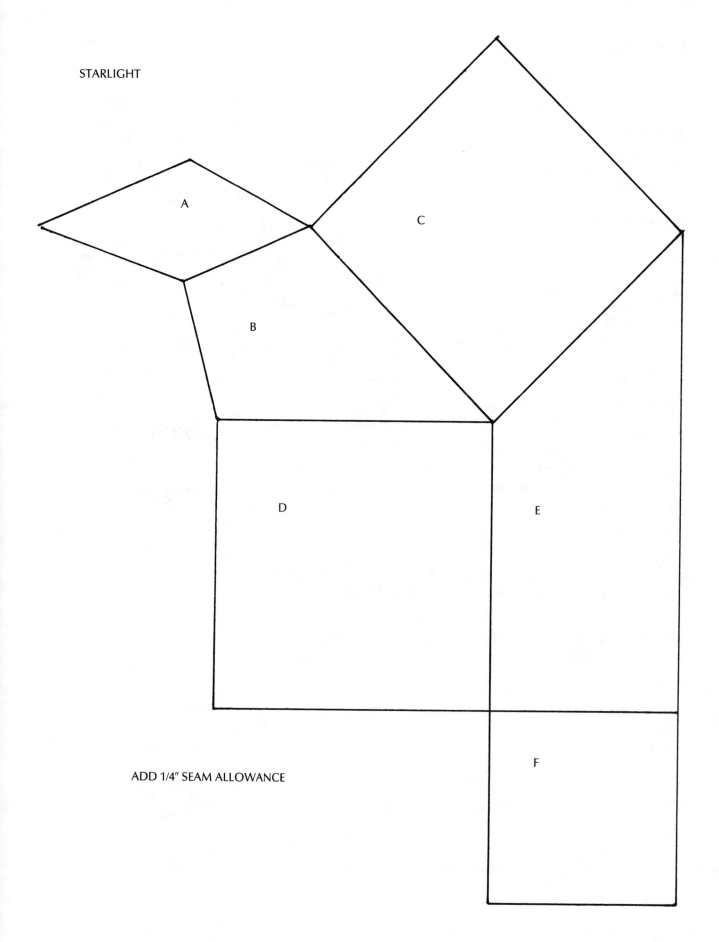

ADD 1/4″ SEAM ALLOWANCE

in color p. 7

BLOCK SIZE: 12″

QUILT SIZE: 72″ × 84″

NO. OF BLOCKS: 42

PIECES PER BLOCK:			**PER QUILT:**
A	1	Plain	42
B	8	Print	336
	8	Plain	336
C	4	White	168
	4	Print	168
D	4	White	168

FABRIC REQUIREMENTS:

Plain—2 yards
Print—2 yards
White—5 yards

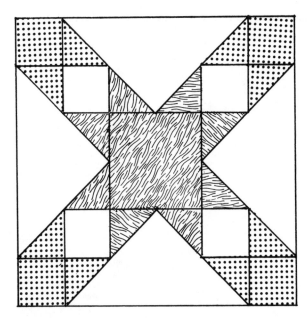

This pattern appeared in *American Needle-woman* in 1926.

This pattern requires a bit of care in the piecing because you have several corners to pivot. Accuracy is extremely important if you want the block to lay flat. Pattern pieces are on p. 198.

Piece the diagonal corners and set in the large white triangle, Part D. Work around the outer edges and then set in the center square Part A.

Because of the size of the individual pieces, this quilt would be better if quilted with an overall design such as squares or diamonds.

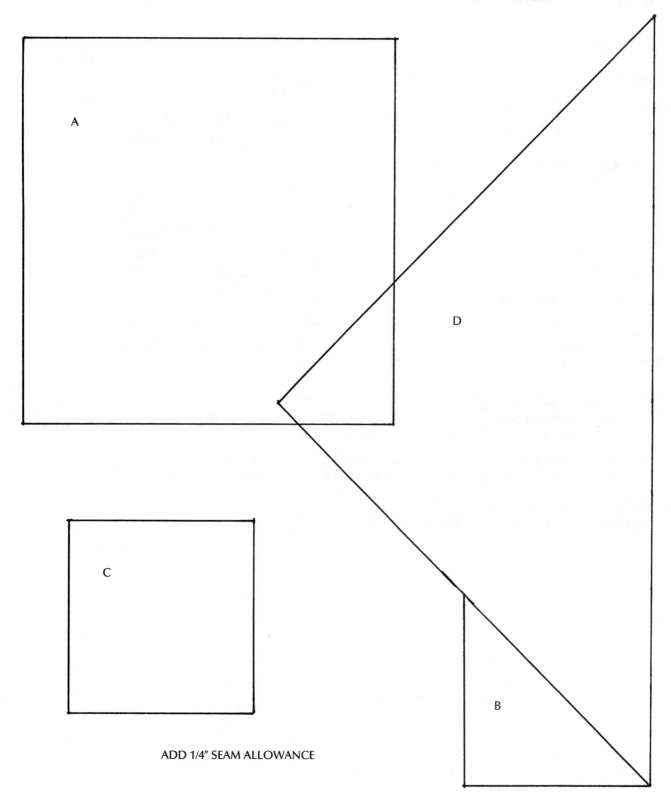

A

D

C

B

ADD 1/4" SEAM ALLOWANCE

in color p. 16

BLOCK SIZE: 12″

QUILT SIZE: 84″ × 84″

NO. OF BLOCKS: 49

PIECES PER BLOCK:			PER QUILT:
A	4	Assorted Prints	196
B	4	Assorted Prints	196
C	4	White	196
D	4	White	196

FABRIC REQUIREMENTS:

White—6 2/3 yards
Assorted Prints

This interlaced design is easier to piece than it appears. Pattern pieces are on p. 200.

Divide the block into four sections diagonally. While piecing, do be sure to keep the color sequence correct.

Piece white C to print #1 A and add white D. Below this unit, sew on print #2, Part A. Coming down the right side, piece white C, to print #2, B. Sew print #3, Part A to the bottom of this unit. Join these two units together to form 1/2 of the block. Across the bottom join white C to print #3, B, add white D. Finish this section with print #4, Part A. The left-hand side is white C to print #4, B to white D. Again join these two units to form the other half of the block. Join the two halves.

Set the completed blocks together seven across and seven down. The blocks could also be set with lattice strips or alternate place blocks.

Quilting should emphasize the diagonal flow of the block.

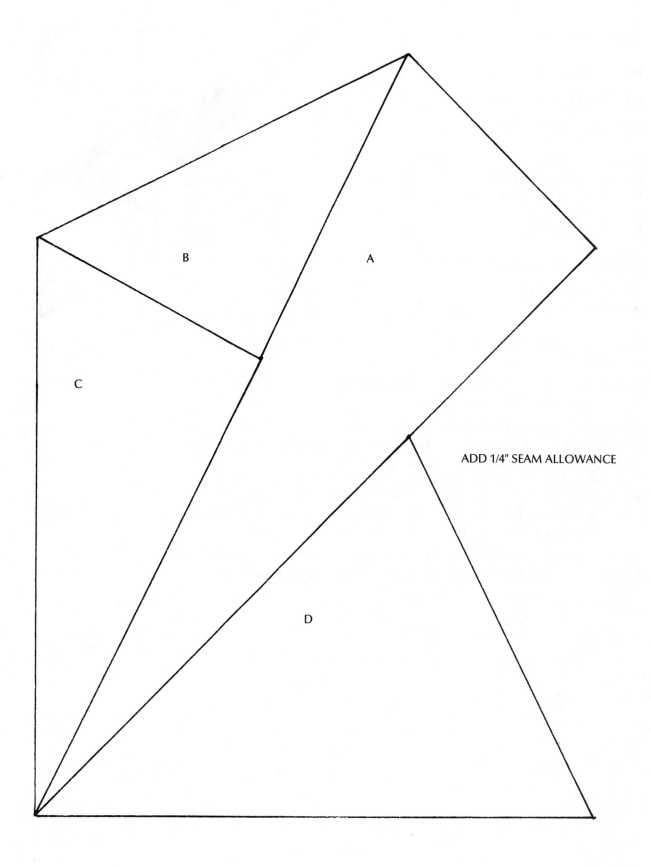

ADD 1/4" SEAM ALLOWANCE

in color p. 12

BLOCK SIZE: 12″

QUILT SIZE: 84″ × 84″

NO. OF BLOCKS: 36
with a 6″ border

PIECES PER BLOCK:			PER QUILT:
A	8	White	288
	4	Dark Blue	144
B	4	Medium Blue Print	144
C	4	Light Blue Print	144
D	8	Dark Blue Print	288
E	4	Medium Blue Print	144
F	4	Medium Blue Print	144
G	1	Light Blue Print	36

FABRIC REQUIREMENTS:

White—1 1/2 yards
Dark Blue—3/4 yard
Medium Blue Print—3 1/4 yards
Light Blue Print—2 1/2 yards
Dark Blue Print—2 1/2 yards

This pattern was published by Old Chelsea Station Needlecraft Service and it falls into the difficult class.

This is a nine-patch design, and can be broken down into three rows of three units: Pattern pieces are on pp. 202 and 203.

For the center unit, set in the E pieces to the G center.

Sew D to the diagonal line on each side of an F piece.

For the corner square, sew B to C, then add an A piece to the three sides.

Set these completed units together in rows of corner unit, DF unit, corner; center—DF unit, EG unit, DF unit. Be especially careful when pivoting the corners of the DF units that the piece will lie flat.

BORDER: Fabric required—1 1/4 yards of color of your choice.

Cut two strips 6 1/2″ × 73″ and two strips 6 1/2″ × 85″. Sew to edges of completed top.

Outline quilt along each seam.

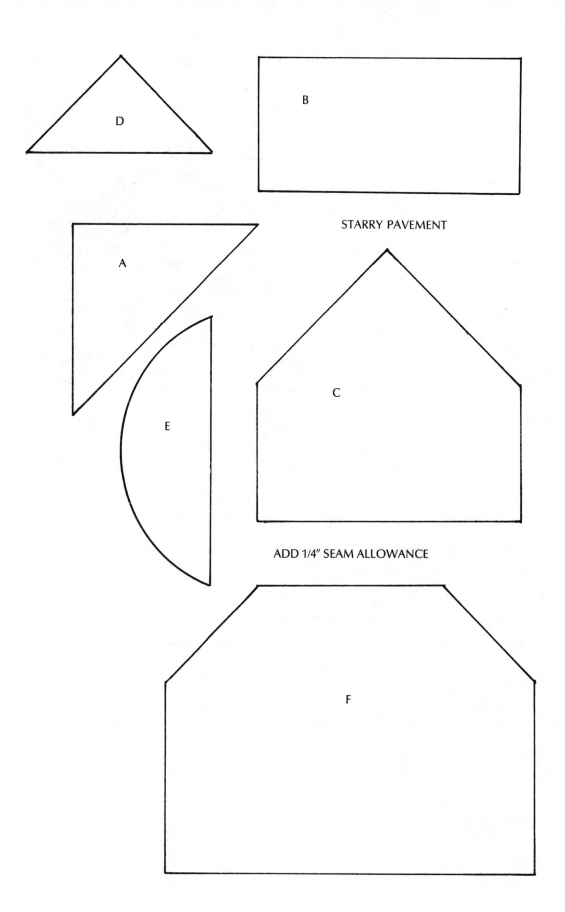

STARRY PAVEMENT

ADD 1/4" SEAM ALLOWANCE

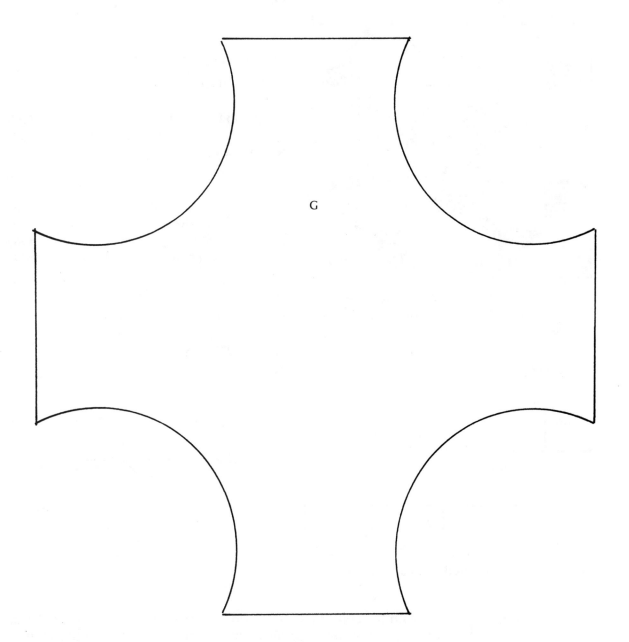

G

ADD 1/4" SEAM ALLOWANCE

103. State Fair

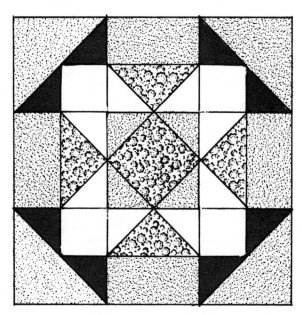

This is another Nancy Cabot pattern, which appeared in the *Chicago Tribune* during the 1930's.

TO ASSEMBLE:

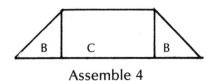

Assemble 4

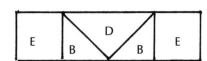

Assemble 2, and 2 BDB only

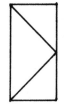

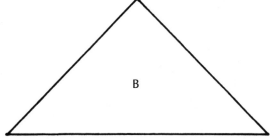

B

EASY

in color p. 12

BLOCK SIZE: 12″

QUILT SIZE: 84″ × 84″

NO. OF BLOCKS: 49

PIECES PER BLOCK:			PER QUILT:
A	4	Blue on White Print	198
B	8	Red	392
	8	White	392
	4	Blue	198
C	4	Blue on White Print	198
D	4	Red Print	198
E	4	White	198
F	1	Red Print	49

FABRIC REQUIREMENTS:

Blue on White Print—4 3/4 yards
Red—2 yards
White—2 3/4 yards
Red Print—2 1/3 yards
Blue—1 yard

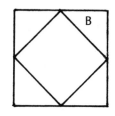

Assemble 1

Start with the center FB units, add BDB to each side. Stitch EBDBE units to top and bottom. Add BCB unit to all four sides. Stitch Unit A to each corner to complete.

Outline quilt the inner pattern. Where the blocks meet you will have an 8″ square for a quilting motif.

Other pattern pieces p. 205.

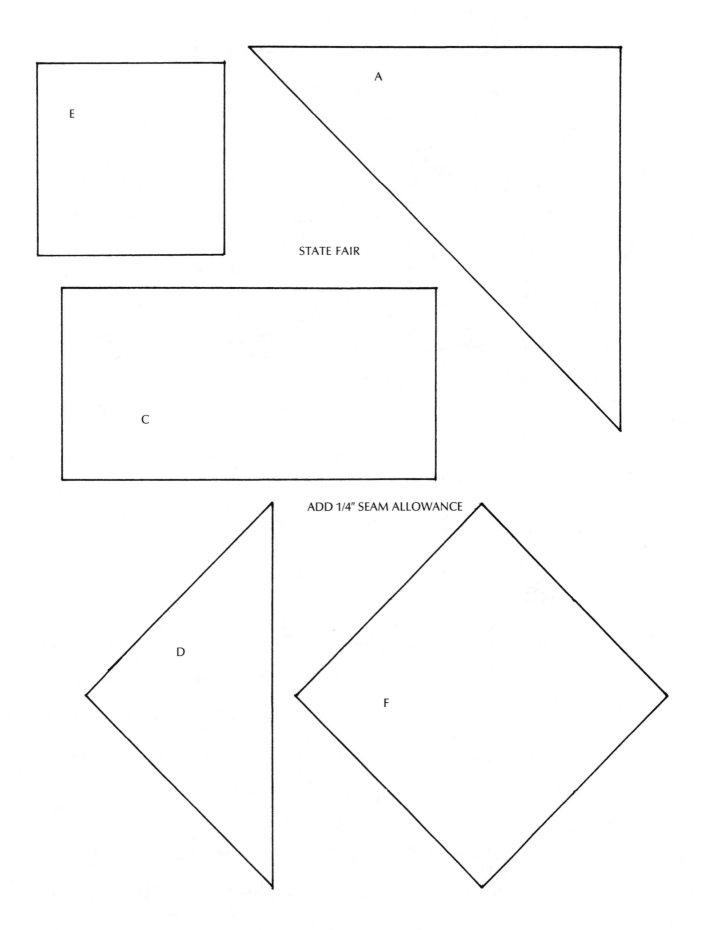

E

A

STATE FAIR

C

ADD 1/4″ SEAM ALLOWANCE

D

F

104. State Fair Block

MODERATE

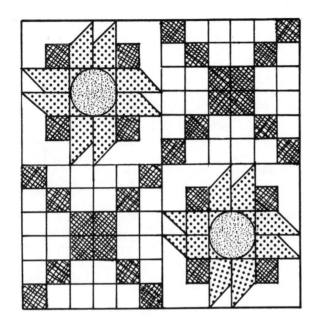

in color p. 4

BLOCK SIZE: 12″

QUILT SIZE: 84″ × 84″

NO. OF BLOCKS: 25 A Blocks, 24 B Blocks

PIECES PER BLOCK:			PER QUILT:
BLOCK A:			
A	4	White	100
B	8	Yellow Print	200
C	4	White	100
	4	Green	100
D	8	White	200
E	4	Yellow Print	100
F	1	Orange	25
BLOCK B:			
A	4	White	96
C	8	Green	192
	4	White	96
G	1	Green	24
H	4	White	96

FABRIC REQUIREMENTS:

White—4 1/3 yards
Yellow Print—2 yards
Green—1 2/3 yards
Orange—1/3 yard

BLOCK A: Following the diagram above and the pattern layout on p. 207, break the block down into three rows: top, middle and bottom. Sew together the following units: white and green C; white D and yellow print B; white D and yellow print B; white and green C. Join these in a strip in the order shown.

Row Two: Make two units of white D and yellow print B; one unit of four E yellow print joined to orange F. Two more units of white D and yellow print B. Join two each of these DB units, then sew on each side of the EF unit.

Row Three: Repeat Row One.

BLOCK B: Follow the diagram for color placement.

Beginning with Block A, join the completed blocks; alternating A and B seven across and seven down.

To quilt Block A, outline quilt 1/8″ from each seam. This pattern can be repeated in Block B or you can outline quilt it, following the seams.

BLOCK A

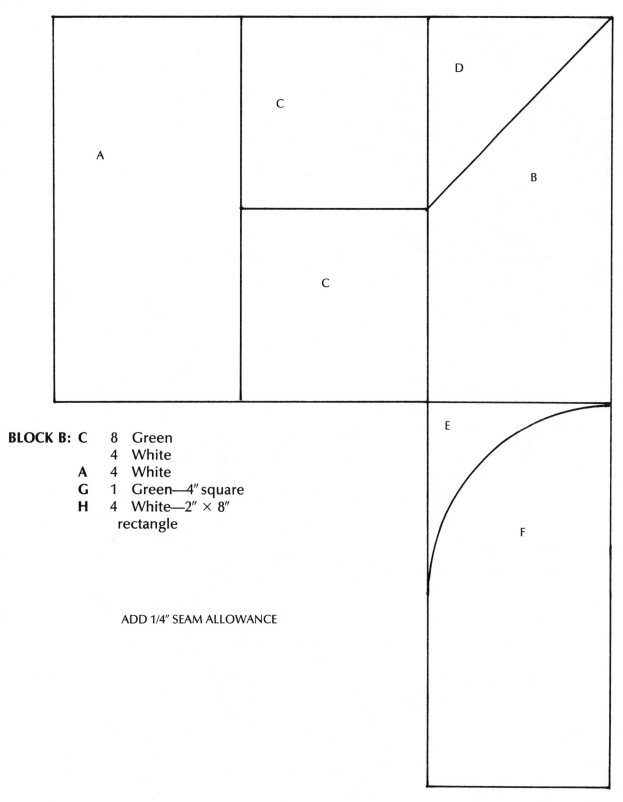

BLOCK B: C 8 Green
4 White
A 4 White
G 1 Green—4″ square
H 4 White—2″ × 8″
rectangle

ADD 1/4″ SEAM ALLOWANCE

105. Storm at Sea

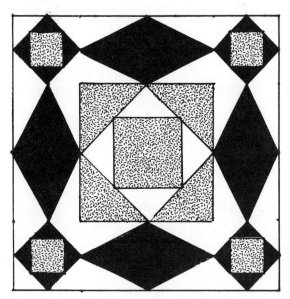

A Ladies Art Company pattern.

3	2	3	2	3	2	3
2	1	2	1	2	1	2
3	2	3	2	3	2	3
2	1	2	1	2	1	2

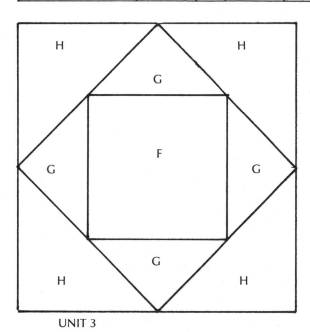

UNIT 3

MODERATE

in color p. 2

QUILT SIZE: 84″ × 84″

PIECES PER UNIT:				PER QUILT:
UNIT 1:				
A	1	Medium Print		81
B	4	Light Plain		324
C	4	Medium Print		324
UNIT 2:				
D	1	Dark Print		180
E	4	Light Plain		720
UNIT 3:				
F	1	Medium Print		100
G	4	Light Plain		400
H	4	Dark Print		400

FABRIC REQUIREMENTS:

Light—8 1/2 yards
Medium—3 1/4 yards
Dark—4 1/8 yards

The outer row serves as a joining strip for the center square. When the blocks are set together you create an impression of intertwining circles.

You will need the following number of units:
Unit 1: Center Square   81
Unit 2: 3″ × 6″ Joining Strip 180
Unit 3: 3″ × 3″ Square   100

To assemble the units, just follow the layout of the patterns on p. 207.

To set the quilt, beginning at left top, join a strip of 3, 2, 3 and stitch to a strip of 2, 1, 2. Continue across row using 9 Unit 1. End with a 3, 2, 3 strip.

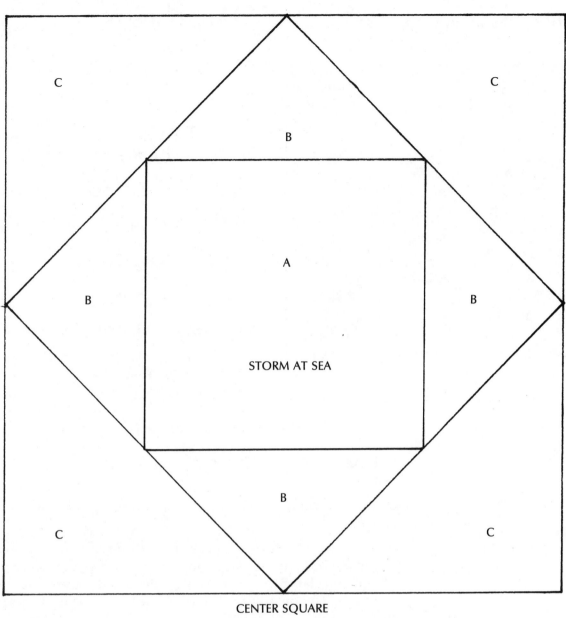

CENTER SQUARE

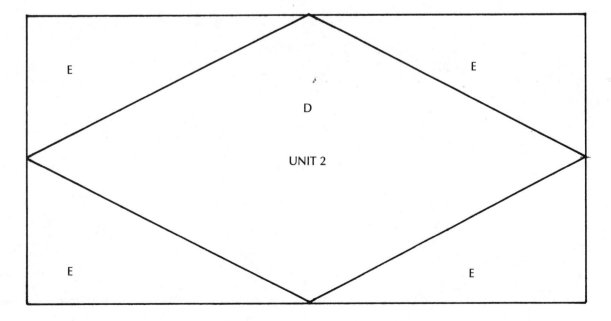

106.   Swing in the Center

MODERATE

in color p. 3

BLOCK SIZE: 12″

QUILT SIZE: 72″ × 84″

NO. OF BLOCKS: 42

PIECES PER BLOCK:			PER QUILT:
A	1	Dark	42
	4	White	168
B	4	Dark	168
C	8	White	336
D	8	Medium	336
E	4	White	168

FABRIC REQUIREMENTS:

White—4 1/4 yards
Medium—2 2/3 yards
Dark—1 2/3 yards

A Ladies Art Company pattern. Pattern pieces are on p. 211.

TO PIECE THE BLOCK: The block is broken on the diagonal into three units.

Unit 1: One center diagonal unit made up of dark B, light A, dark A, light A, and dark B.

Unit 2: Need two. Beginning at the upper left-hand side, piece white C to medium D. Skip the E piece now and add another medium D, and a white C. Join dark B to light A, then join this unit to the previous unit. Join white C, medium D, medium D, white C. Join to the previously completed unit. Set in Part E.

Join two of these sections on either side of the center diagonal unit.

Outline quilt 1/8″ from all seams.

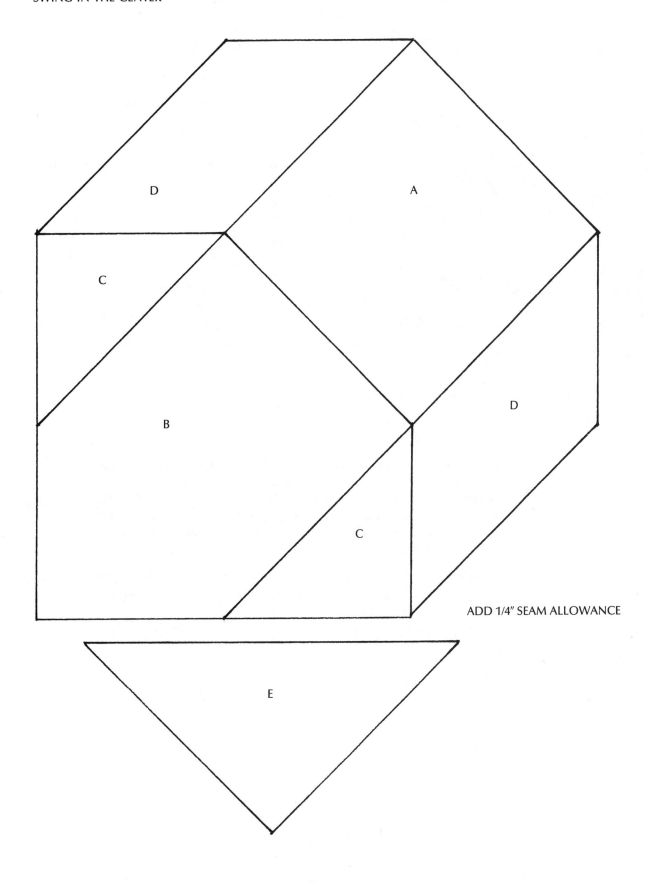

ADD 1/4″ SEAM ALLOWANCE

107. Tangled Garter

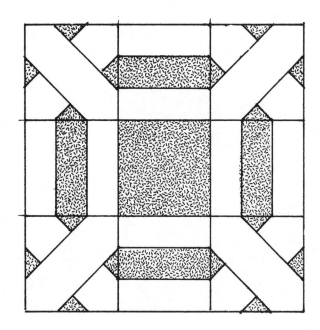

MODERATE

in color p. 15

BLOCK SIZE: 18″

QUILT SIZE: 90″ × 90″

NO. OF BLOCKS: 25

PIECES PER BLOCK:			PER QUILT:
A	4	Light	100
B	8	Light	200
C	16	Dark	400
D	4	Dark	100
	8	Light	200
E	1	Dark	25

FABRIC REQUIREMENTS:

Light—6 1/2 yards
Dark—3 1/4 yards

A Ladies Art Company pattern. Pattern pieces are on p. 213.

This is basically a nine-patch pattern. There are three variations within the block: the corner squares, the middle squares and the center.

To piece the corners make two units by piecing CBC, as shown on the pattern page. Join these two units to each side of Part A. The middle squares are simply alternating colors of Part D. Join completed units together in rows as shown in the above diagram. Do not use lattice strips or alternate plain blocks with this quilt as you will lose the overall pattern of the quilt when it is set together.

Outline quilt 1/8″ from each seam. Shadow quilt into the larger units of the design. Use a small quilting motif for the 6″ center square.

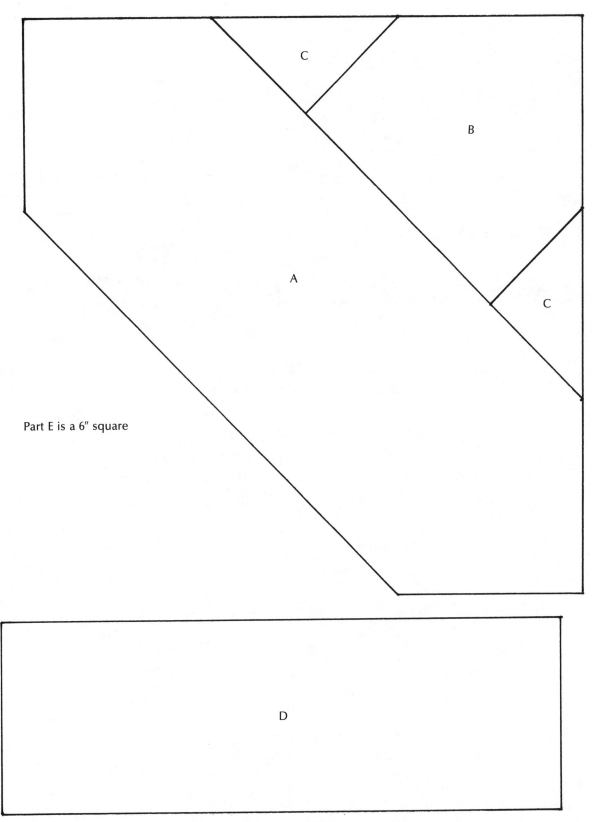

C

B

C

A

Part E is a 6″ square

D

ADD 1/4″ SEAM ALLOWANCE

108. Tangled Lines

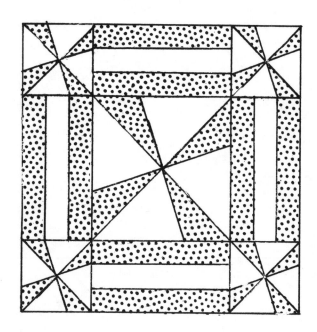

EASY

in color p. 12

BLOCK SIZE: 12"

QUILT SIZE: 84" × 84"

NO. OF BLOCKS: 49

PIECES PER BLOCK:			PER QUILT:
A	16	Print	784
B	16	Plain	784
C	8	Print	392
	4	Plain	196
D	4	Print	196
	4	Plain	196

FABRIC REQUIREMENTS:

Print—5 1/2 yards
Plain—6 yards

This pattern was published by the Ladies Art Company in their 1922 catalog. Pattern pieces are on p. 215.

Break this design into three units for assembling: the four corner squares, the four inner strips and the center square.

For the corner square piece AB, AB, to form a triangle. Make a second triangle and sew these two together to form a square. Make four.

The inner strip is Part C. Make four.

For the center, follow the same procedure as for the corner squares, using Parts E and D.

No border is necessary.

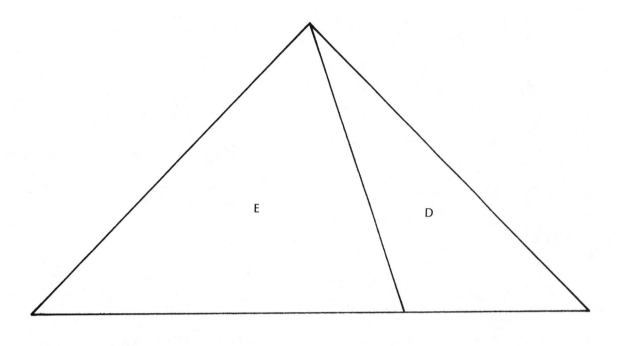

E   D

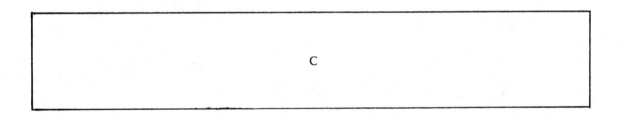

C

ADD 1/4″ SEAM ALLOWANCE

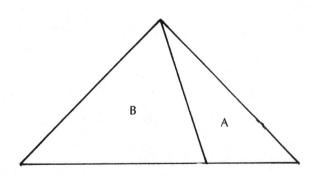

B   A

109. Three Cheers

This pattern appeared in *Farm Journal Magazine*. Pattern pieces are on p. 217.

TO ASSEMBLE BLOCK:

 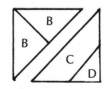

Need 4   Need 8 each

To assemble the completed units, visualize the block in three rows: top, bottom and center. The center will equal two rows.

Stitch A, B, CD units together to form top and bottom row.

MODERATE

in color p. 10

BLOCK SIZE: 12″

QUILT SIZE: 72″ × 84″

NO. OF BLOCKS: 42

PIECES PER BLOCK:

			PER QUILT:
A	4	White	168
	4	Red	168
B	8	Red	336
	8	White	336
C	8	Red	336
D	8	White	336
E	4	Blue	168
	4	White	168
F	4	White	336

FABRIC REQUIREMENTS:

Red—3 2/3 yards
White—5 1/4 yards
Blue—1/4 yard

Sew the F pieces, then set the E pieces into the corners to form center square.

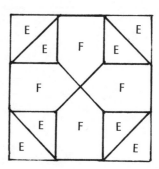

For center row, stitch two sets of B, CD to form side. Attach to each side of center square EF units.

Outline quilt 1/4″ from each seam.

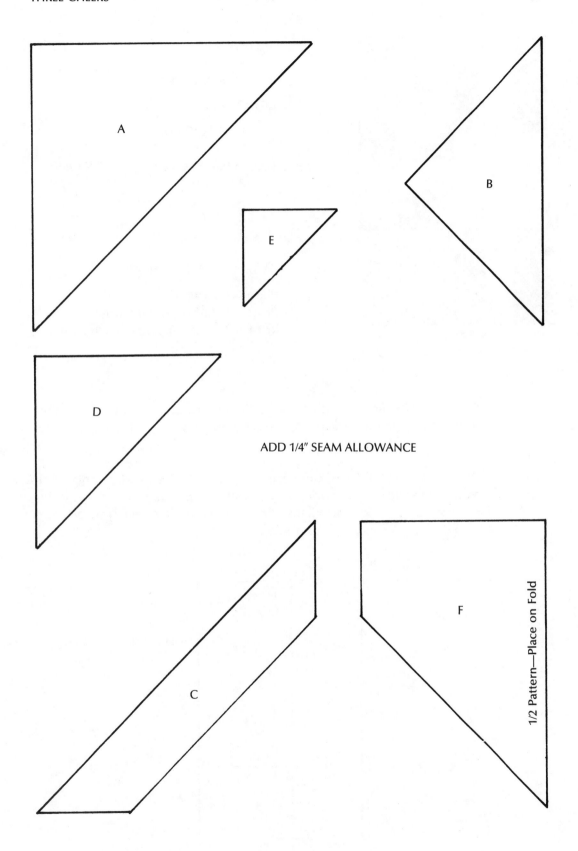

A

B

E

D

ADD 1/4″ SEAM ALLOWANCE

C

F

1/2 Pattern—Place on Fold

110. Tic Tac Toe

This is another easy pattern for the beginning quilter.

EASY

in color p. 12

BLOCK SIZE: 9″

QUILT SIZE: 81″ × 81″

NO. OF BLOCKS: 81

PIECES PER BLOCK:			PER QUILT:
A	1	Plain	81
	4	Print	324
B	4	Plain	324
	8	Dark Print	648

FABRIC REQUIREMENTS:

Plain—2 3/4 yards
Print #1 (light)—3 1/4 yards
Print #2 (dark) or plain—3 1/4 yards

Cut out pattern pieces adding 1/4″ seam allowance. Stitch together Part B; dark print, plain, dark print. Assemble the block following the diagram.

SIMPLIFIED PIECING: Cut out Parts A, adding 1/4″ seam allowance. Cut remaining fabric into 2″ wide strips. Seam strips together; dark, light, dark. Press strips and lay on flat surface. Measure down each strip 4″ and cut apart. Assemble block as above.

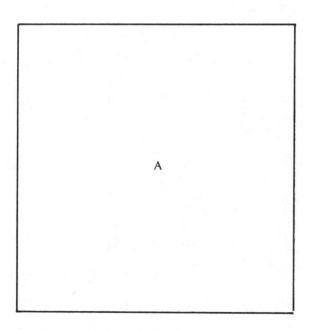

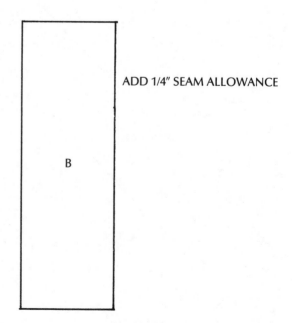

ADD 1/4″ SEAM ALLOWANCE

in color p. 16

BLOCK SIZE: 9″

QUILT SIZE: 81″ × 90″

NO. OF BLOCKS: 90
(45 Block A, 45 Block B)

PIECES PER BLOCK: **PER QUILT:**
BLOCK A:
A   4   Dark   180
        1   Light   45
B   4   Dark   180
        4   Light   180

BLOCK B:
A   5   Light   225
        4   Dark   180

FABRIC REQUIREMENTS:

Light—4 yards
Dark—4 1/2 yards

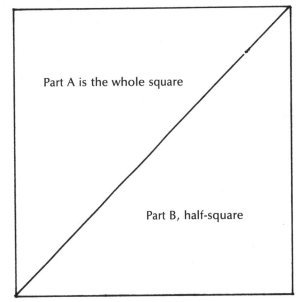

A Ladies Art Company pattern.

BLOCK A: Join light and dark Part B's to form a square. Row One of the block—join the completed B unit to each side of A. Row Two is two dark A's joined to either side of a light A.

BLOCK B: A simple nine-patch, alternating light and dark.

Completed blocks are joined in rows, alternating A and B blocks nine across and ten down.

Outline quilt 1/8″ from all seams.

Part A is the whole square

Part B, half-square

112. Topsy Turvy

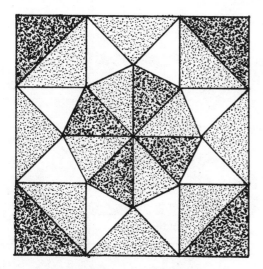

Pattern pieces are on p. 221.

DIFFICULT

in color p. 13

BLOCK SIZE: 10″

QUILT SIZE: 70″ × 80″

NO. OF BLOCKS: 56

PIECES PER BLOCK:			PER QUILT:
BLOCK A:			
A	8	White	224
	4	Light	112
	4	Dark	112
B	4	Light	112
	4	Dark	112
C	4	Light	112

BLOCK B:			
A	8	White	224
	4	Light	112
	4	Dark	112
B	4	Light	112
	4	Dark	112
C	4	Dark	112

FABRIC REQUIREMENTS:

Light—3 yards
Dark—3 3/4 yards
White—2 1/2 yards

The quilt top is set so that the dark and light within each block alternates from block to block. Blocks A and B use the same pieces and number of pieces; just alternate the placement.

By following the above diagram you shouldn't have any trouble piecing this block. It is a little more difficult because of the angles that must be turned.

Outline quilt 1/8″ from all seams.

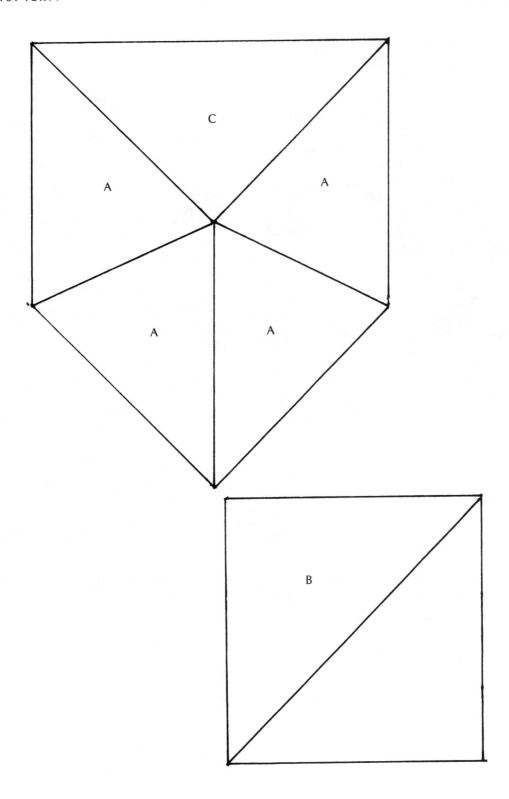

113. Triple Irish Chain

EASY

in color p. 6

BLOCK SIZE: 14"

QUILT SIZE: 98" × 98"

NO. OF BLOCKS: 49
(25 Block A, 24 Block B)

PIECES PER BLOCK:			PER QUILT:
BLOCK A: 25			
C	4	White	100
	13	Light	325
	20	Medium	500
	12	Dark	300
BLOCK B: 24			
A	1	White	24
B	4	White	96
C	8	Medium	192
	8	Dark	192

FABRIC REQUIREMENTS:

White—2 3/4 yards
Light—1 1/3 yards
Medium—2 3/4 yards
Dark—2 yards

This pattern is very easy to piece by just following the color placement shown. Pattern pieces are on p. 223.

Outline quilt each part, quilting 1/8" on each side of all seams. Use a fancy quilting motif for the plain blocks.

A border may be added if desired. In this case, use fewer blocks for the quilt top.

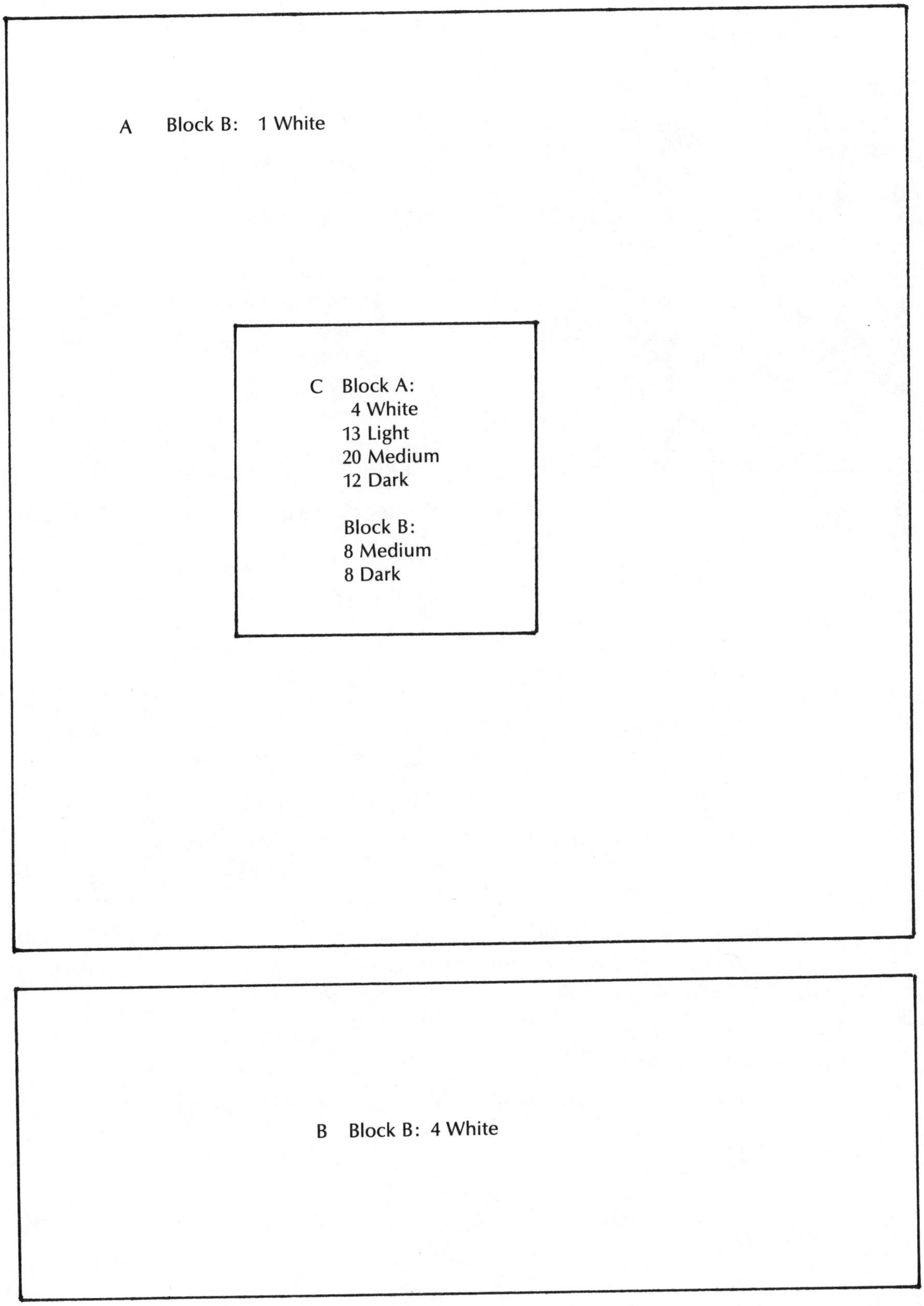

A   Block B: 1 White

C   Block A:
     4 White
    13 Light
    20 Medium
    12 Dark

    Block B:
    8 Medium
    8 Dark

B   Block B: 4 White

114. Tulip & Star

DIFFICULT

in color p. 12

BLOCK SIZE: 12″

QUILT SIZE: 72″ × 84″

NO. OF BLOCKS: 42

PIECES PER BLOCK:			PER QUILT:
A	8	White	336
B	8	Dark	336
C	4	Medium Print	168
D	4	Light Print	168
E	4	White	168
F	4	White	168
G	1	White	42

FABRIC REQUIREMENTS:

White—3 yards
Dark—2 yards
Medium Print—3 1/2 yards
Light Print—1/2 yard

Pattern pieces are on p. 225.

This is a fairly difficult pattern to piece. I've increased the number of pieces to allow for as many straight seams as possible.

For Parts A and B, reverse half the pieces when you cut the fabric.

Unit 1: I've divided the corner diagonally to make this a straight seam. Sew white A to dark B. Sew this to medium print C. Using the reversed pattern, make another A, B and sew to the other side of C. Make four.

Unit 2: Center—seam F to G to F to form a diagonal strip. Seam an E piece to each side of one of the remaining F pieces. Repeat with other E and F pieces. Stitch these to the FGF unit.

Set Part D into Part C. Sew the outer assembled strips to the center to complete the block.

No border is necessary. Outline quilt along each seam.

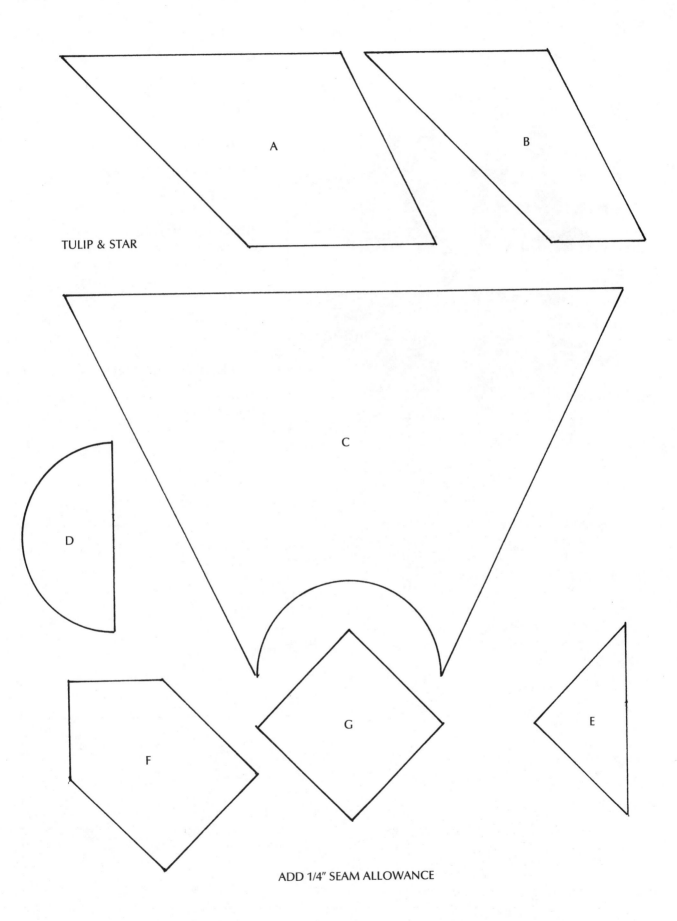

TULIP & STAR

A

B

C

D

G

F

E

ADD 1/4" SEAM ALLOWANCE

115. Turkey Tracks

EASY

in color p. 6

BLOCK SIZE: 9″

QUILT SIZE: 81″ × 81″

NO. OF BLOCKS: 81

PIECES PER BLOCK:			PER QUILT:
A	1	Print	81
B	4	White	324
C	16	White	1296
	16	Print	1296
D	4	White	324
	4	Print	324

FABRIC REQUIREMENTS:

Print—3 5/8 yards
White—5 yards

A Ladies Art Company pattern.

This pattern is very easy to piece. Break the block down into the four corner units and the center strips. Piece four print and plain C's for each section. Join these two units together then join to a plain D and a print D. Join these to form the corner square. Complete all corner squares in the same manner. Stitch together one unit of BAB. To assemble the block, join two corner squares to one Part B. Need two. Join these two units to each side of the completed BAB unit.

Outline quilt 1/8″ from each seam.

in color p. 1

QUILT SIZE: 81″ × 108″

NO. OF STARS—12

FABRIC REQUIREMENTS:

White—10 1/4 yards

Each star requires the following
number of diamonds:
Row 1—8 Print #1		96
Row 2—16 White		192
Row 3—24 Print #2		288
Row 4—32 White		384
Row 5—24 Print #3		288
Row 6—16 White		192
Row 7—8 Print # 4		96

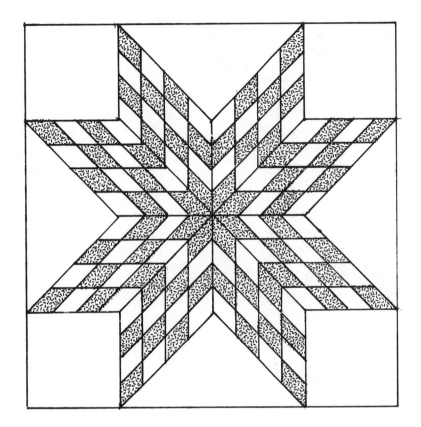

There are a large number of patterns using this star design. The main
difference seems to be color placement. In this case, there are two more
rows than normal and an intriguing pattern emerges because of the
white and print at the point. The points appear to be circular when joined
with other blocks.

Cut out the required number of diamonds for each block. Piece the eight
points of the diamond following your chosen color scheme. (The rec-
ommended fabric uses four different prints, but you could also use only
one carried throughout the star.) Piece two completed points together,
sew these to two more completed points and press. Repeat with the
other four points, then join them all together.

The corner squares will be approximately
8″ with the center triangle half of this
square. Measure the edges of the point
to ensure complete accuracy before cutting these blocks. Set the corner squares
and the triangle into the points of the
star.

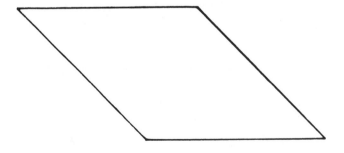

117. Waste Not

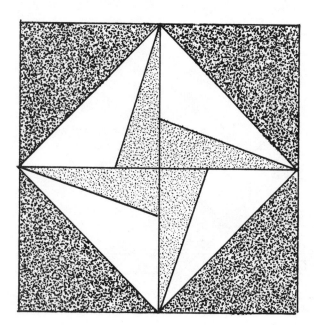

in color p. 3

BLOCK SIZE: 8″

UNITS PER BLOCK: **A** 4 Print or Plain
B 4 Print or Plain
C 4 Print or Plain

This quilt is made entirely of scraps, varying the fabric from block to block.

You have several options in setting the quilt. You can alternate plain blocks with the pieced or set the quilt with lattice strips, adding a harmonizing border. With a little planning you can arrange the blocks side by side, shading the quilt from top to bottom or designing the quilt into blocks of color. Play with the design before you finally decide on the final setting.

TO PIECE THE BLOCK: Join four units made up of ABC. Join two such units following the diagram, then two more. Join these four units at the center seam.

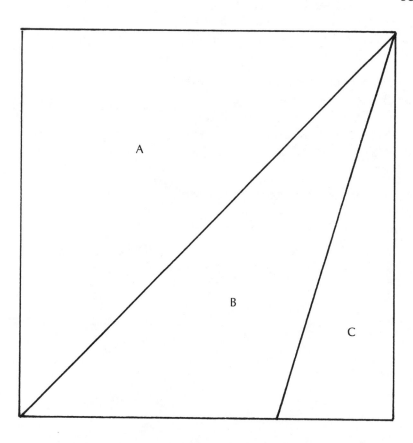

BLOCK A

in color p. 4

BLOCK SIZE: 12″

QUILT SIZE: 84″ × 96″

NO. OF BLOCKS: 42

6″ border

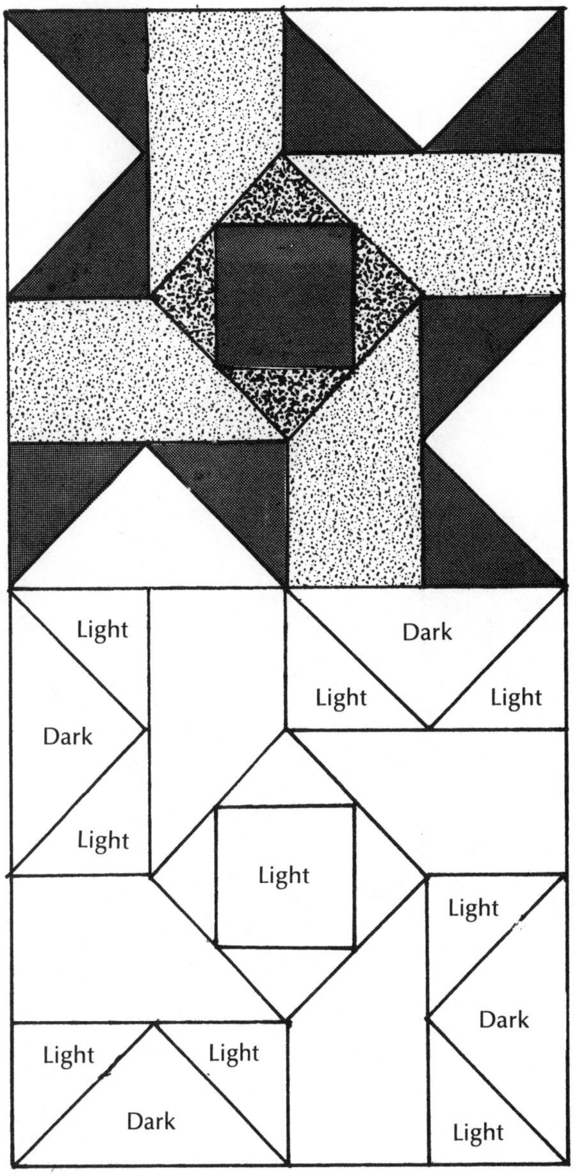

PIECES PER BLOCK:			PER QUILT:
BLOCK A: 21			
A	1	Dark	21
B	4	Scrap Plain	84
C	4	Scrap Print	84
D	8	Dark	168
E	4	Light	84
BLOCK B: 21			
A	1	Light	21
B	4	Scrap Plain	84
C	4	Scrap Print	84
D	8	Light	168
E	4	Dark	84

FABRIC REQUIREMENTS:

Assorted Scraps
Dark Plain—3 1/4 yards
Light Plain—3 1/4 yards
Print for Border—1 1/2 yards

Pattern pieces are on p. 230.

BLOCK B

TO PIECE THE BLOCK: Begin in the center by piecing Part A and four Part B's as shown in the diagram. Piece DED and join to C. Following the diagram, join these completed units to the center unit.

For Block B, alternate the light and dark pieces as shown.

Cut two border strips 6 1/2″ wide by 84 1/2″ long. Join to sides of quilt. Cut two more strips 6 1/2″ wide by 84 1/2″ long. Join to top and bottom of quilt.

Outline quilt 1/8″ from all seams.

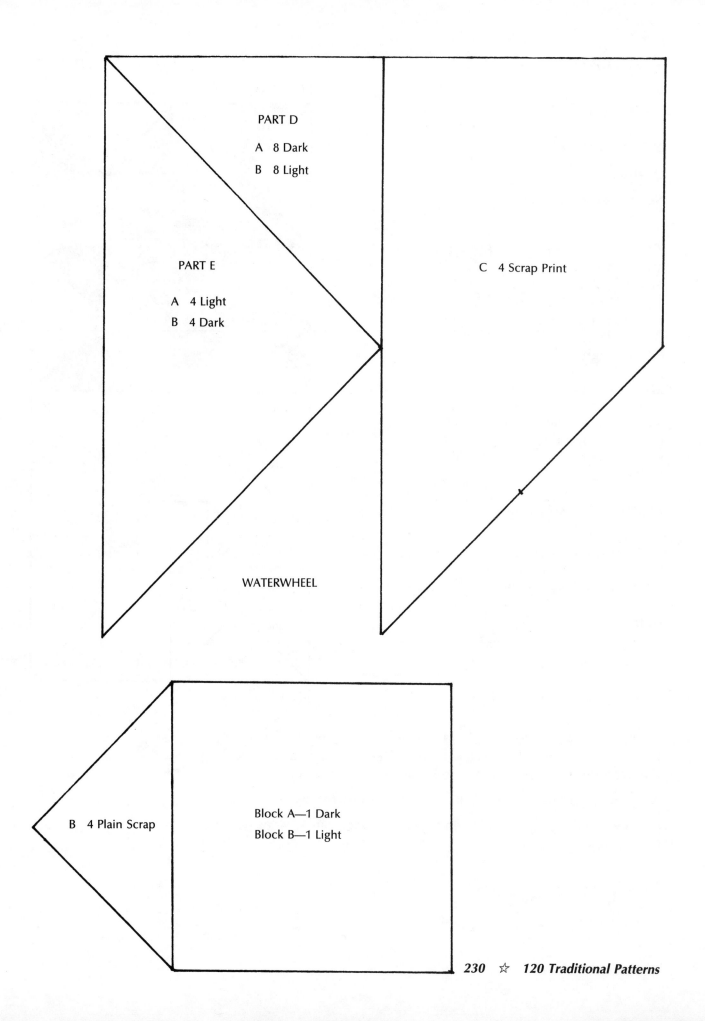

PART D

A   8 Dark

B   8 Light

PART E

A   4 Light

B   4 Dark

C   4 Scrap Print

WATERWHEEL

B   4 Plain Scrap

Block A—1 Dark

Block B—1 Light

in color p. 4

BLOCK SIZE: 11″

QUILT SIZE: 77″ × 88″

NO. OF BLOCKS: 56

PIECES PER BLOCK:			PER QUILT:
A	2	Dark Plain	112
B	8	Light Plain	448
	20	Print #1	1120
	20	Print #2	1120
C	2	Dark Plain	112
	14	Light Plain	784
D	10	Dark Plain	560
	3	Print #1	168
	7	Print #2	392

FABRIC REQUIREMENTS:

Dark Plain—1 3/4 yards
Print #1—3 yards
Light Plain—4 1/4 yards
Print #2—3 1/4 yards

Break the block down into three sections following the diagonal lines. Using the diagram on the pattern page, piece each section then join them together to form the block.

Outline quilt 1/8″ from all seams.

A Nancy Cabot design.

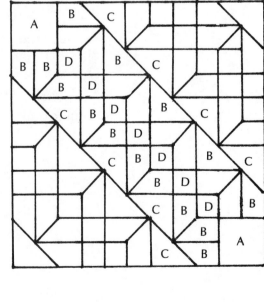

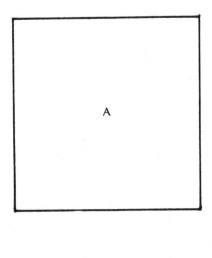

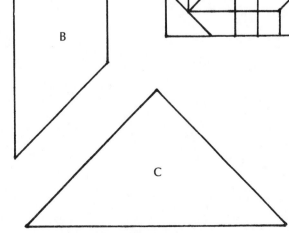

120. Wheel of Fortune

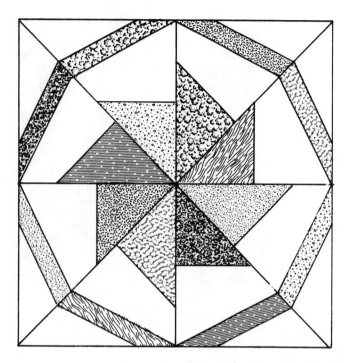

DIFFICULT

in color p. 14

BLOCK SIZE: 16″

QUILT SIZE: 80″ × 96″

NO. OF BLOCKS: 30

PIECES PER BLOCK:			PER QUILT:
A	8	Scrap fabric	240
B	4	White	120
C	4	White	120
D	8	Scrap fabric	240
E	8	White	240

FABRIC REQUIREMENTS:

Assorted scrap fabrics
White—7 yards

Pattern pieces are on p. 233.

From what my research turned up, this pattern appears to be an adaptation, using elements from a Pinwheel design and Water Wheel. It's an excellent quilt to use up scraps. Most scrap quilts require some forethought in the use of color, but for this one the scraps can be used almost at random because of the large areas of white.

To piece the design, divide the block into eight sections following the diagonal, horizontal and vertical lines. Unit A is made up of Parts A, B, D and E. Unit B is made up of parts A, C, D and E. After the units are pieced, sew them together alternating Units A and B.

Outline quilt 1/8″ from each seam; shadow quilt the larger areas to fill in.

A border can be added if desired.

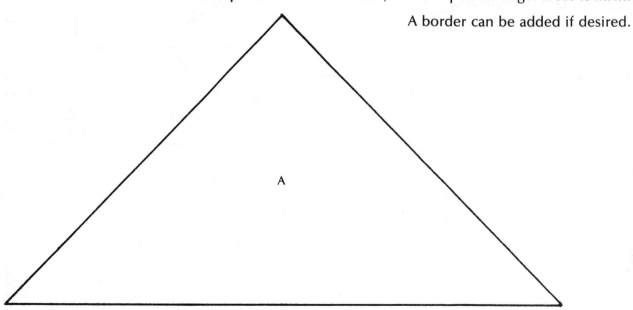

A

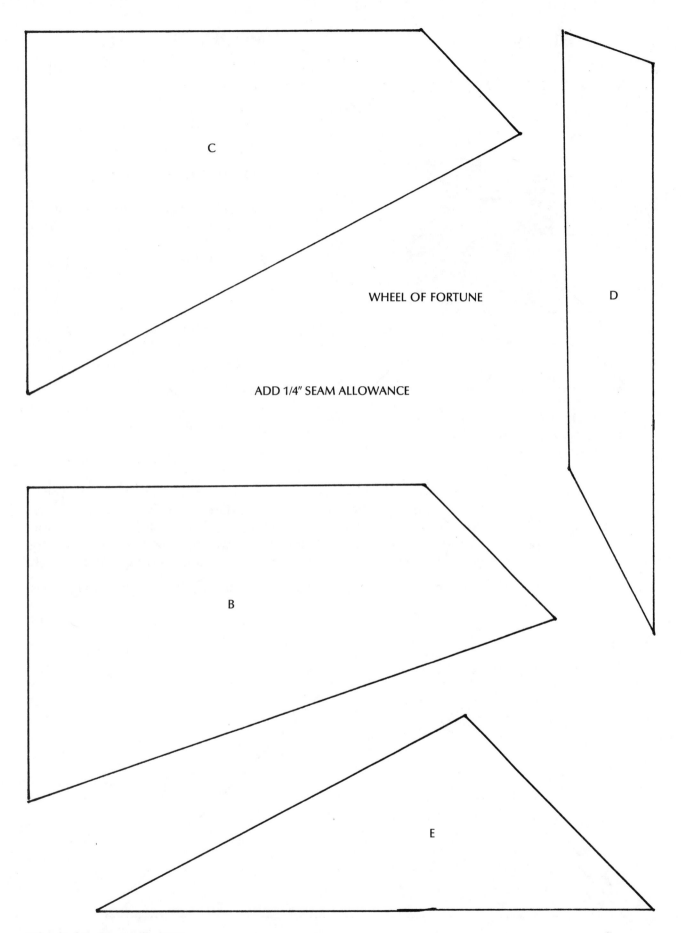

C

WHEEL OF FORTUNE

ADD 1/4" SEAM ALLOWANCE

D

B

E

121. Whirligig

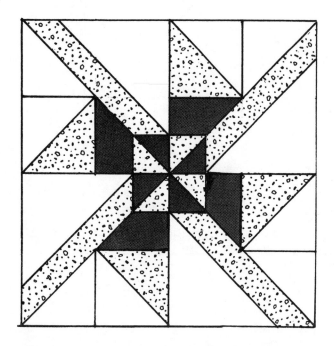

This pattern dates to at latest the 1930's. It's also known as Double Pinwheel and Jack in the Box.

MODERATE

in color p. 11

BLOCK SIZE: 16″

QUILT SIZE: 80″ × 80″

NO. OF BLOCKS: 25

PIECES PER BLOCK:			**PER QUILT:**
A	4	Plain	100
	4	Print	100
B	4	White	100
C	4	Print	100
D	4	Plain	100
E	4	Print	100
	8	White	200

FABRIC REQUIREMENTS:

Plain—1 1/2 yards
Print—2 3/4 yards
White—6 yards

To piece the block, break it down into four sections along the center lines. For each section, piece B, C and dark A. This forms 1/2 of the section. For the other half of the section, piece white E to white E to print E. Add dark D and print A. Join these two diagonal units for 1/4 of the block. Piece the other 3/4 in the same way. Join to complete the block.

Outline quilt 1/8″ from each seam. Shadow quilt inside the larger areas.

Other pattern pieces on p. 235.

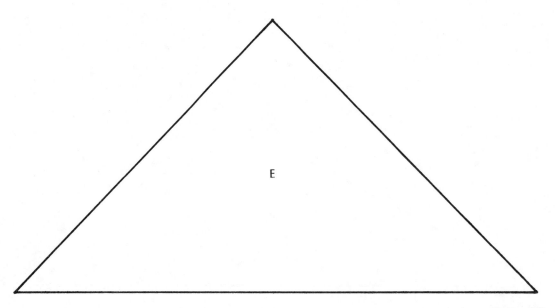

E

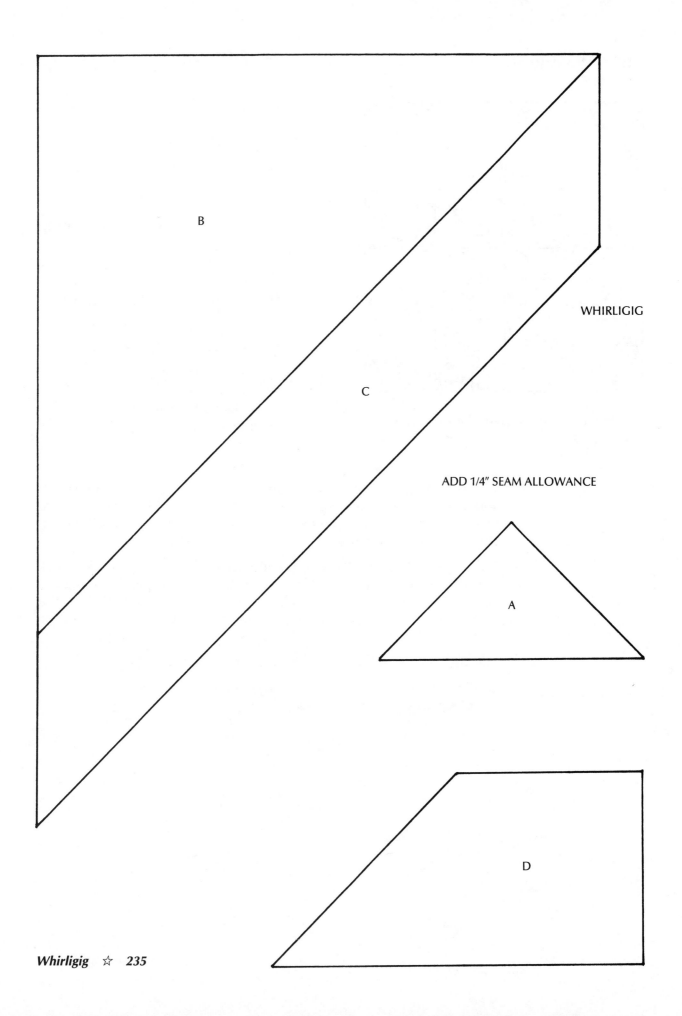

B

WHIRLIGIG

C

ADD 1/4" SEAM ALLOWANCE

A

D

122. Windflower

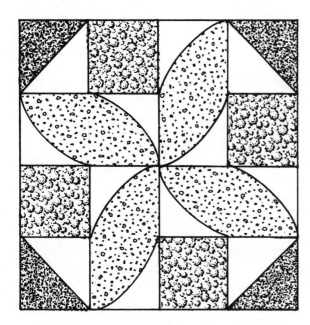

A Laura Wheeler Design. Pattern pieces are on p. 237.

MODERATE

in color p. 3

BLOCK SIZE: 12″

QUILT SIZE: 72″ × 84″

NO. OF BLOCKS: 42

PIECES PER BLOCK:			PER QUILT:
A	4	Print #1	168
B	8	White	336
C	4	Print #2	168
D	4	Dark Plain	168
	4	White	168

FABRIC REQUIREMENTS:

Print #1—2 1/2 yards
White—3 1/4 yards
Print #2—1 1/2 yards
Dark Plain—1 1/2 yards

This is a moderately difficult pattern because of the curved pieces. If you feel hesitant about piecing curves, press under the seam allowance on Part A and lay the piece over the seam allowance on Part B. Whipstitch the two together as you would in appliqué.

Cut and sew together Parts A, B and D. To assemble the block, break it down into four parts. Join unit DD to C, then add AB, following the above diagram. In the upper-left corner, AB goes under DC; in the upper-right corner, AB is seamed to the side of DD. Continue with the other two corners.

Join the four completed units to form the block.

Outline quilt around each part. If desired, a small motif can be used in the 6″ squares where the blocks join together.

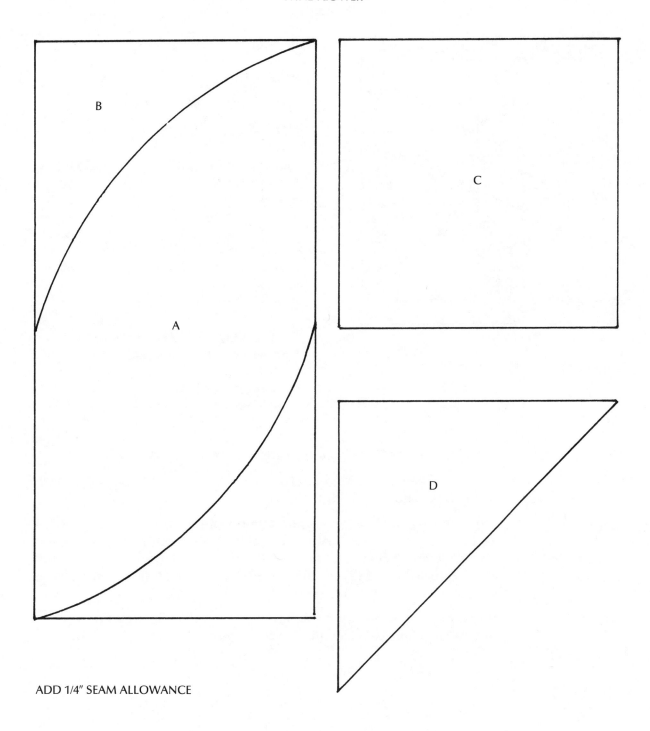

ADD 1/4″ SEAM ALLOWANCE

123. World's Fair

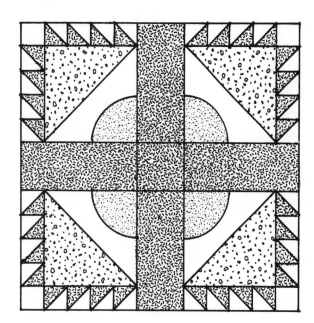

MODERATE

in color p. 15

BLOCK SIZE: 18:

QUILT SIZE: 90: × 90:

NO. OF BLOCKS: 25

PIECES PER BLOCK:			PER QUILT:
A	4	Dark	100
B	1	Dark	25
C	4	White	100
D	32	Dark	800
	32	White	800
E	4	Medium Print	100
F	4	White	100
G	4	Light Print	100

FABRIC REQUIREMENTS:
Dark Print or Plain—5 yards
White—4 1/4 yards
Medium Print—3 1/3 yards
Light Print—1 yard

A Ladies Art Company pattern. Pattern pieces are on p. 239.

This is a time-consuming pattern because of the many pieces in each block, but is not overly difficult.

Break the block down into four sections and the center strip. Piece each of the corner sections following the above diagram. When completed, sew two sections to each side of Part A. Piece the center strip using Parts ABA and sew to the completed upper portion of the block. Repeat for the bottom of the block.

No border is required for this block. Simple outline quilting 1/8: on each side of all seams will accentuate the pattern.

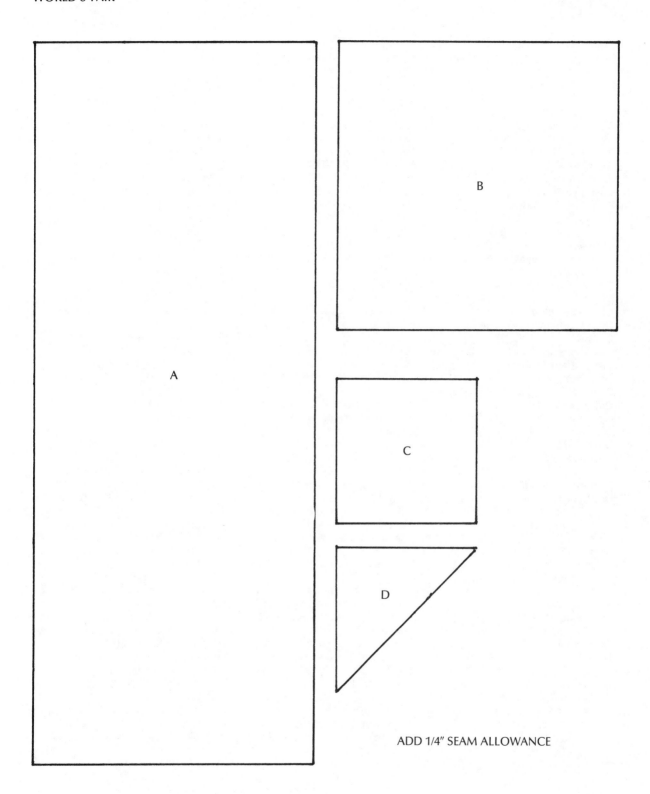

A

B

C

D

ADD 1/4" SEAM ALLOWANCE

Index